MW00479642

"With this book Emma O'Donnell est
in the conversation that is comparativ
only for her comprehensive treatmen.
liturgy in Judaism and Christianity and her adroit handling of
methodological issues but also for the real people that she brings into the
mix. The experience of time is a most important issue in liturgical studies,
and O'Donnell's work is an important contribution to our understanding
of how they relate to one another."

—John F. Baldovin, SJ
Boston College School of Theology and Ministry

"O'Donnell's path-breaking volume successfully presents a compelling
and nuanced explanation of liturgical time as it is experienced both
similarly and also differently by Catholic and Jewish worshipers.
Mobilizing a rich and interdisciplinary range of theoretical perspectives,
she deftly weaves together insights from the liturgical theologies of these
two traditions, ritual studies, comparative theology, and more. Applying
these to her own field work, she broadens and deepens our understanding
of the purpose of the anamnetic memories of past and future constructed
by regular participation in liturgical life. Readers of all religions will find
themselves not only enlightened but also motivated to reflect on their
own prayer practices."

—Ruth Langer, Rabbi, PhD
Associate Director, Center for Christian-Jewish Learning
Boston College

"This book—both scholarly and highly personal—analyzes how the
practice of liturgy redefines and enriches the experience of time in its
spiritual dimensions. Emma O'Donnell performs a feat that few can equal,
bringing together Jewish and Christian practices and understandings so
that both sides can feel that she has their own interests and sympathies at
heart. Strong on both theology and critical theory, this book draws
particularly on sensitive interviews with those deeply engaged in the
liturgical lives of their respective communities. The spirit of Vatican II is
alive and well in this remarkable book, which must be read and meditated
on as a prolegomenon to liturgical studies in a comparative setting."

—Theodore A. Perry, PhD
Emeritus Professor of Hebrew Bible and Comparative Literature
University of Connecticut

"In this excellent book, Emma O'Donnell considers the experience of time in the ritual contexts of Jewish and Christian liturgy. Convinced as she is that religiously formed experience of time is part and parcel of both Jewish and Christian faith, O'Donnell embarks on a journey exploring the subjective realm of experience in both liturgical traditions. This detailed comparative and empirical research contributes not only to the domain of liturgical theology but also to the fields of comparative theology and interreligious studies. O'Donnell's understanding of liturgy as a site for interreligious learning especially will be welcomed by scholars interested in the ritual dimension of interreligious encounters."

—Marianne Moyaert
Vrije Universiteit Amsterdam
The Netherlands

Emma O'Donnell

Remembering the Future

The Experience of Time in Jewish and Christian Liturgy

A PUEBLO BOOK

Liturgical Press   Collegeville, Minnesota

www.litpress.org

A Pueblo Book published by Liturgical Press

Cover design by Monica Bokinskie. Photo courtesy of Thinkstock.

1   2   3   4   5   6   7   8   9

Library of Congress Cataloging-in-Publication Data

O'Donnell, Emma.
    Remembering the future : the experience of time in Jewish and Christian liturgy / Emma O'Donnell.
       pages cm.
    "A Pueblo book."
    Includes bibliographical references.
    ISBN 978-0-8146-6317-2 — ISBN 978-0-8146-6342-4 (ebook)
      1. Liturgics.   2. Judaism—Liturgy.   3. Time—Religious aspects—Christianity.   4. Time—Religious aspects—Judaism.   5. Memory—Religious aspects—Christianity.   6. Memory—Religious aspects—Judaism.
I. Title.

BV178.O36 2015
264.001—dc23   2015017069

So teach us to count our days that we may gain a wise heart.

Psalm 90:12

Contents

Preface

I awake to utter silence. It is a still night, and through the windows I see the brilliant stars sliding in their slow and steady journey across the arc of the sky. The time is 2:00 a.m., and I know that at this hour, across the field under the star-scattered sky, in the chapel nestled inside the monastic cloister, they are chanting. Through the silence, I imagine I hear the voices steadfastly chanting the psalms in Latin, their measured rhythm patiently marking the passage of time.

The next day there is hay to be bailed and brought into the barns. All afternoon we labor under the sun, heaving bails high onto trucks, the fields ringing with laughter and the clatter of engines. After the last bail is in, the clamor subsides and silence slowly settles back onto the fields and barns. And into this silence enters one of the monastery bells, intoning the hour of prayer. It is 5:00 p.m., and Vespers is about to begin.

In the monastery church, a new order of time drifts in and rests upon the tired bodies whose muscles still ache, skin still warm from the sun. With each intonation of the bell, as steady as a heartbeat at rest, time takes on a new shape. Jagged breath and spinning thoughts come to rest with the rhythm of the bell. As one, the community inhales and exhales in chant, finding the pitch and rhythm that will sustain this time of prayer, this unique hour existing only here and now and measured by the ritual and the rhythm of chant. Existing only in this point of the present, yet also dwelling in all spaces of the remembered past and anticipated future. As the ancient poetry of the psalms remembers and announces the stories of the past, the liturgy is held aloft by hope, ritually performing the anticipation of a new world.

It was during visits to a Benedictine monastery over the course of a number of years that I began to see the relationship between liturgy and time. As I looked deeper into it, the particular aspects of the correspondence between liturgy and time that unfolded proved to be subtle and elusive, but very real. I began to see that ritual performance, especially in the contexts of the highly temporal narratives and time-focused theologies of Judaism and Christianity, has the capacity to transform the way that time is experienced.

This book explores the experience of time in the ritual contexts of Jewish and Christian liturgy. Many studies have addressed the relationship of liturgy to time, both in terms of the annual calendar and daily scheduling, yet this one is different. This book examines the *experience* of time in liturgy, and, in doing so, it addresses the existential human condition of being located in time and the fundamental awareness of time as it is informed by religious tradition and practice.

Jewish and Christian narratives of the religiously envisioned past and future are embodied liturgically, and this book charts the ways that liturgical communities perform the temporal orientations of the religious tradition, clothing themselves in the memory and hope embedded in their narratives. It argues that the ritual enactment of collective religious memory and hope evokes a unique landscape of time, the contours of which are determined by the ritually remembered past and the anticipated eschatological future.

The title of this book evokes a complex temporality—indeed, an interpenetration of the past, present, and future—evident in both Jewish and Christian thought and ritually performed in liturgy. Since its earliest beginnings, Christian thought has envisioned a reshaped temporality, a virtual temporal interpenetration. As Louie-Marie Chauvet observes, "As the ancient anaphoras show, in the recalling—the anamnesis—of the *second* coming of the Lord Jesus, as well as of his death and resurrection, the Christian memory is eschatological: it is memory of the future."[1]

---

[1] Louis-Marie Chauvet, *Symbol and Sacrament: A Sacramental Reinterpretation of Christian Existence*, trans. Patrick Madigan and Madeleine Beaumont (Collegeville, MN: Liturgical Press, 1995), 239.

A similar virtual reshaping of time, in which the boundaries of the past, present, and future stretch and become porous, is seen in Jewish thought. Jewish thought evidences none of the radical reworking of time characteristic of Christian thought, however, the latter of which arises out of belief in the divine identity of Jesus Christ and the need to formulate the role of the paschal mystery in history. The vision of time and history in Jewish thought, while less radically reshaped, is flexible and interactive, determined not by the straight ruler of chronology but by the narratives of religious tradition and the emphases of religious memory. In an analogy offered by Yosef Hayim Yerushalmi, rabbinical thought seems to "play with time as though with an accordion, expanding and collapsing it at will."[2] In Jewish practice, moreover, the sense of communal identification and collective memory is central within a tradition which is both intensely memorial and eschatological. In the words of Orthodox Rabbi Joseph B. Soloveitchik, "To exist as a Jew means to be at the juncture of past and future, of that which is no longer real and that which is not yet real. Our mission is to live in both dimensions."[3]

In the temporal landscape of both Jewish and Christian liturgies, time is experienced as multidimensional; memory is eschatological and hope remembers. Hope, as the anticipation of a religiously envisioned future, engages the remembered past and takes from it promises for the future. It sees God's intervention in history, in time, to be a promise for the "future history." Memory speaks to hope and hope speaks to memory. This, in other words, is eschatological memory; this is remembering the future.

Part 1 introduces the concept of the disintegration and subsequent reintegration of the boundaries of the past, present, and future in the context of liturgical performance and lays the methodological foundation for this book. Part 2 takes an ethnographic

---

[2] Yosef Hayim Yerushalmi, *Zakhor: Jewish History and Jewish Memory* (Seattle: University of Washington Press, 1982), 17.

[3] Joseph B. Soloveitchik, *Festival of Freedom: Essays on Pesah and the Haggadah*, ed. Joel B. Wolowesky and Reuven Ziegler (Jersey City, NJ: Ktav Publishing House, 2006), 177.

turn and presents interviews conducted with Jewish and Christian individuals who reflect on their own experiences of time in the contexts of halakhic Jewish practice or as members of Catholic religious orders. Part 3 addresses the Jewish experience of time, beginning with an investigation into time in Jewish thought and followed by an exploration of the experience of time in Jewish liturgy. Part 4 addresses the experience of time in the Christian context, following the same format as part 3. Finally, part 5 examines the ritual, performed nature of liturgy and considers the ways in which ritual performance shapes the experience of time.

In the Christian liturgical context, this book focuses on the Catholic celebration of the Liturgy of the Hours. The Liturgy of the Hours performs the Christian narrative of salvation history within the setting of liturgical services that regularly punctuate the hours of day and night. In the Jewish liturgical context, it addresses a wider range of liturgies, for although the Jewish daily services are celebrated at intervals throughout the hours of the day like the Liturgy of the Hours, the intensely memorial and eschatological holidays of Passover, Tish'ah b'Av, and Shabbat are highly influential in shaping the liturgical experience of time.

This study moves beyond the most readily observable elements of liturgy, such as history, text, and rubrics and enters into the subjective realm of experience, which offers no clear platform for observation and interpretation. It does so in the attempt to better understand an element intrinsic to human experience, i.e., the experience of time. It embarks on this journey motivated by the conviction that the religiously formed experience of time is an integral part of the experience of faith in both Jewish and Christian contexts.

I wish to thank all those who participated in the interviews for part 2 of this book, giving their time and sharing so openly their intimate experiences of liturgy and time. I am particularly grateful to the community of the Abbey of Regina Laudis, for their participation and also for teaching me about community, tradition, and the practice of living in time.

I would like to acknowledge and thank the members of my doctoral committee, whose guidance was invaluable when this project was in its earliest form: John F. Baldovin, SJ, for his support and clear vision of the path forward; Ruth Langer, for her indefatigable attention to detail and scholarly accountability; and Liam Bergin, for his generosity, his precise attention to language, and his warm support. I also wish to thank Hans Christoffersen, Patrick McGowan, and their colleagues at Liturgical Press; my academic community at Boston College; Mary Troxell, for her friendship and for that invaluable necessity, a room in which to write; Tony Perry and Marc Epstein, for their insistence that my out-of-the-box ideas matter; and Catherine Cornille and Marianne Moyaert, for paving the way with their own work and for supporting mine. I would also like to thank Arvo Pärt for his musical compositions which kept me company as I wrote this book, and the work of the Paleolithic artists who painted the walls of the Chauvet Cave, whose paintings ignited in me thoughts on time, memory, and the divine.

The discussions of collective memory in this book are dedicated to the memory of the members of my family whose lives were taken in the Holocaust—my great-grandparents and many of their children and grandchildren, killed at Auschwitz in 1944—and to the memory of my grandmother, Sheindl, and the others who survived, each of whom passed on the gift of collective memory and hope across the generations. And to all the members of my family, with love.

I especially want to thank two people to whom my gratitude knows no bounds: Valery, for being my companion every step of the way, for listening tirelessly, and for his incomparable generosity; and finally, my mother, Patricia O'Donnell, for everything—for the gift of life, for laughter, and for inspiring me with her own writing.

Part 1

The Liturgical Experience
of Time

Chapter 1

Liturgical Time

These are the set times of the LORD, *the sacred occasions, which you shall celebrate each at its appointed time. (Lev 23:4)*[1]

The immediate event—the liturgy—makes sense and has a meaning for our lives only because it contains the other two dimensions. Past, present, and future interpenetrate and touch upon eternity.

—Joseph Ratzinger[2]

INTRODUCTION

The traditions of both Christianity and Judaism are intimately related to the element of time. The religious narratives speak of a world in which time is created and determined by God, in which the unfolding through time of a mythologized history expresses God's will, and in which the future is given shape by the expectation of eschatological redemption. In this atmosphere of time, Christians and Jews return time and again to cycles of prayer, in which they gather to ritually perform these temporal narratives. They perform the memory of the past, the experience of the present, and the anticipation of the future. This book examines the interaction of communal religious memory and eschatological anticipation within Jewish and Christian liturgical performance. It illustrates how communal memory and anticipation, operating together in ritual performances infused with the awareness of time, contribute to a liturgical reshaping of the experience of time.

---

[1] New Jewish Publication Society translation.

[2] Joseph Cardinal Ratzinger, *The Spirit of the Liturgy* (San Francisco: Ignatius Press, 2000), 60.

Religious traditions provide metanarratives that shape the way that one's experience in the world is interpreted, and this interpretation is ingrained through religious ritual, from the simplest rituals of daily life to the most complex rituals of liturgical performance. Liturgy thus has the capacity to influence the way its participants formulate even the most fundamental elements of human experience, such as the experience of time. The centrality of time—including time measurement, time consciousness, and notions of historical progression—to Jewish and Christian thought and religious practice suggests that the elemental human experience of the passing of time is taken up and experientially transformed in these traditions.

Jewish and Christian traditions each understand the biblical narrative of the past to inform the way that the present world is interpreted and the present time experienced. The memorialized narrative of the past also indicates a shape for the future, and inversely, the contours of the envisioned eschatological future influence the perception of the present in each tradition. This dynamic lends a particular texture to the sense of the present, formed in the tension between a communally remembered narrative of the past and a communally anticipated vision of the future. Informed by the narratives and conceptual structures of each religion, this particular texture, or temporal landscape, constitutes a unique sense of the present. This book investigates this sense of the present, referred to here as the "liturgical present," and charts the ways in which Jewish and Christian narratives and liturgical practices inform the experience of existing within time.

The motivation for this book arose from a fascination with the experience of time. Our lives are so encased by time that it seems we are held captive within its inescapable structure. Yet time cannot be grasped, and it perpetually recedes. This condition has long inspired wonder and despair in many, as expressed by Saint Augustine's plaintive observation in *Confessions* that "time flies so quickly from future into past that it is an interval with no duration. If it has duration, it is divisible into past and future. But the present occupies no space."[3] And present in both Jewish and Christian

[3] Augustine, *Confessions*, trans. Henry Chadwick (Oxford: Oxford University Press, 1992), 11.15.20.

liturgical practices is a preoccupation with measuring and contemplating time: the daily, weekly, and annual cycles of prayer require precise measurements of time, and Jewish and Christian liturgical celebrations are infused with expressions of memory and hope, repeatedly gesturing toward the past and the future.

According to sociologist Daniele Hervieu-Leger, religious rituals are defined by their enactments of memory, hope, and the marking of time. "And what characterizes a religious rite in relation to all other forms of social ritualization," Hervieu-Leger proposes, "is that the regular repetition of a ritually set pattern of word and gesture exists in order to mark the passage of time (as well as the transience of each individual life incorporated in the chain) with the recall of the foundational events."[4] In marking the transience of the lives of individuals, ritual meditates on cyclical time as experienced through the cycles of birth and death. And, in the recollection of religious or primordial history, ritual also contemplates historical time, experienced as the imagined ancient past.[5]

The ways in which this ritual marking of time is *experienced* in liturgy have not been thoroughly explored. While there are many studies of the role of time in Jewish and Christian liturgies, with few exceptions the main focus of discourse on the relationship between time and liturgy is the liturgical calendar, including studies of the development of the liturgical calendar, the relationship of cosmic cycles to liturgical practices, and the particular times of day when certain liturgies are performed. This means that, of the great wealth of theological work addressing the relationship between liturgy and time, the vast majority discusses the time within which liturgy is performed. This may seem to be a self-evident observation, for what else would be the focus of reflection on the relationship between liturgy and time other than the time within which liturgies are performed?

---

[4] Daniele Hervieu-Leger, *Religion as a Chain of Memory* (New Brunswick, NJ: Rutgers University Press, 2000), 125.

[5] Anthropologist Paul Connerton argues for increased attention to the transmission of collective memory through "commemorative ceremonies and bodily practices" and investigates how "images of the past are conveyed and sustained by (more or less ritual) performances." Paul Connerton, *How Societies Remember* (Cambridge, UK: Cambridge University Press, 1989), 40.

This book proposes, however, that the time within which liturgy is performed is only one element of the relationship between liturgy and time, and that a great and largely untapped wealth of meaning can be found in exploring the way in which time is molded and experienced within liturgy. The relationship between liturgy and time encompasses not only the time within which liturgies are performed but also the *liturgies within which time is performed*. This book demonstrates how the religious narratives and theological traditions of Judaism and Christianity allow the performance of liturgy to transform the sense of time, bringing the past and the future into dialogue with the present; in other words, it examines the liturgical performance of time.

THE BIBLICAL CREATION OF TIME

Christianity and Judaism are each built around the notion of historical time; each was born out of the shared landscape of the narrative of the Hebrew Bible, and each is shaped by a biblical understanding of the progression of history. The biblical narrative paints a temporal landscape in which the unfolding of history is of utmost importance. That one event was followed by another bears great significance in biblical thought: God's voice was heard in history, and the divine promises were fulfilled.

The Hebrew Bible tells a story bound by time, beginning with the creation of time and continuing with the development of a people through time. The opening word of Genesis, which serves as the first line of both the Jewish and Christian sacred texts, is the Hebrew word *bereshit*, "in the beginning." The *bet* at the beginning of this word has multiple connotations, meaning alternately "in," "with," or "when." In the context of Genesis 1:1, it has been translated and interpreted in multiple ways. The King James Bible translates the *bet* as "in": "In the beginning God created the heaven and the earth." The New Revised Standard Version, on the other hand, maintains the "in," but includes the temporal designation "when": "In the beginning when God created the heavens and the earth . . ." Reflecting rabbinic interpretations of this verse, the New Jewish Publication Society translation favors the temporal indicator and translates the line as "When God began to create heaven and earth . . ." As in the Hebrew original, each of these diverse translations introduces the sacred text with an evocation of time.

The first chapter of Genesis offers a narration about the creation of the world, and significantly, about the establishment of night and day to mark time. The first thing to be introduced after the creation of heaven and earth is the division between night and day: "Then God said, 'Let there be light'; and there was light. And God saw that the light was good; and God separated the light from the darkness. God called the light Day, and the darkness he called Night. And there was evening and there was morning, the first day" (Gen 1:3-5). The creation of undifferentiated light is immediately followed by the division of light from darkness, establishing the foundational temporal distinction of day and night. The categorization of time into day and night is developed further in the narration of the fourth day:

> And God said, "Let there be lights in the dome of the sky to separate the day from the night; and let them be for signs and for seasons and for days and years, and let them be lights in the dome of the sky to give light upon the earth." And it was so. God made the two great lights—the greater light to rule the day and the lesser light to rule the night—and the stars. God set them in the dome of the sky to give light upon the earth, to rule over the day and over the night, and to separate the light from the darkness. And God saw that it was good. (Gen 1:14-18)

Here, the categorization of time is celebrated; time is divided and put in order. No longer a meaningless void of timelessness, the world becomes organized in a system of days and nights. It is given order, and this order redeems it from the chaos from which the world was created. The creation of day and night gives form and definition to the passing of time, and as indicated in Genesis 1:14, this definition of time is intended to separate time into even more specific divisions. It is to be not only for the division of day and night but also "for signs and for seasons and for days and years." In this opening narrative, the passing of time is sanctified; the element of time is introduced as a medium of God's work in the world. Time is equated with progress, and in the progression of time, the idea of past, present, and future arises.

The Hebrew Bible introduced a new sense of time, transforming the cultures that received it with a sense of time as an ongoing continuum of great breadth. In his Haggadah commentary, Rabbi Jonathan Sacks notes that while a sense of cyclical time is innate to animals who observe the cycles of night and day and the changing seasons, the sense of a distant past and a distant future is unique to humans, and it is this sense of the broad reach of the past and future that was introduced and developed in the Hebrew Bible.[6] The shape of time that developed in the Hebrew Bible marked a major departure from the cyclical understandings of time prevalent in the polytheistic traditions out of which the biblical tradition emerged. Within the biblical narrative, Sacks observes, the exodus is one of the first narratives to exert a sizable impact in the development of the idea of time: "For the first time an abyss opened up between the past and the future, Egypt and the promised land. The journey through space, across the wilderness, came to symbolize a journey through time, whose destination is something new, unprecedented, a tomorrow radically unlike yesterday."[7] The narrative of the exodus entails a shift from a vision of time as that which is experienced in the moment and encased within a larger cyclical pattern of seasons into a vision of great chronological breadth.

The vision of time introduced in Scripture provides a structure for understanding change, development, loss, birth, and death. It gives meaning to these processes, revealing an image of time that is ultimately and spiritually meaningful. The biblical conception of time lends itself to understanding that a particular time can be quantitatively like any other time and yet qualitatively different. Through the intervention of divine action, it can be transformed into something entirely unique. It is no longer seen as an endless cycle, mirroring the cycles of the seasons. Nor is it seen as simply a meaningless stream of events moving forward in a linear motion, each moment disappearing into the past without leaving a mark. Rather, in the biblical landscape, the progression of time is given shape and meaning.

---

[6] Jonathan Sacks, "Time as a Narrative of Hope," in *Rabbi Jonathan Sacks' Haggadah* (New York: Continuum, 2006), 76.
    [7] Ibid., 77.

This meaning is also forward looking, as the idea of time indicates that the historical precedents point to future events and a future goal. In the biblical narrative, God's action in history functions as a promise that God will act in the future. The history of divine intervention, as it is preserved and kept alive in communal memory, indicates that the future is no longer entirely unknown and shapeless. In this way, the religious imagination is focused both on the past and the future.

Arising from the biblical text is the notion that memory is a fundamentally religious act.[8] The remembrance of the work of God in history becomes an act of faith—as a thanksgiving for divine action and a hope for future action. The past anticipates the future, and so, just as memory is a religious act, so too is the anticipation of the future. Religious memory provides a shape for the future. The contemplation of the past, present, and future through ritual acts of memory and hope is central to both Jewish and Christian practice.

A CHRISTIAN-JEWISH COMPARATIVE STUDY

Christianity and Judaism each hold visions of time that are notably different in many regards and yet nonetheless very similar. The concept of time in both traditions is based in the narrative of the Hebrew Bible, which introduces time as a linear progression from the distant past to the distant future, imbued with the significance of memory and eschatological hope. Yet despite the similarities, the perception of time is articulated differently in each tradition, reflecting the distinct temporal narrative of each. The distinction is

---

[8] E.g., "That was for the LORD a night of vigil, to bring them out of the land of Egypt. That same night is a vigil to be kept for the LORD by all the Israelites throughout their generations" (Exod 12:42); "Let the Israelites keep the passover at its appointed time. On the fourteenth day of this month, at twilight, you shall keep it at its appointed time; according to all its statutes and all its regulations you shall keep it" (Num 9:2-3); "You must not eat with it anything leavened. For seven days you shall eat unleavened bread with it—the bread of affliction—because you came out of the land of Egypt in great haste, so that all the days of your life you may remember the day of your departure from the land of Egypt" (Deut 16:3); "Then he took a loaf of bread, and when he had given thanks, he broke it and gave it to them, saying, 'This is my body, which is given for you. Do this in remembrance of me'" (Luke 22:19).

9

even evidenced in the computation of years, for while the Gregorian calendar counts time forward and backward from the date of the birth of Jesus Christ, the Jewish calendar counts the years based on the date of creation according to rabbinic tradition. The computation of months also differs, as the Gregorian computation is solar whereas the Jewish calendar computes months based on the lunar cycle, set within a calendar that takes account of both lunar and solar cycles.

Christianity and Judaism each maintain distinct emphases of memory and anticipation within their respective visions of time. For Judaism, the sense of memory and historical consciousness is rooted in the narrative of the exodus from Egypt and entrance into the land of Israel, guided by the covenantal relationship between God and Israel. In contrast, the Christian sense of memory, while also understanding itself to be rooted in the narrative of the Hebrew Bible, is based primarily in the life, death, and resurrection of Jesus Christ.

A disparity is also seen in their eschatological visions: For Judaism, the final redemptive vision is of a messianic future yet to come. In contrast, the Christian eschatological vision is considered to be already partially inaugurated, growing out of the tension between the redemption already brought about by Christ and the fullness of the kingdom yet to come. At the same time, both traditions share a vision of earthly time in which the seven-day week serves as the building block of the calendar, bounded by the Sabbath in each tradition and enunciated within the weekly cycles of the Liturgy of the Hours and the Jewish daily services. Accordingly, this book examines the experience of time as it is shaped and expressed by Jewish and Christian liturgies, each reflecting a temporal narrative unique to its religious tradition.

The comparative study rests on the conviction that the experiential quality of liturgical performance and the complex content of that experience—as subjective, elusive, individual, or collective as it may be—has much to contribute to interreligious learning. Religious identity and belief take root in religious practice and ritual participation, and it follows that a comparative study of liturgical experience may yield unforeseen insights in interreligious learning. This comparative study is intended to provide a new path for understanding the relationships between Judaism and Christianity, based not on the familiar precedents of historical interaction or doctrinal comparison but on the liturgical experience of memory, hope, and time in each tradition.

METHODOLOGICAL CHALLENGES

The notion that the experience of time is transformed in liturgical performance may seem to be evident to the liturgical participant, yet there is nothing *self-evident* in this claim. It is only a sense. Likewise, the suggestion that the experience of time might be a vehicle for religious understanding rests on the experiential. Even in the highly structured ritual form of liturgy, the experience of time is just that: experience. It is inescapably subjective, and what is absolutely clear to experience is, paradoxically, seemingly impossible to demonstrate objectively.

The claim that the experience of time is transformed in liturgical enactment leads to a unique methodological challenge: liturgy speaks in a language that transcends the verbal and objective. The language of liturgical enactment is symbolic and performative and is more experiential than propositional. This language is not communicated by words alone but through physical gesture, vocalization, repetition, and an engaged involvement of the person acting in time. Because of the experiential nature of liturgical performance, the full range of its content cannot be objectively determined. Thus, its study defies standard systematic, textual, and historical methodologies. For this reason, a methodology that "reads" liturgy as it is *experienced*, grasping its complex extraverbal content, may be capable of shedding light on elements of faith inaccessible through the traditional propositional mode of theology.

The claim that the experience of time is altered through the liturgical performance of memory and hope is suggested indirectly in diverse sources and is touched on by a number of scholars.[9] Yet

---

[9] E.g., Jeremy S. Begbie, *Theology, Music and Time* (Cambridge, UK: Cambridge University Press, 2000); Abraham Joshua Heschel, *The Sabbath: Its Meaning for Modern Man* (New York: Farrar, Straus and Giroux, 2005); Yehuda Kurtzer, *Shuva: The Future of the Jewish Past* (Waltham, MA: Brandeis University Press, 2012); Bruce T. Morrill, *Anamnesis as Dangerous Memory:*

despite the fact that support for the thesis is implied in many sources, it has not been explored substantially. It remains a "sense" that people experience. The task of this book, then, is to draw together these various sources, each of which suggests that the perception of time is transformed in liturgy, and to construct from them a cohesive proposal on this particular function of liturgical performance.

The arguments presented here rest on a few claims about the nature of liturgical experience. This book claims, first, that experience matters. Experience is not just a by-product or reflection of liturgy. It is not secondary in relation to an ontological primacy of liturgy; liturgy is inherently experiential. Second, it claims that experience is not always and only individual. Experience is, by nature, subjective, but that does not preclude the possibility of shared or communal experience. Third, experience is real. That is, that which one experiences and perceives constitutes one's vision of reality; the experiential functions as the real.

This book challenges the notion that a comparative liturgical theology limited to a study of readily observable elements such as text, rite, history, and creed is sufficient to understand the full dimensions of liturgical experience. It departs from the standard methods of liturgical theology and engages in the paradoxical activity of observing that which cannot be isolated or directly apprehended. It seeks to uncover phenomena under the radar of the observable and measurable, with confidence that this phenomenon

Political and Liturgical Theology in Dialogue (Collegeville, MN: Liturgical Press, 2000); Franz Rosenzweig, *The Star of Redemption*, trans. William W. Hallo (Notre Dame, IN: University of Notre Dame Press, 1985); Alexander Schmemann, *Introduction to Liturgical Theology*, trans. Asheleigh E. Moorhouse (Crestwood, NY: St. Vladimir's Seminary Press, 1966); Alexander Schmemann, "Liturgy and Eschatology," *Sobornost* 7, no. 1 (1985): 6–14; Eliezer Schweid, *The Jewish Experience of Time: Philosophical Dimensions of the Jewish Holy Days*, trans. Amnon Hadary (Northvale, NJ: Jason Aronson, Inc., 2000); Joseph B. Soloveitchik, *Festival of Freedom: Essays on Pesah and the Haggadah*, ed. Joel B. Wolowesky and Reuven Ziegler (Jersey City, NJ: Ktav Publishing House, 2006); Yosef Hayim Yerushalmi, *Zakhor: Jewish History and Jewish Memory* (Seattle: University of Washington Press, 1982).

can indeed be perceived and understood, albeit through nonconventional methods.

POSTMODERNITY AND LITURGICAL REASONING

This book approaches the notion of the experience of time with a postmodern understanding of subjectivity. Following twentieth-century hermeneutics, it begins from the theory that experience is always a process of interpretation and that nothing can be perceived directly and without the mediation of culture, language, and symbols. The search for objective reality becomes a moot point, not due to any *a priori* conclusion about its existence, but because subjectivity mediates all experience.

The main task of postmodern thought has been to deconstruct the metaphysical foundations that were seen to undergird the intellectual structure of modernity. Whereas modernity had attempted to master and control, postmodernity attempts to deconstruct in order to reveal. For most postmodern thought, however, the "object" to be revealed by undoing the layers of modernity is not, in fact, objective. No foundational core remains intact after the postmodern unveiling of the structures of modernity.

From this perspective, faith seems to be an anomaly, if not absurd. Theology and the faith of which it speaks are understood to rest on the foundation of revelation in both the Jewish and Christian traditions, and the rejection of foundations and certitude proposed by postmodern philosophy poses a substantial obstacle to theology. If everything is contingent on yet another layer of shifting, ephemeral appearance, and if there is no certitude in an ultimate foundation of truth, then faith becomes a delusional activity, presupposing a core of reality where none exists and doomed to be nothing more than a reflection on contingent cultural constructions.

Postmodern thought, however, also invites a renewed turn toward the liturgical. In the postmodern intellectual atmosphere, metaphysical categories of "being" no longer hold as they once did, and we are invited to renew and rethink "doing." That is, we are invited to focus on religious experience rather than on religious truth claims and to contemplate processes of becoming rather than states of being. This leads us to liturgy, and even more specifically, to liturgical experience.

This book examines both Jewish and Christian liturgical experience, not as expressions of individual spirituality, but as communal phenomena shaped by religious traditions that function as dense cultural and semiotic systems. A similar approach is taken by the movement of Liturgical Reasoning, described by Steven Kepnes in *Jewish Liturgical Reasoning* as "a postcritical attempt to rebuild after postmodernity."[10] Inspired by George Lindbeck's cultural-linguistic theoretical framework, Kepnes claims, "Judaism is not based on spontaneous insights and personal 'religious' experiences. Judaism is not invented anew by every Jew but is already there, a given, objective system that individual Jews need to internalize."[11] The current study also builds on Lindbeck's theoretical foundations, seeing religions as structures that shape the experience and worldview of its participants similar to the way that language shapes the formulation and expression of thought.

This book recognizes the importance in today's world of a theology that looks to ritual and experience as resources, reading the language of liturgical performance rather than a type of theology predicated on the systematization of knowledge, the process of "mapping all knowledge onto a manipulable grid."[12] Cognizant of the bold declarations and invitations of postmodern thought, the current study turns toward the ritual and experiential, searching for the experiential phenomenon of the liturgical sense of time.

This turn toward the experiential and liturgical suggests that postmodern thought and theology are not as incompatible as they may initially seem. In the intellectual climate of postmodernity, where it seems that the rejection of metaphysics and the so-called deconstruction of the metanarrative have made theology irrelevant, new theologies and methodologies have emerged out of the

---

[10] Steven Kepnes, *Jewish Liturgical Reasoning* (New York: Oxford University Press, 2007), 9.

[11] Ibid.,15.

[12] Catherine Pickstock, *After Writing: On the Liturgical Consummation of Philosophy* (Oxford: Blackwell Publishers, 1998), xiii.

very elements that seemed to threaten. The leap that this book takes, namely, examining an elusive experiential phenomenon as it manifests in communal, tradition-bound ritual structures, tracing it to scriptural and philosophical roots and proposing that it alters the experience of time—all within a Jewish-Christian comparative context—is an unusual venture, but it joins the work of others exploring similar directions and identifies with those who find in a new wave of liturgical studies a renewal of theology after postmodernity.

MEASURING AND DEFINING TIME

Two types of time are addressed in this study, both of which involve the phenomenon of time as experienced from the human perspective. The first is the passage of the kind of time that is marked by the earth's cosmic cycles as the sun rises and sets and the seasons pass. The second is the concept of historical time, which involves notions of the distant past and future. The first is cyclical and evident in nature; the second is linear and requires the cognitive maintenance of a sense of past and future.[13] Yet the two are intimately related in liturgical experience. When the historical narratives of religious tradition are performed liturgically, the temporal cycles and schedules of prayer, measured by cosmic motion, interact with the historical notion of time, which is fed by the narratives of religious tradition and brought to life through memory and hope. Reflecting this interaction, this book does not strictly compartmentalize these two types of time but explores them together as they relate to each other.

Given the significance of time to Jewish and Christian tradition, both in its cyclical and historical expressions, it is not surprising that the development of time-measurement methods was crucial to early Jewish and Christian communities. Prior to the regular

---

[13] Paul Ricoeur develops a related distinction between cosmological time, experienced as a continuous flow of time, and phenomenological time, experienced through the concepts of the past, present, and future. Paul Ricoeur, *Time and Narrative*, vol. 3, trans. Kathleen Blamey and David Pellauer (Chicago: University of Chicago Press, 1988).

systematization of calendars, Jewish communities developed complex methods of calendrical computation to systematize liturgical celebrations. In later centuries, both Christians and Jews developed regulated times of daily prayer. The focus on timekeeping continued into the Middle Ages, as the development of early time-keeping devices, referred to under the blanket term "horologia," was largely centered in monasteries.

> It seems probable that the [modern] clock was invented by monks, because of the temporal regimentation of monastic life, but whether or not this is true, it certainly owed its development to the Catholic Church. The mathematics required to construct gear trains required a high level of education, which was provided only by the Church during that period. Also, the alarm mechanisms of the most sophisticated monastic water clocks were weight-driven devices that are the most likely forerunners of the clock's escapement.[14]

The maintenance of daily prayer services, at least in Christian monastic contexts, was highly influential in the development of timekeeping mechanisms.[15] The capacity to measure time with greater accuracy, therefore, increased in connection to liturgical

[14] Jo Ellen Barnett, *Time's Pendulum: The Quest to Capture Time—From Sundials to Atomic Clocks* (New York: Plenum Trade, 1998), 79. Eviatar Zerubavel also addresses the monastic development of timekeeping devices in "The Benedictine Ethic and the Modern Spirit of Scheduling: On Schedules and Social Organization," where he claims that the need for temporal regulation within Benedictine monasteries contributed to the development of the clock. Eviatar Zerubavel, "The Benedictine Ethic and the Modern Spirit of Scheduling: On Schedules and Social Organization," *Sociological Inquiry* 50 (1980): 157–69. Gerhard Dohrn-van Rossum criticizes this claim, however, in *History of the Hour: Clocks and Modern Temporal Orders*, noting that Zerubavel fails to distinguish between clocks and alarm devices, the latter of which were used by Benedictine monasteries to regulate the times of prayer. Gerhard Dohrn-van Rossum, *History of the Hour: Clocks and Modern Temporal Orders*, trans. Thomas Dunlap (Chicago: University of Chicago Press, 1996), 34.

[15] Barnett, *Time's Pendulum*, 80. Early clocks were also often found in cathedrals, and the earliest records of clocks are of those in cathedral towers. The first known public clock was in the tower of the church of St. Eustorgio in Milan in 1309, followed by other early mechanical clocks in cathedrals at Caen (1314), Norwich (1321), Florence (1325), London (1335), Milan (1335), Modena

practice. Here we see the close relationship between the measurement of cyclical cosmic time and the practice of contemplating the sequential time span of the religious narrative: as the monastic communities regulated the daily celebrations of the office, they engaged in the practice of communal memory of the religious narrative and hope in the eschatological future within a carefully measured passage of cyclical hours. An early precedence for the role of time measurement in the regulation of liturgical observance can also be seen in the Jewish tradition. In the first chapter of the Mishnah, the ancient rabbis discuss the appropriate times for saying the Shema and argue over whether the morning recitation of the prayer may be said once there is enough light to distinguish between blue and white, or between blue and green.[16] This passage evidences the necessity of measuring time to the proper observation of liturgical traditions in a time before the development of mechanical timekeeping devices.

Yet, what *is* this time that Jews and Christians have sought to chart and measure? Time is famously difficult to define; various proposed definitions are offered by physicists, philosophers, and psychologists, but none is conclusive. In Aristotelian physics, taken up again by medieval scholasticism, time was understood as a measure of motion. This theory was altered during the course of the seventeenth-century scientific revolution as time became seen as a universal background against which properties such as motion can be measured. In other words, time became separated from physical properties. As defined by Isaac Newton in his 1687 *Philosophiae Naturalis Principia Mathematica*, "Absolute, true, and mathematical time, of itself, and from its own nature, flows equably without relation to anything external, and by another name is called duration."[17]

For Newton, time was absolute and was the same from all points of observation. Yet, this was overturned in the twentieth century

---

(1343), Padua (1344), Monza (1347), Strasbourg (1352), Genoa (1354), Bologna (1356), Siena (1359), and Ferrara (1362).

[16] Mishnah Berachot, 1.2.

[17] Iaian Nicolson, "Mutable Time," in *The Book of Time*, ed. John Grant and Colin Wilson (North Pomfret, VT: Westbridge Books, 1980), 157.

by Albert Einstein, who began yet another revolution in the understanding of time. Einstein challenged the Newtonian concept of absolute, objective time by claiming that the objective observation of time is impossible. That is, because we cannot escape observations of time based on our position in space, we are able only to observe the appearance of time. Due to this condition, time can only be determined in the relationship between the observer and the universe.[18]

In a letter of condolence to his friend Michele Besso, Einstein wrote, "People like us, who believe in physics, know that the distinction between past, present, and future is only a stubbornly persistent illusion."[19] In fact, contemporary physicists also find that "the laws of nature do not appear to prohibit the possibility of time running backwards, and the reason why time should appear to us to flow uniquely in one direction is by no means obvious; indeed the whole concept of the 'flow' of time seems to be highly unsatisfactory."[20]

The idea of time as a linear progression relies on a particular mental state. Time is measured in relation to space and motion. The past and the future appear in the domain of the imagination, held into two distinct camps not by any rigid laws of temporality but by our perception.[21] Here we reach the central focus of this work. A state of temporal awareness is required for the mind to preserve the idea of time as linear and evenly measured; when this awareness shifts, the perception of time is altered too. It is no stretch, then, to claim that ritual performance, and Jewish and Christian liturgical performance in particular, contributes to a transformation in the perception of time. The past and future are

---

[18] Abhay Ashtekar, "Space and Time: From Antiquity to Einstein and Beyond," *Resonance* 11, no. 9 (2006): 4–19.

[19] Pierre Speziali, ed., *Einstein-Besso Correspondence* (Paris: Hermann, 1972), 32.

[20] Nicolson, "Mutable Time," 157.

[21] Gerald M. Edelman, *Wider than the Sky: A Revolutionary View of Consciousness* (London: Penguin, 2005), 102–3. Edelman, a Nobel Prize–winning neuroscientist, defines higher-order consciousness as "having the awareness of the past, the future and the self."

already conceptually present in ritual acts of memory and anticipation, and as the temporal orientation of the liturgical community shifts in the performance of the religious narrative, so too does the perception of time.

DISINTEGRATION AND INTEGRATION: CREATING LITURGICAL TIME

The idea of time requires maintaining the concept of the past, present, and future. Yet temporal consciousness can also function to disintegrate the boundaries between those temporal markers. When time is perceived in the mind and held onto through memory and anticipation, its measured chronology tends to become less regular. Certain events of the past hold more weight than others and seem to expand, taking up a larger portion of remembered time. Or, a projected future event may be anticipated to such a degree that it seems to dwell already in the memory. In this way, sequential time and the distinctions between the temporal markers of the past, present, and future have a tendency to stretch, condense, and disintegrate within the imagination.

It is my contention, developed in the following chapters, that this *disintegration* of temporal boundaries is actually an *integration* of time. The disintegration of past, present, and future creates a special quality of reintegrated time. In this new integration of time, the temporal markers of past, present, and future interpenetrate. The past bears influence on the present and the future, and likewise, the anticipated future informs the remembered past as the vision of the eschatological future exerts an interpretive influence on the time that precedes it.[22] This is counterintuitive, for in the

---

[22] This concept is clarified by Egyptologist Jan Assmann's concept of mnemohistory and the permeability of the present and the past in the memory: "Unlike history proper, mnemohistory is concerned not with the past as such but only with the past as it is remembered. It surveys the story-lines of tradition, the webs of intertextuality, the diachronic continuities and discontinuities of reading the past. . . . Mnemohistory is reception theory applied to history. But 'reception' is not to be understood here merely in the narrow sense of transmitting and receiving. The past is not simply 'received' by the present. The present is 'haunted' by the past and the past is modeled, invented,

simple linear vision of time, the past may influence the present, but the reverse cannot be possible. Yet this work argues that the religious vision of time, first introduced in the Hebrew Bible and then developed in Jewish and Christian traditions, not only involves but also requires a perceived interpenetration of the past, present, and future.

The liturgical enactment of memory transcends the simple recollection of chronological events of the past and allows the community to engage in an activity that draws the past into the present. At the same time, this engagement with memory is oriented toward a vision of the eschatological future in which the present is known and understood in relation to the promises of the anticipated future. Thus, through liturgy, the present time is envisioned to be impacted by the past and future, ritually remembered, and anticipated. In this unique quality of time, the distinction between past, present, and future is made porous, or even collapsed, in the perception and experience of the participants. Religious time is fluid; it reaches from the distant past to the distant future and flows in many directions and crosscurrents on its way, and it is in liturgical performance that the disintegration and subsequent reintegration of time into a new present is experienced most fully.

---

reinvented, and reconstructed by the present." Jan Assmann, *Moses the Egyptian: The Memory of Egypt in Western Monotheism* (Cambridge, MA: Harvard University Press, 1997), 8–9.

Chapter 2

The Elusiveness of Experience

We ought to experience time simultaneously in its two dimensions, as recollection and anticipation, as review and meditation, and as quest and search. Time is the experiential memory that reaches out for the as yet non-real future.

—Rabbi Joseph B. Soloveitchik[1]

LITURGY AS *THEOLOGIA PRIMA*

Liturgical studies are often approached through the methods of historical research, with attention to the development of liturgical rites and texts over time in social and political contexts. While textual and historical studies are crucial elements of liturgical studies, they do not in every case have the final word; liturgical texts, rites, and history alone are unable to sufficiently communicate the depths of meaning in liturgy. This textual trend is prevalent in studies of both Christian and Jewish liturgy, and liturgical scholar Uri Ehrlich comments on this tendency in the latter:

> But this primary focus on liturgical formulas . . . ultimately leads to the neglect of additional aspects of prayer. A tacit assumption shared by these studies is that the main aspect of the prayer phenomenon, and in many instances its totality, lies in textual formulas. Whether explicit or implicit, this assumption narrows the scope of

[1] Joseph B. Soloveitchik, *Festival of Freedom: Essays on Pesah and the Haggadah*, ed. Joel B. Wolowesky and Reuven Ziegler (Jersey City, NJ: Ktav Publishing House, 2006), 177.

research and, in some respects, even distorts the research topic itself.[2]

The current study challenges liturgists to develop a way to handle "prayer qua prayer, not just prayer qua literature," echoing the words of Jewish liturgical theologian Lawrence Hoffman; i.e., to address phenomena which emerge in the performance of prayer.[3] The phenomenon of a liturgically transformed sense of time is *connected* to liturgical history and texts but is not *contained* entirely in these resources.

Catholic liturgical theologian Aidan Kavanagh argues that real liturgical theology happens not in books or universities but in the growth of liturgy, in the act of liturgical performance by communities in prayer: "This is how liturgies grow. Their growth is a function of adjustment to deep change caused in the assembly by its being brought regularly to the brink of chaos in the presence of the living God. It is the adjustment which is theological in all this. I hold that it is theology being born, theology in the first instance. It is what tradition has called *theologia prima*.[4] For Kavanagh, theology arises through ritual performance. He identifies a rupture that occurs in the fabric of reality, as perceived by the liturgical community, when it is brought to a liminal place of spiritual transformation. The community must then adjust; that is, it must navigate a path between this "brink of chaos" and the regular mode of life. This is where theology happens.

This concept is borrowed by Richard D. McCall, who categorizes methods of liturgical theology by differentiating between *theology of the liturgy* and *theology from the liturgy*. He uses the phrase *theology of the liturgy* to refer to a liturgical theology, characteristic of scholasticism, that involves "a systematic analysis of sacraments

---

[2] Uri Ehrlich, *The Nonverbal Language of Prayer*, trans. Dena Ordan (Tubingen, Germany: Mohr Siebeck, 2004), 2–3.

[3] Lawrence A. Hoffman, *Beyond the Text: A Holistic Approach to Liturgy* (Bloomington, IN: Indiana University Press, 1989), 6.

[4] Aidan Kavanagh, *On Liturgical Theology: The Hale Memorial Lectures of Seabury-Western Theological Seminary* (New York: Pueblo Publishing Company, 1984), 74.

derived from prior systematic reflection."[5] McCall identifies the second type of liturgical theology, *theology from the liturgy*, as a discipline that uses liturgy itself as the primary source of theology, or *theologia prima*. In this method, "actual Christian worship, as enfleshed in the rites of the Church, is the primary way in which Christians *do* theology."[6]

Maintaining that the meaning of liturgical performance exceeds its verbal content and that its full significance comes to be in the enactment of liturgy, this project favors the second method. Rather than reading only the liturgical text, it reads the "text" of liturgical experience. This book, however, is not in itself theological in the sense that Kavanagh discusses. It does not navigate from a position on the "brink of chaos in the presence of the living God," but rather, explores that brink as others have experienced it. It examines liturgical experience and the theology that implicitly flows from it and makes secondary, objective observations about primary, subjective experience.

Recognizing that the search for meaning can sometimes obscure the essentially performative nature of liturgy, much liturgical theology in recent decades has expressed a preference for what liturgy "does" rather than what liturgy "means."[7] The search for a theological meaning abstracted from the embodied performance of liturgy has become less relevant to the nature of liturgy than an examination of liturgy as a lived, experienced, performance of "doing." Behind this notion is the concept that liturgy communicates a process of becoming, and therefore, it expresses "doing" rather than the "being" addressed in metaphysics.

---

[5] Richard D. McCall, "Liturgical Theopoetic: The Acts of God in the Act of Liturgy," *Worship* 71, no. 5 (S 1997): 400.

[6] McCall, "Liturgical Theopoetic," 400.

[7] David W. Fagerberg, *What Is Liturgical Theology? A Study in Methodology* (Collegeville, MN: Liturgical Press, 1992); Kavanagh, *On Liturgical Theology*; Hoffman, *Beyond the Text*; Jean-Luc Marion, *God without Being: Hors-Texte* (Chicago: University of Chicago Press, 1991); Richard McCall, *Do This: Liturgy as Performance* (Notre Dame, IN: University of Notre Dame Press, 2007); Catherine Pickstock, *After Writing: On the Liturgical Consummation of Philosophy* (Oxford: Blackwell Publishers, 1998).

The current study shares this preference for a liturgical theology which is "'description' more than 'definition' for it is, above all, a search for words and concepts adequate to and expressive of the living experience."[8] It eschews conclusions about the definitive meaning of liturgy and rejects the notion that a unified theory can be found concerning the nature of God, prayer, or the theological relationship between Christianity and Judaism. Rather, it very simply observes what liturgy "does" and traces the effect that liturgical performance has on the way that its participants experience and envision time.

These concepts have a number of implications for this project. First, while a study of liturgy that aims to study "prayer qua prayer" may begin with a textual study, it must also move beyond it. The phenomenon of liturgical experience, particularly the experience of time in liturgy, cannot be found in texts alone. Second, a methodology that explores the performance of liturgy, as in the category of *theology from the liturgy*, is better suited to the purposes of this study than a *theology of the liturgy* that reads into liturgy conclusions gained from systematic theology, for this book examines experiential phenomena of liturgical performance. Finally, the real question raised by liturgy is not about what liturgy means but about what liturgy does. For this book, this implies that the transformation of the perception of time in liturgical performance must be examined through a reflection on prayer as it is prayed and liturgy as it is performed and experienced.

ISOLATING THE NATURE OF EXPERIENCE

The notion that meaning is not inherent and fully formed in the texts and rubrics of liturgy alone but is developed and reaches its full depth in liturgical experience points to the significance of the experience of the participants in liturgical theology. This book, in short, claims that the meaning of liturgy comes into fullness in the experience, or subjectivity, of the liturgical community. The following discussion visits theological, anthropological, and philosophi-

---

[8] Alexander Schmemann, "Theology and Liturgy," in *Church, World, and Mission* (Crestwood, NY: St. Vladimir's Seminary Press, 1979), 133–24.

cal treatments of the category of experience and constructs an understanding of liturgical experience as a dialogue between the liturgical subject's primary, individual experience and the formative influence of religious tradition.

The meaning of the term "experience," however, is open to many varied understandings, necessitating a clarification of the use of the term in this study. A good place to begin is with a definition offered in the introduction to a volume entitled *On Sharing Religious Experience: Possibilities of Interfaith Mutuality*, a collection of essays that grapples with the inherent subjectivity of religious experience in general and with the difficulty of attempting to transcend one's hermeneutical circle in order to let experience be shared, particularly across the borders of religious traditions: "'Experience' concerns the subject's conscious perception of reality through which the subject makes sense of, actively responds to, and undergoes reality."[9] At the center of this definition is the notion that reality is given shape by its perception.

The concept of reality here refers neither to a fixed state of the world nor to the experience of an uninterpreted, raw reaction to an objective situation. Rather, both experience and the vision of reality are formed in a constant, reciprocal flow of interpretation in which the vision of reality comes into being through experience, and experience itself is interpreted even as it occurs.

This notion is discussed by anthropologist Clifford Geertz, who holds that experience is never "mere experience," i.e., raw or uninterpreted, but is "an experience," i.e., an "interpretive replay [of an experienced event] as we recollect it to ourselves and recount it to others."[10] Observing the embedded interpretive activity within all experience, Geertz writes, "All experience is construed experience,

---

[9] Hendrick M. Vroom, "Can Religious Experience be Shared? Introduction to the Theme 'Sharing Religious Experience,'" in *On Sharing Religious Experience: Possibilities of Interfaith Mutuality*, ed. Jerald D. Gort, Hendrik M. Vroom, Rein Fernhout, and Anton Wessels (Grand Rapids, MI: Eerdmans, 1992), 6.

[10] Clifford Geertz, "Making Experience, Authoring Selves," in *The Anthropology of Experience*, ed. Victor Turner and Edward Bruner (Urbana: University of Illinois Press, 1986), 380.

and the symbolic forms in terms of which it is construed thus determine . . . . its intrinsic nature."[11] This is in line with much postmodern thought, which holds that the concept of a foundational, unchanging reality is an illusion. The experience of that which is perceived as the real inevitably passes through the filter of perception, and because of this, knowledge cannot be gained in an absolute state, freed from the interpretive lens through which it is perceived. Everything is mediated by the filter of subjectivity, and the reflexivity of the subject is such that no "pure" knowledge of reality is possible.

This means that the fundamental "truth" of reality is irrelevant not because it doesn't matter but because it categorically cannot be known except through the mediation of subjectivity. This understanding does not assert that a foundational reality cannot exist, nor does it challenge the validity of the idea of truth; it claims only that reality cannot be directly perceived without mediation. Within this hermeneutical circle, primary reality cannot be extracted from the perception of reality, in which nothing escapes the mediation of symbols.

These general theoretical positions on perception and mediation bear on the perception of time too, for the perception of time is an integral part of the mediated perception of reality. If no foundation of reality can be apprehended directly, then no unchanging structure of time can be directly observed without the mediating filter of one's perception. Essentially, if reality appears to be fluid, so too does time.

Recognizing the inescapable mediation of symbols and the hermeneutical circle of subjectivity is key for an investigation into the meaning of experience, for experience is reality forming in the most basic sense. Experience shapes reality because it shapes the *experience of reality*, and we cannot pass beyond the experience of reality to perceive an ultimate or unmediated reality. Experience, then, is the medium through which reality is formed and reformu-

---

[11] Clifford Geertz, "Person, Time, and Conduct in Bali," in *The Interpretation of Cultures: Selected Essays* (New York: Basic Books, 1973), 405.

lated, and this coming-to-be is as fluid as the changing perception of the subject.

As discussed above, religious experience shares the basic traits of general experience but introduces the element of the transcendent. While experience concerns the processing and creating of a vision of reality, specifically religious experience is the processing of reality in relation to the transcendent, communicated through tradition. This allows for a particular kind of interpretation of reality, in which the metanarratives of the religious tradition interact with immediate experience.

Geertz discusses the reality-shaping function of religious experience in the context of ritual, which he claims allows that which is experienced firsthand and that which is religiously "imagined" to intersect:

> For it is in ritual—that is, consecrated behavior—that this conviction that religious conceptions are veridical and that religious directives are sound is somehow generated. It is in some sort of ceremonial form—even if that form be hardly more than the recitation of a myth, the consultation of an oracle, or the decoration of a grave—that the moods and motivations which sacred symbols induce in men and the general conceptions of the order of existence which they formulate for men meet and reinforce one another. In a ritual, the world as lived and the world as imagined, fused under the agency of a single set of symbolic forms, turn out to be the same world, producing thus that idiosyncratic transformation in one's sense of reality.[12]

In specifically religious experience, reality is not only perceived through the lens of subjectivity but also shaped by the concept of a transcendent "other." Whereas experience in general is understood to be the process of interpreting the perception of reality, the introduction of an "other" in religious experience creates an atmosphere of interacting influences in the perception of reality. For monotheistic traditions, the relation to transcendence is identified as a

---

[12] Clifford Geertz, "Religion as a Cultural System," in *The Interpretation of Cultures: Selected Essays* (New York: Basic Books, 1973), 112.

relationship with God, which implies that religious experience is the processing and negotiating of a relationship. The interpretation of reality then becomes a dialogical process of negotiating reality through the conversation between one's immediate experience and religious metanarrative. This lends multidimensionality to the way that the world is perceived. It is negotiated within a relational structure and no longer created by individual perception alone. Rather, reality is now created through a dialogical push and pull between the self and the "other" through the structure of religious tradition.

In religious experience, the subject is confronted with the transcendent "other." This encounter is a meeting of different horizons, to borrow Hans Georg Gadamer's concept of the fusion of horizons. Gadamer identifies the fusion of horizons as the process through which understanding occurs, as the horizons of the reader and text meet.[13] The present study borrows Gadamer's notion of horizons and adapts it to represent the encounter between the liturgical subject and the religious tradition. In the present context, the two horizons are not that of the reader and the text, as in the Gadamerian context, but that of the liturgical participant and the transcendent, mediated through religious tradition. In this meeting of horizons, the subject encounters a force of otherness that challenges everything to redefinition. The encounter with the transcendent acts as a destabilizing force in the processing of reality, introducing an element of otherness that shifts the course of the formulation of reality. Like a meeting of thunder clouds, this meeting of disjunctive horizons makes religious experience a site of rupture.

The rupture created in this encounter introduces an element of volatility. As the subject shifts and adapts to the worldview communicated by religious tradition, the perception of reality, which had previously seemed self-evident to the subject, encounters a set of new elements. In this rupture, the subject's perception shifts in a state of what some social scientists call liminality.[14] The dialogical

---

[13] Hans Georg Gadamer, *Truth and Method*, trans. Joel Weinsheimer and Donald G. Marshall (New York: Crossroad, 1991), 306.

[14] See Turner, *Ritual Process: Structure and Anti-Structure* (New York: Aldine, 1969). The understanding of liminality in ritual studies is explored in more depth later in this chapter.

encounter between the subject and the transcendent becomes a site of transformation as the encounter with another worldview alters the perception of reality.

This process of rupture, liminality, and transformation is essential to the phenomenon of the liturgical experience of time, for with the transformation of the perception of reality comes a shift in the perception of time. The perception of time is thus formed by the encounter with the transcendent "other," communicated through the liturgical performance of faith.

THE MEDIATION OF TRADITION

In the dialogical relationship of religious experience, the transcendent "other" is communicated through the mediation of tradition. Religious tradition provides the symbolic framework through which the transcendent is perceived. The framework of tradition acts as a language, giving shape to the experience of transcendence and enunciating it within a form capable of being transmitted.

The role of tradition in mediating religious experience is especially evident in Judaism and Christianity, in which even the elements considered to communicate the most immediate experience of God are in actuality mediated by tradition. Consider as an example the narrative of the revelation on Mt. Sinai in which Moses encounters God. The Israelites fear direct encounter themselves and beg Moses not to let God speak to them directly, for fear that they will die (Exod 20:19); even the voice of God cautions that those who look upon him will die (Exod 19:21). Moses communicates the divine revelation, and it is his communication that becomes authoritative. He acts as the mediator, and in doing so, becomes the voice of tradition. The transmission through tradition happens on a number of levels: first, through the narrative of God's communication to Moses; second, through the narrative of Moses' retelling to the community; third, through the process of oral and textual transmission of the narrative; fourth, through the process of canonization which establishes the texts as scriptural and authoritative; fifth, through the interpretation and celebration of the texts by religious communities, and so forth.

The notion of tradition may be defined in many ways, and for the purposes of this exploration, a definition offered by Gerhard

Oberhammer provides a good place to begin. "What exactly is the phenomenon of tradition? For the moment suffice it to say that tradition is the process of the "mythologization" of "transcendence," a process which obtains supra-individual validity insofar as it comprises the adoption by others of the testimony of an actual personal experience of transcendence as "mythical," i.e., as an articulate pattern of one's own experience of the transcendent."[15]

Oberhammer identifies tradition as the process through which the experience of the transcendent becomes transmitted, a process he calls mythologization. This process of mythologization occurs when a personal experience of the transcendent becomes normative for the religious community and takes on the status of myth. In this process, a religious experience, i.e., an encounter between a subject and the transcendent "other," becomes foundational for a community. It is adopted by the community as authentic and is thus transformed from a purely individual experience into one with communal significance. The perception of reality is now formed not only by individual experiences but also by collectively acknowledged, mythologized experience. As the experience becomes foundational for the community, its meaning becomes systematized within the framework of the tradition.

A shift occurs as the experience is transferred from the individual to the communal: The mythologized religious experience begins to act as a pattern for the personal religious experience of each person within the tradition. The phenomenon of tradition is thus comprised of a process through which the individual experience informs communal experience, and in exchange, the individual becomes formed by the communal. The mythologization of religious experience acts as a formative influence, imprinting the individuals within the community with the stamp of tradition.

Sociologist Daniele Hervieu-Leger argues that religious tradition, experienced as a "continuity of the lineage of believers," is at

---

[15] Gerhard Oberhammer, "Hermeneutics of Religious Experience," in *On Sharing Religious Experience: Possibilities of Interfaith Mutuality*, ed. Jerald D. Gort, Hendrik M. Vroom, Rein Fernhout, and Anton Wessels (Grand Rapids, MI: Eerdmans, 1992).

the core of religious belief: "At the source of all religious belief, as we have seen, there is belief in the continuity of the lineage of believers. This continuity transcends history. It is affirmed and manifested in the essentially religious act of recalling a past that gives meaning to the present and contains the future."[16] This continuity, which is in essence religious tradition, is here identified with the religious memory of the past and anticipation of the future. The ritual acts of memory and anticipation shape and give meaning to the past, present, and future, and in doing so, fortify and reify the continuity of religious tradition.

Within ritual studies, the notion of tradition has been defined in relation to the interplay of stability and mutability. As contemporary ritual theorist Catherine Bell notes in *Ritual Theory, Ritual Practice*, some scholars of ritual studies consider tradition to be categorically conservative and unchanging, while others see tradition as an interplay between unchanging and evolving elements. "Many scholars designate as 'tradition' that which does not change; others attempt to combine change and continuity within the notion of tradition. Taking the latter position, Paul Mus, [Stanley] Tambiah, and J. C. Heesterman have all advanced an understanding of tradition as constituted by a paradox, an 'inner conflict' so to speak, between an ideal atemporal order (unchanging structure) on the one hand, and the profane world of temporal change and compromise (changing history) on the other."[17]

This understanding of tradition as constituted by a tension between timelessness and temporal change bears great relevance to the study of the perception of time and its formation through tradition. If, as the latter scholars suggest, the phenomenon of tradition consists of a tension between change and unchangeability, between time and timelessness, then that tension is held as well within the religious imagination. The conflict between the ideal of an unchanging eternal order and the temporal world of change is such

---

[16] Daniele Hervieu-Leger, *Religion as a Chain of Memory* (New Brunswick, NJ: Rutgers University Press, 2000), 125.

[17] Catherine Bell, *Ritual Theory, Ritual Practice* (New York: Oxford University Press, 1992), 119.

that the tension it weaves becomes the fabric of tradition. Using the analogy of a loom, if the concept of an eternal unchanging order is represented by the vertical threads and the changing world by the horizontal threads, then tradition would consist of the woven fabric itself, built of the tension between the warp and woof. This suggests that tradition is formed through the experience of the passing of time. Religious experience, mediated by tradition, is thus entirely imbued with the experience of the passing of time and the tension between change and the ideal of the eternal.

THE CULTURAL-LINGUISTIC FORMATION OF EXPERIENCE

The methodology developed here, particularly as it concerns the formation of the individual by the framework of religious tradition, is indebted to George Lindbeck's cultural-linguistic theory, which proposes that religions function like cultures and languages in shaping a person's understanding. The cultural-linguistic model serves as a basic theoretical foundation for the methodology developed in this book inasmuch as it addresses the process by which a person's experience and understanding of reality are formed by religious tradition. The understanding of religion operative in this study is also indebted to Geertz, whose work was influential to Lindbeck as well.

In *The Nature of Doctrine*, Lindbeck proposes a set of theoretical models for understanding how religion and doctrines function. His cultural-linguistic theory proposes that belief and identity are formed through the structures of religious tradition, which are as all-encompassing and formative as language. Summarizing the cultural-linguistic model, he writes, "In the account that I shall give, religions are seen as comprehensive interpretive schemes, usually embodied in myths or narratives and heavily ritualized, which structure human experience and understanding of self and world."[18]

Lindbeck's theory acts as a theoretical starting point in this project, which begins with the notion that religious tradition shapes

---

[18] George Lindbeck, *The Nature of Doctrine: Religion and Theology in a Postliberal Age* (Philadelphia: Westminster, 1984), 32.

subjectivity. He claims that religions resemble cultures and languages in the way they exert a formative influence on subjectivity, shaping the experience of the person. He writes, "Like a culture or language, it is a communal phenomenon that shapes the subjectivities of individuals rather than being primarily a manifestation of those subjectivities."[19]

Lindbeck defines the cultural-linguistic theory in contrast to two other main theoretical understandings about the nature of doctrines, namely, the propositional-cognitivist and the experiential-expressivist models. In the propositional-cognitivist model, "doctrines function as informative propositions or truth claims about objective realities."[20] In this model, truth is conceived propositionally, and statements of religious truth are believed to have an epistemological and ontological correspondence to reality. That is, this model attributes a correspondence between "the structure of knowing and the structure of the known."[21] The experiential-expressivist model, in contrast, "interprets doctrines as noninformative and nondiscursive symbols of inner feelings, attitudes, or existential orientations."[22] In this model, the meanings of a religious tradition may change while the formulation of doctrines remains unchanged. Likewise, if doctrines change, the meanings may remain the same. As Lindbeck explains, "The general principle is that insofar as doctrines function as nondiscursive symbols, they are polyvalent in import and therefore subject to changes of meaning or even to a total loss of meaningfulness."[23]

One of the main differences between the cultural-linguistic model and the experiential-expressivist model is the way that each understands the causal relationship between internal experience and the external form of a religion. While the experiential-expressivist model understands internal experience to shape doctrine, the cultural-linguistic model understands the causality to be

[19] Ibid., 33.
[20] Ibid., 16.
[21] Ibid., 47.
[22] Ibid., 16.
[23] Ibid., 17.

reversed. In the cultural-linguistic model, inner experiences are derived from the external structure of religion and formed by its doctrinal system.[24]

The theoretical framework of this book is more closely related to the cultural-linguistic than to the experiential-expressivist model, but it is nuanced in such a way that it contains elements of both. The methodology developed here examines liturgical experience, but unlike the experiential-expressivist model, which sees experience to be an expression of a spiritual impulse springing directly from the heart, this book understands religious experience to be shaped by tradition; the cultural linguistic theory helps define the relationship of individuals to their received tradition.

The double causality in which belief shapes experience and experience shapes belief is reminiscent of the dual meaning of the ancient adage *lex orandi, lex credendi*.[25] The adage can be interpreted in reverse ways, meaning either that liturgy forms belief, or that belief forms liturgy.[26] Yet the adage most commonly refers to liturgy's formation of belief, and it is this meaning that has endured.

Similarly, in the theoretical framework developed here, religious experience is shaped by tradition, yet it also exists in an interactive dynamic with the structure of the religious tradition. The subjectivity of experience takes on a shape that conforms to the tradition in which it arises, and yet it also contributes to the shape of tradition. Religious experience enriches tradition with multiple shades of meaning, all the while being formed by the structures of meaning communicated by the established tradition.

[24] Ibid., 34.

[25] Originally formulated by Prosper of Aquitaine as *ut legem credendi lex statuat supplicandi*, in its original context the adage was directed against semi-pelagians and referred specifically to liturgical intercessions. In later usage the phrase was reworded as *lex orandi, lex credendi* and took on a broader meaning, signifying the more general idea that belief is formed through liturgy. See Paul De Clerck, "'Lex Orandi, Lex Credendi': The Original Sense and Historical Avatars of an Equivocal Adage," *Studia Liturgica* 24 (1994): 178–200.

[26] This dual meaning was taken up in the 1947 encyclical *Mediator Dei*, which rejected the absolute and unequivocal formation of belief by prayer, favoring a reciprocal relationship between liturgy and doctrine.

This book addresses the experience of time with a postmodern, hermeneutical understanding of subjectivity. The notion that liturgical performance influences the experience of time rests upon an interpretive lens attuned to the formative influence of subjectivity on the perceived world. In other words, it is based on the concept that time is experienced only as it relates to the subject who perceives it. In this understanding, time takes shape in our perception of it as it relates to our experience.

The turn to subjectivity problematizes the study of religions, however, particularly interreligious learning and comparative religious studies. The study of religions can no longer approach a religion as an objective system capable of being fully observed and understood; rather, the study of religions must be hermeneutical, attuned to the layers of meaning embedded in experience and interpretation. A hermeneutical awareness that recognizes the formative influence of subjectivity on perception and interpretation may also lead to an increased respect for the alterity of the "other," whose experience is by nature incommensurable with one's own. Thus, if the study of religions hopes to maintain integrity with the nature of its subject, a degree of untranslatability must be acknowledged.

The impenetrability of religions to objective observation and complete understanding has been increasingly recognized. This approach, however, can also lead to a sense of the futility of understanding the "other." Comparative theologian Catherine Cornille notes this trend: "Whereas early scholars of religion were quite optimistic about the possibility of understanding the religious other, this optimism has waned through the course of the twentieth century, turning to a radical pessimism fed by postmodern notions of the fundamental incommensurability of religions and cultures and the radical alterity and incomprehensibility of the other."[27]

One of the central proponents of the notion of the untranslatability of religious truths is Lindbeck. A number of comparative

[27] Catherine Cornille, "Introduction," in *Interreligious Hermeneutics*, ed. Catherine Cornille and Christopher Conway (Eugene, OR: Cascade Books, 2010), xiii.

theologians have pointed to the limitations of Lindbeck's theory, arguing that it places overly severe restrictions on the possibility of interreligious understanding.[28] Although the methodology and general philosophical underpinning of the present study borrow heavily from Lindbeck's work, it joins the voices of those who argue that religious identity is often less bounded than Lindbeck proposes, allowing for a greater possibility of understanding through and into other religious traditions or systems. This study proposes that the experience of time is shaped by the metanarratives of religious tradition, but it also maintains that religious identity and experience are not necessarily static or firmly bounded. The mediating structure of tradition is experienced and interpreted differently by each person and may be continually reevaluated and reinterpreted in each new context. Furthermore, religious traditions and narratives are themselves porous, evolving in relation to other narratives and situations, both religious and secular. Particularly in today's pluralistic world, religious traditions and religious identities are in continuous negotiation with other worldviews and characterized more by evolution than by stasis.

[28] One example comes from constructive theologian Jeannine Hill Fletcher, who argues that Lindbeck's theory presupposes an unlikely fixity of religious identity, and that religious identity tends to be more hybrid than Lindbeck assumes. See Jeannine Hill Fletcher, "Religious Pluralism in an Era of Globalization: The Making of Modern Religious Identity," *Theological Studies* 69, no. 2 (2008): 402; Jeannine Hill Fletcher, "Shifting Identity: The Contribution of Feminist Thought to Theologies of Religious Pluralism," *Journal of Feminist Studies in Religion* (2003): 7. A related critique is raised by the Belgian theologian Marianne Moyaert, who argues that all religions are not irreducibly incommensurable and untranslatable, as Lindbeck claims. She juxtaposes Lindbeck's theory with Paul Ricoeur's notion of linguistic hospitality and argues that neither our selves nor our religious identities are so static as not to shift and evolve in the process of learning about and communicating with the religious other. See Marianne Moyaert, "Absorption or Hospitality: Two Approaches to the Tension between Identity and Alterity," in *Interreligious Hermeneutics*, ed. Catherine Cornille and Christopher Conway (Eugene, OR: Cascade Books, 2010), 68–69; 82–88; See also Marianne Moyaert, "Postliberalism, Religious Diversity and Interreligious Dialogue: A Critical Analysis of Lindbeck's Fiduciary Interests," *Journal of Ecumenical Studies* 47, no. 1 (2012): 64–87.

In conclusion, the methodology developed in this chapter arises from a theoretical position concerning the way in which experiences are formed and the way they function in the perception of reality. Essentially, this chapter is about how experience *forms* and how it is *formed*. Experience shapes the perception of reality, but experience is not direct and unmediated by culture and language. Rather, experience itself is shaped by the cultural worldview in which it occurs.

In the context of religious experience, the worldview that informs the perception of reality is the body of religious tradition. Tradition is comprised of narratives, collective memory, ethical guidelines, embodied practices, and so on, yet tradition also comprises the very atmosphere in which a person lives and acts. Tradition gives us a collective memory, and "of its essence fluid and evolutionary, collective memory functions as a regulator of individual memory at any one moment."[29]

Given that the real is always and only mediated through the lens of perception and the mediation of symbols, liturgical experience forms the way that reality is perceived. In liturgical performance, the participant formulates a vision of reality and negotiates an understanding of the nature of time; this is what allows the liturgical experience of time to be unique. And, as tradition informs the experience of time, the liturgically created vision of time in turn enriches and adds to the tradition.

[29] Hervieu-Leger, *Religion as a Chain of Memory*, 124. Hervieu-Leger's work builds on that of Maurice Halbwachs, who observes "Often we deem ourselves the originators of thoughts and ideas, feelings and passions, actually inspired by some group. Our agreement with those about us is so complete that we vibrate in unison, ignorant of the real source of the vibrations. How often do we present, as deeply held convictions, thoughts borrowed from a newspaper, book, or conversation? . . . We are unaware that we are but an echo." Maurice Halbwachs, *The Collective Memory*, trans. Francis J. Ditter and Vida Yazdi Ditter (New York: Harper and Row, 1980), 45.

Part 2

In Their Words

Chapter 3

Be-Khol Dor Va-Dor:
In Every Generation

In every generation a person is obligated to regard himself as if he had come out of Egypt, as it is said: "You shall tell your child on that day, it is because of this that the Lord did for me when I left Egypt." (Ex. 13:8) The Holy One, blessed be He, redeemed not only our ancestors from Egypt, but He redeemed also us with him, as it is said: "It was us that He brought out from there, so that He might bring us to give us the land that He swore to our ancestors."

—Passover Haggadah[1]

INTRODUCTION

This chapter is the product of a series of conversations reflecting on personal experiences of liturgy and time. A select group of people, each of whom has a rich practice of Jewish prayer and ritual observance, participated in this study, offering to share their own experiences of memory, hope, and the experience of time in their liturgical practices. In the context of interviews, each lasting an hour or longer, the participants contemplated questions that often addressed issues they had not previously considered in the context of liturgical experience. Responding to questions such as "Do you find that your liturgical practice affects the way you experience the duration and quality of hours in the day?" "Have you experienced in liturgy anything that you would call communal

---

[1] Translation of the Passover Haggadah, Joseph B. Soloveitchik, *The Seder Night: An Exalted Evening: The Passover Haggadah*, ed. Menachem Genak (New York: Orthodox Union Press, 2009), 101.

memory, and if so, in what specific liturgical contexts?" and "Do you find that your liturgical practice gives you a sense of experiencing the past as if it were in the present?" the participants gradually unfolded many layers of their liturgical experience, often struggling to finds words to express intimate, spiritual, and nearly indescribable experiences.

The six people who participated in this study range in age from their twenties to their seventies and live in Boston, New York City, Connecticut, and Maine. While each person speaks from a unique place and personal experience, the participants also have much in common. Each is highly educated, with a rich knowledge of Judaism; one is a rabbi, two are rabbinical students, two are professors of languages and literature, and another is a doctoral student in religious studies. Their denominational affiliations and liturgical practices vary, but all share a deep respect for Orthodox Judaism and halakhic observance.[2] In the pages that follow, reflections on diverse liturgical experiences are woven together to present a picture of the complex, elusive experience of time within Jewish liturgical practice in which memory and hope are intimate and personal, and yet also collective, transmitted from generation to generation.

IN EVERY GENERATION

The conversations reflected in this chapter express a wide range of experiences of Jewish life and liturgy, yet each of the people interviewed in this study agree that Jewish liturgy is intrinsically wedded to time. The participants understand Judaism to be a religion of time; their ritual practices shape their experience of time

---

[2] The similarity in religious practices is not coincidental, for the study requires that the participants observe liturgical and ritual practices on a daily basis, allowing the practices to be interiorized and become integral to a person's identity and existential experience. Most secular Jews and members of progressive denominations such as Reform Judaism do not experience liturgy in this way. A number of people with intensely disciplined and devotional practices, such as Hassidic and other Haredi Jews, were also invited to participate but declined.

and give them a sense of being situated within a meaningful vision of history and time that incorporates the past, present, and future.

We begin with a description offered by Rabbi Michael, a rabbi of a Conservative synagogue in the Boston area.[3] As a leader of a large and active Jewish congregation, Rabbi Michael's responses tend to reflect on Jewish practice as experienced by his community. Beginning from a general perspective, he notes, "Judaism, from the standpoint of being a religion of time, is extremely attuned to how to garnish moments with meaning. I think when we stop and think about how much at the mercy we are to time . . . [we feel a] sense of significance of the time that we have."

Rabbi Michael finds that liturgical practice, which he describes as involving a "discipline of pause and focus," attunes him to the significance of time. Referring to the repeated practice of punctuating the hours of the day and the days of the week with prayer, particularly through the daily services, he remarks, "It profoundly shapes how I reorient the twenty-four hour cycle." He finds that it gives him "an opportunity to pause and focus, like the discipline of ritual itself." He acknowledges that the extent to which liturgy influences his experience of time varies, depending on the focus and intensity that he brings to prayer each time. He concedes, "I would also say that [prayer] doesn't always work. And so, when it really is profound . . . it totally changes the way I look at time." When it does "work," it affects his experience of time distinctly; he says "we can see the texture of time." Describing the sense of transformed time following a Friday evening Shabbat service, he continues, "From our stride to the expressions on our faces, it's qualitatively different."

This idea is explored by Adira, a young Orthodox woman, who finds that her liturgical practice heightens her awareness of time. Adira is a student at an Orthodox rabbinic seminary for women, the first of its kind in a denomination that has traditionally ordained

---

[3] All first names in this chapter have been changed to protect the anonymity of the participants. A biographical description is provided for each participant, however, to allow the reader to situate the participant within his or her religious and professional context.

only men. The daily services shape the schedule of her days and influence the way she understands the passage of the week: "Prayers on Mondays and Thursdays are different than prayers on other days of the week, and there's a different psalm for every day. I find that I never lose track of track what day of the week it is, in part because the prayers every day are different."

Liturgy acts as a clock and calendar for Adira, helping her keep track of her place within time. She appreciates this quality and seeks to heighten it by praying the services with a community in synagogue, rather than praying them alone at a convenient time: "When I've gone to synagogue and prayed with a community of people, it's a very different prayer experience and a very different time experience than it is praying by myself. When I'm praying by myself in my apartment, it's just another thing on my to-do list . . . but if you go to synagogue, it's a whole event, and that event has a half-an-hour time slot appointed to it that's inviolable."

The connection between liturgy and time, in Adira's experience, also involves a specific texture or pace that time has during liturgy. She expresses this as a sense of slowness, saying "I think liturgical time . . . certainly feels separate [from nonliturgical time]. . . . It's a time and a space where it's better to slow down." In Adira's experience, this slowness is particularly characteristic of Shabbat. She states, "Shabbat is slower and sweeter than any other day of the week." She finds that the weekdays are oriented toward Shabbat, and she spends most of the week looking forward to and planning for Shabbat. When Shabbat begins, for Adira, the pace of time suddenly changes.

The sense that time during Shabbat is different than time during the weekdays is shared by most of the participants in this study, all of whom observe Shabbat as a day of complete abstention from work of any kind, according to halakhic guidelines. This is the case for Hannah, a graduate student in religious studies, who has spent time studying in a Conservative yeshiva and currently identifies as a nondenominational halakhic Jew. Like Adira, Hannah finds that the weekdays are directed toward Shabbat and increase in intensity as Shabbat approaches: "My experience of time in the week is very much structured around the Shabbat experience, and really everything feels very much in reference to Shabbat. How much time is left until Shabbat comes, how much time since Shabbat. Shabbat will end, and the first few days of the week have a great expansiveness of time to get stuff done, and as the week narrows toward Shabbat, time feels like it compresses, and what needs to be done or what I imagine could be accomplished before the next Shabbat is squeezed."

Hannah identifies a radical break in time that occurs at the beginning of Shabbat, after the intensity of the weekday work has peaked: "Shabbat becomes a barrier, a wall that you run into, and as soon as I cross that barrier, I can't even remember what I needed to do and didn't get done. I can't even remember it, it's a different space." After this abrupt shift in time, she describes an experiential loosening of time: "[The time of Shabbat] feels incredibly long. The fact that there's nothing that has to be done means that there's infinite possibility. . . . It feels like the time is radically unstructured and there's profound possibility."

The sense of possibility and the loosening of restraints during Shabbat is also observed by David, a retired professor of Hebrew Scripture who identifies himself as Modern Orthodox. Describing this unique sense of time, David chooses words that allude to the indescribable nature of time during Shabbat: "When you get to Shabbos and you get to davening . . . there's a kind of *kiddushah*, it's there, it kind of has vibes."[4] The *kiddushah*, or holiness, of time during Shabbat eludes direct description.

David connects this sense of holiness in time with space, *makom*, evoking a liminal realm where time and space are spiritually connected: "When you get in that place where you daven, that *makom*, it's an opportunity to get out of the box. So Shabbos is an opportunity to get out of the box, the box of the six days, it's an opportunity to release my thinking."

---

[4] "Daven" is a Yiddish word for prayer, commonly incorporated into English, which refers specifically to the recitation of the prayer text in Hebrew. Following the Ashkenazi Yiddish tradition, David also refers to Shabbat as "Shabbos."

Further exploring the relationship between time and space, David observes that liturgical time is connected to space, and that liturgy gives one a "place" in life: "Space has the same existential definition that time has. . . . A glass jar has its place in the cupboard, just like a tomato has its own time for ripening. . . . Whatever you do, it has its place and it has its time. I think liturgy helps to do that. You know where you are. Not that you have control. It's better than having control; you know what to expect, and you have patience." From this "place" of prayer, according to David, one understands one's own position in time. He is careful to note, however, that he is using the concept of liturgy in a broad sense, encompassing not only the recitation of liturgical texts but also a way of life: "I want to emphasize that it's not only liturgy; I think that 'liturgy' here is another way of saying the way that makes sense for me to live and to get through all the tasks." He does not understand liturgy to be something that one does only at certain times but as a mode of living that pervades all aspects of his life. In his words, "The distinction between my living and my liturgical living is very thin; one is like the other."

Naomi, a professor of literature who also identities primarily as Modern Orthodox, experiences a similar permeability between her liturgical practice and her fundamental experience of living. She speaks of a state of heightened awareness during liturgy, in which her participation in ritual sharpens her awareness of her existential condition.

> I would say it's a heightened awareness of existence, and of your place in time. How infinitely small it is, really, because it's just a speck in this long connection and string . . . and [it heightens] the awareness of the minuteness of oneself, which can be a relief at times. But at the same time, because the moment is so holy, and it has to do with the spirit of the moment, it also heightens or intensifies my experience of my own life. It actually makes it bigger. In one way it makes it smaller feeling, the infinitesimal string of meaning, and then on the other hand it also inflates and gives meaning and purpose to life.

The state of awareness that Naomi describes experiencing through liturgy attunes her to her existential place in life and in time. The sense of a unique liturgical time is so intense for Naomi that she describes it as a tangible experience: "It's palpable on a cellular level, to the extent that you can call your awareness of your existence at a given moment palpable." Here, Naomi is describing a distinct sense of reality that arises during liturgy; it's a transformed sense of reality and a heightened awareness of existence brought about through participation in communal ritual action. She finds that liturgy reorients her and transforms her sense of position within life and within time.

Like David, Naomi is careful to qualify that this awareness of time occurs not only in formal liturgical celebrations but also during any aspect of life that is shaped by her Jewish identity and practice: "For me, it's less about personal prayer than it is about observing traditions on a cyclical yearly, weekly, and daily basis. I could probably count on two hands the times that I remember, that stand out to me, when the actual moment of [personal] prayer has given me the same kind of intense feeling of connection in time, forward and backward . . . as these things that are just ritual traditions that we don't think of as prayer. Actually, I think these things are a form of prayer."

As an example of the capacity of communal rituals to orient a person within time and space, she tells of a Jewish wedding that she recently attended. "To be there, and to be part of that, such an intense shared experience, it's not like I'm just an onlooker. It didn't feel like I was just an onlooker. . . . There's a tradition that a highway to heaven is open during the time of the *chuppah* (wedding canopy). It's again, palpable, you could sense that the bride and groom were so aware of that and were so into maximizing on that moment, and it spilled over. And that's an [example of the] acute sense of connection with time and place." In Naomi's description, the wedding liturgy lent a deeper layer of multidimensionality to time and space, as she felt that she was not simply an onlooker but a participant in a mystery which connects heaven and earth and past generations to the present and future generations.

She finds this in a variety of Jewish ritual practices which alter her perception of time: "I think it's about a perception of time. As much as it puts you as an individual as into a relative perspective historically and mythologically, in doing that it also places you firmly within that context." When asked to clarify what she means by "that context," she explains that the specific sense of time that she experiences within liturgy is part of the context of Jewish tradition in general: "You could call it a mythology, you could call it a tradition, you could call it a time span. And I think that that's part of what, for me, has been the most meaningful. . . . Over time, and having lived and experienced these things again and again, I've come to realize that—because it is palpable, it's extremely palpable in the moment—for someone who has those antennas out, [this sense of a mythology, tradition, and time span] is so vertical in its experience. It's so deep."

Another participant in the study, a young man named Jacob, offers his own interpretation of the awareness of time that Jewish liturgy awakens in him. Jacob is a student in a transdenominational rabbinic seminary, preparing for ordination to the rabbinate. He describes his religious identity as a transdenominational practice of Jewish renewal theology in conjunction with a deep appreciation for traditional Orthodox practice. His description of his religiously informed understanding of time reflects his own perspective and religious practice, which combines traditional and new approaches to Judaism: "Judaism gives me a model. . . . It's my reference point. The reference point is that time is a spiral, so it's a combination of a more ancient view of time which is very cyclical and a modern view of time which is more linear, and theoretically, Judaism is an integration of these things."

Whereas Naomi finds that Jewish liturgy awakens in her a heightened existential and temporal awareness, Jacob finds that Jewish liturgy encourages him to rethink the conceptual way in which he envisions time: "Each holiday, each year, I feel nudged: 'Think bigger, see the bigger picture.' If you're thinking in days or months, I feel like the tradition is constantly nudging me: 'Think in terms of decades and centuries and millennia.' I think Jewish teachings nudge me to think on bigger time scales."

Jacob's experience of time in liturgy, while it tends toward the conceptual, also includes an element of a spiritual, inexpressible sense of time. In his weekly liturgical practice, he tries to make time to pray the daily services, but he does not do it consistently. Yet he finds an ineffable spiritual sense attached to the times of the daily services, even when he does not complete the prayers. Speaking of this connection to time, he struggles to find words to adequately express this spiritual experience:

> Regardless of whether I do or don't do those [morning, afternoon, and evening] prayers, those periods of time have a certain significance to me. . . . I notice them in a different way. So, whether I pray or not, first thing in the morning I experience—there's a certain kind of . . . it's not a thing that has words—the morning has a specific kind of significance and midday has a specific [kind of significance]. There's a nostalgia for sunrise because this is an ideal time to pray. . . . And the same thing with sunset. I've taken up the practice of saying a piece of the evening liturgy as close to sunset as I can. I can't put words to it, but there's something that happens there . . . something ineffable happens at each of those moments.

The sense of time that Jacob speaks of feeling, particularly during the times of sunrise and sunset, has a mystical quality. It is not a sense of regular chronological time but of something more multidimensional and indescribable. When asked if he would use the term "timeless" to describe it, he reflects, "I don't know if I have that experience [of timelessness] itself. But I do feel that I'm speaking to or reaching for timelessness, as if it's possible for me to have a relationship with timelessness." Exploring what the concept of timelessness means to him, he continues, "I think timelessness to me means that there is a level of reality where what seems like before or after in our physical world doesn't work in that kind of way; that 'before' and 'after' aren't like that."

Jacob concludes that his own experience of time during prayer can best be described as "expansiveness, like in that place [of prayer] more is possible." He is careful to qualify that the sense of timelessness in Jewish tradition, according to his understanding of it, does not entail a rejection of time. "Timelessness doesn't have to do with escaping time," he says, and clarifies that Judaism embraces time and the time-bound world.

Many of the participants in this study expressed a similar valuation of time and a sense of connection with the past through identification with the chain of generations. Adira is particularly attuned to the significance of the past and discusses this at length: "Ultimately, what I find really powerful about Judaism is that connection to the past. I'm not just some fleeting being that is here for, God willing, eighty or ninety years and then disappears. I'm a link in a much larger chain, and if that chain doesn't share memories down the line, then that chain isn't valuable. But if you can pass on those memories and pass on those stories, then the stronger and stronger your chain is."

Adira understands her position in the present to be in continuity with the past and sees the maintenance of this continuity to be of great importance. She feels that the connection with the past gives direction and meaning to her life, and she claims, "[Communal memory] is absolutely central to me." She continues, "I've always felt that when things in my life are really hard . . . even in the little mundane ways of helping you cope with things, but also in the much bigger ways of having a sense of how to give meaning to time . . . I look to the past."

Adira looks to the traditions of the past to justify her actions in the present; this even shapes her understanding of the nature of God and the meaning of prayer. Speaking of the doubts she sometimes has when praying, when she wonders how her prayer could be meaningful and whether God hears her, she expresses how the traditions of the past inform her drive to persevere in prayer: "But, [it's helpful] to think about it as something my community has done for thousands of years, and they earned my place here. It's not because I did anything particularly good that I can stand in conversation with God but because of what my community has been through and how that relationship has developed over many thousands of years."

The continuity between the past and present in Jewish experience is maintained, in part, through communal memory. When asked how she understands and defines communal memory, Adira points to the communal memory both of recent historical events and the ancient biblical past: "In the Jewish community, communal memory is a place for Jews to come together and remember things that we don't individually remember, like the destruction of the Temple, or the exodus, or, for my generation, the Holocaust. I wasn't there, but it still feels like a part of my story. Similarly with the revelation at Sinai. The Jewish tradition says that every soul was there. It's just part of my story. It doesn't matter whether I was physically there; I feel like I was there. That's how relevant the revelation at Sinai feels to my life." Here, Adira moves from speaking of the memory of the past as past to a remembrance that actualizes the past in the present. Adira identifies with the past as an aspect of the present—relevant and real in her own life.

Jacob expresses a similar identification with the past, although he nuances the concepts of time, memory, and history differently: "Even though the word 'memory' is used in the celebrations of Judaism, I don't think of it as memory, and I don't experience it as memory, because I don't think of these events as being historical. . . . It's not about something that did or didn't happen. It's about something that's happening right now." When Jacob says that he doesn't consider the ancient events of the biblical narrative to be historical, he is not implying that the events are fictional. Rather, he considers them to be narratives that express a truth that is happening in the present moment. In conversation, he reflects that, when referring to historical reality, he finds it difficult to conceive of the past as something that exists actively in the present. He readily admits, however, that he considers the past and present to be fully intertwined when speaking of mythical, spiritual reality, and this is the type of reality that he finds the biblical narratives communicate.

Rabbi Michael expresses a similar sentiment about the biblical narratives, but rather than emphasizing the narratives' disconnection from history, he emphasizes the veracity of the stories. He believes this veracity rests on their relevance in today's world rather than on notions of historicity. "The first four stories in the Bible— Adam and Eve, Cain and Abel, Noah, and the Tower of Babel— absolutely happened, I'm absolutely convinced. The reason I'm convinced they happened is because they're happening right now. They happen every day. . . . To me those stories happened because they always do."

In these discussions, the participants are suggesting that the narratives referred to as historical—regardless of whether that history is considered to be mythical or actual—are better conceived of as events occurring in the present. For some, the narratives of the religiously envisioned eschatological future hold a similar quality. In Jacob's words, "[The world to come] doesn't have to do with something that may or may not happen in the future. To me, it's a level of reality that's happening all the time."

The eschatological future is indeterminate in Jewish thought, for despite the multiple strands of messianism that can be found in Judaism, there is no single established vision of the eschatological future that is shared across denominational lines. A similar discrepancy exists within denominations, as well, and many Jews find it difficult to envision a clear picture of the eschatological future. The phrase "the world to come," *haolam haba*, is commonly used to refer to the realm one enters after death, but this phrase and concept also becomes intertwined in the imagination with the time of the messiah on earth, *yemot hamashiach*.[5]

Adira reflects on this indeterminacy and finds the vision of the future difficult to grasp: "The past is much more present to us than the future, and it's more gripable. It comes in story-sized bites." Even though Jewish tradition does have certain fundamental elements that are expected to be present in the eschatological future, these elements do not form a narrative in the same way that the stories of the past lend themselves to joining into a long chain of narratives. As Adira observes, "You can't tell stories about future. . . . We don't have stories about the future, really. We have lots and lots of stories about the past." She continues, "I think our community doesn't talk about [the messianic future] and doesn't have a shared sense of what we want the future to look like." She finds, however, that the indeterminate vision of the future is, in fact, strong enough to provide a tangible sense of hope and strength: "The stories [about the future] aren't as strong or as rich as the stories about the past. Yet, are the stories about the future strong enough that they can give hope in hard times? Yes, I do have that experience." In general, Adira considers herself to be

[5] See the discussion of messianism in chapter 5.

more attuned toward memory of the past than toward anticipation of the future, and remarks, "I think that is characteristic of my greater religious community."

Like Adira, Hannah also finds this tendency to be characteristic of many in her religious community and speculates, "I imagine that most of my friends, if I was to have this conversation with them, would say that what they are most moved by is the past and the connection to their ancestors." In Hannah's own experience, however, the future is far more compelling than the past. In this way, Hannah's temporal orientation is different than the others' in this chapter; she remarks, "I find that what I am most inspired by, and what gives me life, is the future orientation to a world redeemed."

The orientations toward the past and the future that Adira and Hannah each express are also reflected in how each interprets the text of the Amidah.[6] Adira finds in the Amidah a meditation on the continuity between the ancient past and the present:

> [Communal memory is involved] even in daily prayers. The daily Amidah starts out talking about the God of our ancestors, the God of Abraham, Isaac, and Jacob, and what that means is that my connection to God is through that lineage and that history and that chain. And part of the reason why I can stand before God in prayer in this way is because of that history of the relationship between God and the Jewish people. . . . The opening lines of the daily Amidah are really about that connection to the past, and we're a link in that chain going to the past. . . . I'm part of this continuum.

Hannah, on the other hand, interprets the same prayer as an expression of hope for a redeemed future: "In general, I use the daily liturgy, and particularly the Amidah, as a practice in . . . dreaming about redemption rather than as a practice of remembering the past. Although, always in Jewish liturgical life we dream about the future in light of the past."

---

[6] The Amidah is also referred to as the Eighteen Benedictions, recited three times a day, during each of the three daily services.

The very distinct interpretations that each offers of the same prayer reflect the ways in which each is attuned to the past and the future and to the liturgical performance of memory and hope. The prayer text is the same, the liturgical setting is the same, and the broader religious narrative in which the liturgy is situated is the same, and yet the vision of time that the tradition evokes is so complex that each finds her own way through it, navigating the landscape of the past and future in unique ways.

Hannah's experience of faith is heavily anticipatory, and she values the past for its capacity to provide a template for the future. She observes, "There's a sense of justification of the hope because of the past. . . . I remember God's salvation in the past because it gives me hope that God will save me in the future." When Hannah engages in ritual remembrance of the past, such as during Tish'ah b'Av, she draws meaning from the way that the past tragedy becomes transformed into hope for the future:[7] "The only time I spend a lot of time in past sorrows is Tish'ah B'av. . . . When I encounter Tish'ah B'av, I weep over the suffering, and I think I weep even more deeply over the people who went through the suffering and managed to persist in their faith. . . . Again, it's the human capacity for hope in the face of deep darkness, which again has that future structure to it."

Hannah's orientation toward the future finds liturgical expression in Shabbat, which is traditionally considered to provide a taste of the world to come. She finds this association particularly compelling:

> The most profound experience I have on Shabbat is of a mythological future, rather than a mythological past. We talk about Shabbat as a taste of *haolam habah*, and I would say that that's more centrally important to me than [the idea] that past generations did this practice, or that it references the exodus from Egypt or the creation of the world, which are also two big mythological themes that are probably more central in the liturgy of the Sabbath than the foretaste of the world to come. But, I think the foretaste of the world to come is more personally meaningful.

---

[7] Tish'ah b'Av is the annual liturgical commemoration of the destruction of the First and Second Temples and subsequent disasters.

She attributes this experience of anticipation of the future in Shabbat to the blessing after meals on Shabbat, the *birchat hamazon*, which refers to the world to come as a "day which will be all Shabbat," *yom shekulo shabbat*. In reflecting, "I don't think that I would have that experience had I not heard that blessing," Hannah demonstrates how liturgical practice shapes the way she experiences time. Having recited these words many times at the close of a meal during Shabbat, she has begun to experience time during Shabbat as a mystical foretaste of the future.

A number of participants in this study find that liturgy gives them a sense of being connected to the past and the future. Naomi speaks about this in depth, and she finds that it occurs in all ritualized aspects of Jewish life, not just in liturgical prayer. Referring to the particular sense of existential awareness she experiences during ritual, she notes that it involves an incorporation of the past and future into her experience of the present: "I think it incorporates the past and future but not my past or my future. . . . When people ask me what it is about Judaism that is appealing to me, often that is my answer: the experience that what I do isn't just about me here and now, but it connects me and my family to something so much more; it gives responsibility. It's taking on a responsibility of being that connects you to the past and the future."

The connection to the past and future, heightened by ritual participation, does not, in Naomi's experience, involve merely an *awareness* of the past and future; she describes it as a sense of actually being extended across time so that her existence reaches into the past and future: "I would say that the quality of time—especially when thinking of how we experience time as being something connected to a past or a future—is the notion that my time here and now is actually extended beyond me to something before and something after, if that's possible. It sounds very unreal, but if that's possible, then I would say that the moments when that is the most obvious to me, and perhaps also why those moments become as special as they are, is during holidays, or practices that are ritual, that are not part of a secular daily routine."

Here she expresses an experience of temporal interpenetration, in which the past, present, and future seem to be interwoven. For

Naomi, however, this not just an abstract theory; it is experienced through interpersonal relationships, community, and a sense of responsibility born out of a connection to the generations that have gone before and the generations to come. As she puts it, she feels that Jewish ritual life is "crowded" with the past and future generations:

> If I'm lighting candles or gathered around the Shabbat table, or at funeral or at a wedding, there is that awareness in that present time that it's crowded because I'm not the only one that's there. Meaning not just the other guests, but the fact that in the 1930s in Germany people were doing it, in the 1700s in Copenhagen people were doing it. . . . There's a comfort in that notion of sharing in time, in past, present, and future. . . . When I do these rituals, even if I'm alone, or if I have a table full of people around me, it's a way to connect with and feel that I'm sharing the burden of my existence, of our existence, with everyone that came before, and everyone that's going to come after, and that makes it more bearable. That's the bottom line.

She expresses having felt a similar sense of connection with the past and future generations during a funeral she recently attended: "My Jewish experience of that passing and that moment is very acute, and the experience of time then is radically different than any other time. . . . Because it's ritualized and takes place within the traditions that it does, and with the awareness that it does, framed for me in a Jewish context, it feels that you're doing it with all those that preceded before you and that you're actually doing it also with all those who will come after you."

Naomi finds that the sense of being connected to generations through the ages can ease the pain of loss through overcoming the sense of existential isolation. As she says above, she finds "comfort in that notion of sharing in time, in past, present, and future." Essentially, Naomi is identifying a source of spiritual and emotional strength in the consciousness of time. In the memory of the past and the anticipation of the future, she finds a grounding that places her firmly within her religious identity, her family, and her community and grants her a unique perspective on her existential state within time. In her words, "There's a sense of connection which goes above and beyond the isolated individual experience—which can be devastating existentially— of time and existence."

Naomi acknowledges that the sense of a connection to the past and the future is capable of remedying an otherwise frightening existential condition. Without an awareness of the relevance of the past and the future to the present moment, time and existence may be experienced as tragically meaningless, lacking any continuity with the past or the future. Through participation in Jewish liturgy and ritual, however, she recognizes herself as connected to a greater community and tradition with links reaching into the past and future. Bound to the past and to the future through this chain of continuity, she experiences a heightened existential awareness marked not by isolation and devastation but by meaning and hope.

David shares Naomi's sense of being connected to the past and future through the concreteness of interpersonal relationships and community. Speaking of communal memory and of the sense of being connected to a community extending through time, he remarks, "It's what Jews do and are very good at it, but not through philosophy or doctrine or anything like that. . . . We tap the past in that way, so it's a past of the people." His vision of time, community, and God is complex yet practical, and he envisions abstract concepts such as infinity in relation to the concrete world: "This is the only world I have to deal with right now. But, it's infinitely extensive, not only in the past, but in the future. Liturgy, with all the cyclicality and all the repetition and so forth, reinforces that feeling, rather than putting me in another world."

David understands his own life in the present moment to be connected to the past and the future, yet it is not an otherworldly connection; it is a natural and real part of this world, and he becomes more aware of it through liturgy. When he reflects that "the concept of eternity goes in both directions; you can't say only from here on in, because you lose all the possibility of unifying or grabbing onto a much larger human experience," he points to a purpose for this sense of temporal connection. He sees the connection to the past and the future as a human reality and an interpersonal reality; the awareness of the past and the future within the present moment opens up the potential to understand and unify the experience of people in this world, in time.

This unification of the past, present, and future is, for David, also a part of the messianic vision: "Messianism goes back to the original creation of the world as good. Everything was created for a purpose, and nothing will be lost. All of the memories, all of the past, all of the future, everything is there and will always be there. . . . That's a trigger for us reaching in all directions, past, present, and future." In the messianic future, "Everything in this world will be remembered for good." He concludes, "That is the type of liturgical memory that I want."

Chapter 4

As It Was in the Beginning, Is Now, and Ever Shall Be

Gloria Patri, et Filio, et Spiritui Sancto, sicut erat in principio, et nunc, et semper, et in saecula saeculorum. (Glory to the Father, and to the Son, and to the Holy Spirit. As it was in the beginning, is now, and ever shall be, world without end.)

—The Minor Doxology

INTRODUCTION

Like the previous chapter, this chapter is the product of interviews conducted with a select group of individuals who reflect on their personal experiences of memory, hope, and the experience of time in liturgy. The participants in the study conducted for this chapter are all members of Roman Catholic religious orders, and each maintains a daily practice of reciting the Liturgy of the Hours, or the Divine Office.[1]

The first part of this chapter consists of reflections on monastic liturgical practice, as experienced by five Benedictine nuns of the

---

[1] The daily liturgy is referred to as the Liturgy of the Hours in the extended four-week cycle format practiced by most priests and members of "active" religious orders, i.e., orders and communities that practice outreach ministries in society as opposed to contemplative communities dedicated to work and prayer within monasteries. The liturgy is referred to as the Divine Office in the intensive one-week cycle format maintained by the Abbey of Regina Laudis and other communities.

Abbey of Regina Laudis, a community of contemplative Benedictines of the Primitive Observance, who live an agrarian life on nearly four hundred acres of land. These nuns express aspects of a life intensely formed by a rigorous schedule of liturgy and monastic work in a close-knit contemplative community.

This is followed by a discussion of the experiences of three men belonging to the religious orders of the Society of Jesus and the Franciscans. Each of these priests lives in an urban area and works within a university community in theological studies and religious formation. These priests lead very different lives than those of the contemplative Benedictines, and their reflections on their own experiences of liturgy and time highlight the extent to which one's religious community, identity, and daily practices influence the way one experiences and enunciates memory, hope, and the sense of time. The thoughts, feelings, and observations presented here weave together the personal experiences of eight vowed members of religious communities, with the understanding that the experience of each person is deeply personal and yet also reflective of a community, tradition, and spiritual heritage through which each person's experience is filtered and given meaning.

NON RECEDAT LAUS: MONASTIC EXPERIENCES OF LITURGY AND TIME

At the Abbey of Regina Laudis, all eight of the traditional offices of the Divine Office are celebrated: Matins, Lauds, Prime, Terce, Sext, None, Vespers, and Compline, and the celebration of the Office takes up a large portion of the available time of day. The Office is sung in entirety, preserving the traditional Latin language and keeping alive the ancient tradition of Gregorian chant. The members of the community study Latin and the art of Gregorian chant, and the performance of the liturgy is viewed as a very serious work and offering to God, in keeping with the monastery's motto *"non recedat laus,"* "let praise never cease." The liturgy is at the center of the monastic life here. Mother Jacoba, involved in liturgical organization as the mistress of ceremonies, confesses that "Apart from [the liturgy], I don't see that there's a reason to be here [in monastic life]." Another member of the community echoes, "I don't see how we could make it as a community it we didn't have the chant, I really don't."[2]

The monastic community maintains a rigorous schedule of work and prayer, and each community member is engaged in diverse work involving the care of livestock for meat, dairy, and wool; the cultivation of gardens; cheese making; monastic arts such as blacksmithing, stained glass, and pottery, in addition to the work required to cook, clean, care for the ill, and maintain the properties. This work is punctuated at regular intervals by the ringing of the bells, which signal the end of a work period and the beginning of the time for prayer. The hours of each day are divided into multiple segments in this way, and each community member must continually adjust to a structure of daily time determined by the hours of prayer. Mother Valeria, who works in the vegetable gardens, describes the way in which this schedule of work and prayer shapes time at the monastery: "The day is completely structured by what we call the Office. It affects our language. We speak to each other as 'I'll meet you after Lauds,' or 'I'll meet you before Terce,' or 'after Mass,' so, it's really part of our natural way of seeing the day. So it becomes reflexive, rather than reflective. You don't think about it."

The schedule of the Divine Office shapes time throughout the day and remains stable, while the other work and timetables of the day shift. It provides a regular pace, and the times of the Office occasionally function in place of the time indicated by the clock. Indeed, the time of the liturgy often takes precedence over the time of the clock. For example, the daily Mass which is scheduled to begin at 8:00 a.m. may begin at 8:05 or 8:25, but it is still experienced as an

---

[2] All first names in this chapter have been changed to protect the anonymity of the participants. At the Abbey of Regina Laudis, at the point of her investiture into religious life, each woman is given a name that reflects some aspect of her personality or spiritual vision. She is referred to as "sister" until her full profession, at which point she is addressed as Mother; the names and titles used in this study reflect this tradition. A biographical description is also provided for each participant to allow the reader to situate the participant within his or her religious and professional context.

anchor in time, as the point of time marked by the beginning of the liturgy of the Mass.

The precedence of the ritual practices and liturgical schedule in shaping the experience of time in the monastery is also seen in the custom of marking time through the ringing of large bells. The ringing of the bells are the first and the last sounds of the day, breaking and then reestablishing the nighttime Great Silence established in the Rule of St. Benedict.[3] The bells ring in the morning to wake the community for the first liturgy of the morning; they ring shortly before each Office, signaling the appropriate time to set one's physical labor aside; they intone the series of rings of the Angelus at the end of an Office; they ring during the consecration of the Eucharist; and they ring to gather the community to meals. In many ways, the bells take the place of clocks, marking the important times of day. While clocks mark the passage of time in calculated and exact increments, however, the bells mark the passage of time according to the ritual practices of the monastery. What is normative is not the time according to the clock but rather the time of the bells and the time of the prayer.

The liturgical schedule is so ingrained into the pattern of life in this community that it has entered the language and become naturalized as a given structure of time. Sister Revelatia, one of the younger members of the community, observes that the liturgy serves as a stable beacon, around which the rest of time flows: "We pray the hours on a regular basis, every day of the week. . . . Life happens in between the hours; those are the things that are set, and everything else can shift and change in between these very solid things, and those things are solid and concrete every day of the week."

As Mother Valeria observes, this regularity is maintained regardless of any crisis or breakdown of regularity outside of the liturgy: "For instance, no matter what is going on, globally, internally, whatever crisis is going on, no matter what, the Office goes on. . . . No matter what it is, that rhythm continues. . . . So no

---

[3] *Rule of St. Benedict 1980*, ed. Timothy Fry (Collegeville, MN: Liturgical Press, 1981), chapter 42.

matter what it's been, whether it's a natural disaster, or a great moment, or a moment of death, always this bringing it back to the Lord occurs. And it touched me from the very beginning that there was always this rhythm of out and back and out and back, and it's intense."

The regularity of the Office keeps time for the community, and this timekeeping is rhythmic, "out and back and out and back." The eight offices are celebrated every day without fail, and the pace can be exhausting. Mother Valeria sees this as a form of penance: "I would say that we don't really have many classical penances here, except the relentlessness of the Office." She doesn't see it as punishment but as a challenge to use time well, for "the economy of time is essential."

The liturgical schedule requires the monastic community to maintain a heightened consciousness of time, and this consciousness happens on a number of levels. Most practically, the "economy of time" is such that every moment must be utilized well, for time is always delimited by a rigorous schedule of work and prayer. The liturgical schedule also draws awareness to the passage of time as evidenced in nature, from the daily arc of the sun to the passage of seasons. Mother Clara, the cellarer of the monastery, discusses this awareness, noting the connection between the liturgical cycle, the daily and seasonal cycles, and the agricultural cycles: "Living the liturgical cycle here sensitizes me somewhat to the daily passage of the sun—I'm very aware of the key points of the day in that regard—and also to the seasons, which are very prominent here, particularly because the liturgical year is so linked to the agricultural cycle of the year, and they are so interwoven, and we're immersed in both of them."

All of the community members of the Abbey of Regina Laudis who contributed to this study experienced some sense of a particular quality of time during liturgy, but many found it difficult to describe. Mother Valeria claims "there is definitely a qualitative difference" in the sense of time within liturgical celebration, but she finds that this quality cannot be described precisely. Mother Clara also finds it difficult to find words to describe her sense of time during liturgy, but she finds that the Advent liturgy is so rich in temporal associations and sensory experiences that it allows a unique sense of time to be more clearly identified: "This sense experience helps you tune into the mystery of Christ's birth in time, especially at Advent, and again, it's very much a past, present, and future thing because Advent is looking forward to the ultimate coming and how he's coming into your heart at this moment and how he came into history, and I think that's what people love about it. In the Advent liturgy there's so much 'hodie,' today, today, it's happening today, and I think that's very real."

In this monastic community, every liturgy is sung in Gregorian chant, and the music and liturgy are inseparable in the experience of many. Mother Natalina, who is particularly attuned to the musical settings of the liturgy through her role as the community's instructor in chant, experiences a liturgical transformation of the sense of time in connection with this liturgical music. She begins by describing a transformed spiritual state which eludes description: "There's something about the music in the Gregorian chant that just takes you into the mystery." She continues, "It can bring you to a transcendent place, whether you know what they're singing or not, and that's partly the power of a community singing— it's a group; but it's also the power of Gregorian chant, which is timeless." For Mother Natalina, the chant that she sings daily opens up another dimension of anticipatory and proleptic experience within the liturgy. "Great music gives me a taste of that heaven, so I'm not so afraid of the end."

Mother Jacoba also finds that the chant awakens a consciousness of time within her during the liturgy through the time-bound quality of music—particularly the *melismata*: "You might get a whole phrase of notes with this one word, and that word will come out in time, because every word is focused within time. The chant has opened me to time in that way, through how long you to have to savor a word, to understand that meaning in time."

At the Abbey of Regina Laudis, the rich liturgical tradition is paired with an immersion in work, centered in the stewardship of the land, reflecting the Benedictine dedication to *ora et labora*, work and prayer. Work is understood to be prayer, just as prayer is work. Furthermore, the spirituality of this community incorporates an analogical imagination, through which all the work that one does throughout the day is seen as part of each person's spiritual journey. The work is interpreted analogically, as a material symbol of the mysteries of faith. Mother Natalina, a microbiologist and consultant to the monastery's cheese makers, expresses this in relation to her own work.

> I'm dealing with aging cheese and with caves. I do often talk about death, I realize, because we're supposed to keep death always before our eyes, Benedict says. And, that's what you're dealing with when you're dealing with cheese microbiology, it's a process of decomposition that occurs during cheese ripening. The breakdown of carbohydrate, protein, and fat gives you incredible taste and flavor, so it's an incredible experience of death, too, unconsciously. And what goes on in the cave—you think of Christ in the tomb, there's this darkness, and there's this unknowing that goes on in cheese ripening because it's a transformation, and you don't know how it's going to end up. So, I think part of it is because we really choose to pursue our faith in terms of analogy here . . . that you would naturally bring that into the Office.

In this analogical understanding of work and prayer, the consciousness of time takes root. Time is elusive and difficult to conceptualize abstractly. The abstractness of time can find a body through the material world, however, and in the cycles of growth and decay, time can take material form. Mother Natalina finds an analogical body for time in her work, and she speaks of death and transformation in the process of cheese making. She likens it to Christ's transformation in the tomb. This analogy provides an experiential gateway into the contemplation of time as the change, death, and rebirth of the material world speak of memory, hope, and time.

Work and prayer are united, creating a life that is thoroughly liturgical. As Mother Natalina says, "Everything is liturgical here, yes, and for us pressing the cheese and milking a cow are also liturgical." This wholly liturgical life offers an experiential taste of the narratives of the past and the vision of the eschatological future, which comprise the greater religious narrative. Fed by the tangible symbols and physical experience provided by the life of relentless prayer and work, the religious narrative becomes not just an idea but a firsthand experience.

Mother Valeria describes this experiential phenomenon by explaining, "Here, we begin with the incarnational base and move from there into the self-identification with the scriptural narratives. Christ is an encounter, not a story." For Mother Valeria, and for many in this community, the divine is not a concept but an experience. Other members of the community express a similar experiential orientation when describing eschatological hope and the experience of time. Speaking of her tendency toward hope and thoughts of the future, and more specifically, of the eschatological future, Mother Natalina describes an experiential encounter: "I feel like I don't have to talk about it as much as witness it. This experience of resurrection—I feel like I've experienced it." Mother Valeria communicates a preference for the experiential when speaking about the concept of time, as well: "It [the religious narrative of the past, present, and future] is not a painting, it's participatory. It's participatory, or else forget it."

By this logic, liturgy is not the recitation of a concept or the telling of a story. Rather, it is an experience of the mystery communicated by the narrative in one's self, in time. Mother Natalina understands this experiential identification with the religious narrative to happen through the liturgical cycle: "If you're going to decide to join a community like this, then you are going to *live* that liturgical cycle, and you will be plunged into that mystery. If you choose to be a Catholic who follows the liturgical cycle, or you join a community in which you sing the Hours, you're faced with these saints. You are plunged into meditating on the mystery of the saint, or martyr, and you get taken into that. You're choosing freely to enter into a cycle of death and resurrection."

A related concept is discussed in the *General Instruction of the Liturgy of the Hours*, suggesting that the person who recites the psalms undergoes a shift in which she becomes less identified with herself as an individual and more identified with the communal body of the faith. "Whoever sings the psalms in the Liturgy of the Hours sings them not so much in his own person as in the name of the whole Body of Christ, and indeed, in the person of Christ himself. If he keeps this in mind, difficulties will disappear, even if while he is singing the psalms the feelings of his own heart differ from the sentiments expressed in the psalm."[4]

The document suggests that the liturgical participant steps outside of her individual identity to participate in a greater, communal identity. The individual speaks in the voice of the liturgical community and enters into a communal union of identity. The *Directory for the Celebration of the Work of God* expands on this, noting that viewing the Liturgy of the Hours as a communal representation of the Church helps to avoid "the unfortunate error of regarding the celebration of the Divine Office as merely the sum of the prayers of the individual members of the community."[5] Liturgical performance allows one to be clothed in a narrative greater than one's own individual narrative and to experience a spiritual narrative, and a spiritual mystery, beyond that which one imagines alone.

When asked if she has experienced, within liturgy, a sense of sharing in a communal memory held by the entire Church, rather than simply her own personal store of memories, Mother Jacoba immediately nodded. "It's so much bigger than us. Every time we process in [to the choir for liturgy], it's not about us. It's about something much bigger."

This liturgical identification with "something much bigger," or in other words, an identification of the self with a communal, spiritual body, may come readily to a community like the Abbey of Regina Laudis, which has a rich sense of communal identity. The concept of community is central to the spirituality of the monastery, and a sense of community and communal identity pervades the pattern of work and prayer. The identity of each individual is developed and understood in relation to the community, and an identification of the self with the community can be seen in the

[4] *General Instruction on the Liturgy of the Hours* (Collegeville, MN: Liturgical Press, 1975), sec. 108.

[5] *The Monastic Hours: Directory for the Celebration of the Work of God and Directive Norms for the Monastic Liturgy of the Hours*, ed. Anne M. Field (Collegeville, MN: Liturgical Press, 2001), sec. 2.

language, as well. In the conversational interviews transcribed here, the nuns were asked to speak about their own personal experience, and yet the answers often reflected a communal identity and a sense of communal experience.

In considering the relationship between the communal life and the experience of time, Mother Valeria observes, "On any given day, somebody is in darkness, and somebody is in elation, and you're part of this one body that's experiencing all of that at once. . . . Really, the passion, death, and resurrection are going on in one moment." In identifying with the multiplicity of personal experiences occurring within the monastic community, the religious narrative of Christ's passion, death, and resurrection are experienced as a present reality. The paradigmatic events of the past are experienced in the present, and the sequence of passion, death, and resurrection occur together in one unified and complex present.

A number of members of the community speak of finding a connection to time—to the distant reaches of the past and future—through experiencing the death of other community members and loved ones, perhaps reflecting the centrality of interpersonal relationships to the spirituality of this community. Mother Valeria finds that the experience of death gives her a sense of a shift in the dimensions of time: "Going through death with different members of our community, I begin to get a sense of eternity as reaching back into time."

Mother Natalina also speaks of sensing a transformation in time through losing loved ones: "I think when important people have died in your life it puts you into a new sense of time, like there's always a part of you in another place. . . . It changes, to me, your sense of time. Because they're always there beyond you." She senses this shift in time through mourning the dead, she says, through liturgical performance: "For me, probably one of the biggest things about the Office, especially Lauds, is that it puts me in touch with the dead. And that is really important to me." The act of praying the Office puts her in touch with the dead and gives her a "new sense of time." When asked how she envisions "there beyond you" to be situated within time, i.e., whether it is located in the past, as a memory, in the eschatological future, or elsewhere, she responded, "It is the future. It's more anticipation than the past. Absolutely. To me, that is one of the most important parts of the Office. . . . It's something enchanting."

Through the process of holding these conversations about the experience of time with members of the monastic community, it became clear that the vocabulary for experience of time is insufficient. The past and future can mean many different things, in scriptural, liturgical, practical, and imaginative contexts. The eschatological future can refer to many things: the Second Coming, the redemption of the world, the end of the world, or the fate of an individual soul after death. The notion of the past also has many connotations, from the past experiences held within one's personal memory, to the ancient past as it is known through the discipline of history, to the mythological past communicated by Scripture, which includes both the primordial world of Genesis and the paradigmatic "historical" narratives of the Hebrew Bible. This mythological, communally "remembered" sense of the past, like the sense of the eschatological future, is primarily spiritual. While this study uses the terms "past" and "future" to refer to these dimensions of time, they cannot be fit neatly within the concept of chronology. Many see time as practical and sequential, as measured by the clock, yet the past and future discussed in this study—the religiously envisioned mythological and spiritual past and the eschatological future—are not defined by measured chronology.

The conversations represented in this chapter evidence the indeterminacy of the terms "past" and "future." The interview subjects each speak about extraordinarily different concepts when they speak of the future. Some speak of the future within time—that is, the immediate future, or the future of the next generations—and some speak of a religiously envisioned future. Some speak of the afterlife of the dead as existing in the future, while others see it as an aspect of the past. Some do not envision *any* of the various aspects of eschatology to be in the future; rather, they envision it in another dimension, beyond chronology, as exemplified by Sr. Revelatia:

> No, I do not see [the various concepts associated with the eschaton] located in time. . . . It's hard for me to give any form or shape or

place or time to it, but I do know that it's not out there at another time; I don't experience it as something I'm waiting for. . . . I suppose that there are many people of Christian orientation that believe that it's going to happen within time, and they're waiting for a certain year, or it's a very concrete calendar-based reality. That's one way to experience it. . . . I just think that it's so beyond anything that I can comprehend right now.

Mother Natalina, who considers herself generally oriented toward the future, claims that she does not "experience the past as much as the present and the future." When asked if she thinks of the biblical narrative as a part of the past, she reflects, "I don't think of it as the past, when I hear it, because I relate it to what's going on right now." When she thinks of the phrase "the past," she thinks of the historical past and the past memories of her own life. In contrast, for her the biblical narrative is transtemporal; it is set in the historical past, but she experiences it in the present. So, while she initially says that she does not think much about the past, she in fact thinks about the religiously envisioned, biblical past with such immediacy that it seems an aspect of the present. She exclaims, "It's true! I guess I don't think of the past as past. That wouldn't be satisfying enough, because we have to make all things new." Mother Natalina experiences a form of temporal interpenetration, in which the past is so interwoven with the present that it is experienced as part of the present.

Sr. Revelatia experiences a similar sense of temporal interpenetration. She considers herself very attuned to the past and understands it to be interwoven with the present: "Those people in the past are not only in the past, they're still [present] now. So if I'm connected with the people who lived in the past, who are still around now, I feel that something in the past will also be put at peace." She concludes, "So chronological time is only one dimension of time." She understands the past to be present within the current time, and she also understands the present to impact the past: "Yes, I do [think that the afterlife can overlap with this present time], and I do think that the present can affect the past as well." For Sr. Revelatia, the past and present are permeable.

Sr. Revelatia also experiences this temporal permeability within the Office, as she chants the Psalms, contemplating the ancient origins of the text: "When I'm conscious of the words I'm saying [in the Office], it's more of an awareness of being connected to those people at that time [who wrote the psalms and sang them in antiquity]. . . . And, there's an awareness that I would not have the same connection to those people at that time and the truth they're expounding if I did not stop throughout the day to pray the Hours."

Mother Natalina also expresses a mystical sense of the past generations that she feels when praying the Office, exclaiming, "You're standing in the choir, and suddenly all of those generations are there! Wow." She feels a deep sense of the presence of the past during the Office, and she also speaks of having a feeling of eschatological anticipation during the Office. She feels this particularly strongly during the offices of Lauds and Compline, which are the first and last offices of the day, respectively. She attributes her sense of eschatological anticipation during these two offices to the fact that they occur early in the morning and late in the evening and observes that their situation in time influences her sense of anticipation. Here, a distinct experiential connection exists between liturgical rituals connected to the time of day and the sense of the distant reaches of the past and future.

Mother Natalina is able to identify an explicit sense of temporal interpenetration in her conception of time: "I think in general I would feel the past, present, and future [as one], because there's a timelessness about how we live." This temporal sense is shared by Mother Valeria, who, in response to being asked if she experiences an interpenetration of the past, present, and future replies "Oh, yeah! It is there all the time. The only limitation is how conscious of it I can be . . . . It is all there, it's definitely all there."

While Mother Natalina, Mother Valeria, and Sr. Revelatia all express a similar sense of temporal interpenetration in which they sense the presence of the past and the future through their highly liturgical life, Mother Clara experiences it differently. Rather than experiencing the elements of time as already integrated into one, she sees it as a goal: "I suppose in a way I feel like our whole life is about knitting [the past, present, and future] together. It's not so much that we go to Mass or to the Office and that we feel the experience of how it's together, as all day long every day we're in this work of knitting it together, or bringing it together." For Mother Clara, the interpenetration of time is a mission; it is something that she strives to build through a conscientious spiritual life.

Euntes Ergo Docete

The three priests interviewed in this part of the study are each members of religious orders, yet unlike the Benedictine nuns, they do not participate in a regular daily liturgical schedule with members of their community. Each of these priests holds an active career and duties in university education and religious formation, and while they maintain the recitation of the Liturgy of the Hours obligatory for priests, the communal celebration of Liturgy of the Hours within their religious communities is rare.

The greatest discrepancy between the liturgical experiences of the nuns and the priests interviewed in this study is found in the way that liturgy intersects with time on a daily basis. Daily life in the Benedictine monastery is shaped by the liturgical schedule, and all other work is scheduled around the liturgical schedule. As described above, time is sensed and measured in the monastery according to the daily pattern of liturgical celebration. By contrast, the liturgical schedules of each of the priests is adjusted daily to fit into the professional schedules they keep.

This irregularity is described by Fr. Charlie, a Jesuit priest who teaches theology in a university: "I'd say, to be honest, it's a struggle to fit the Liturgy of the Hours into my day. So I fit them in, but often I'll lump them together, or sometimes I'll end up saying Morning Prayer in the afternoon, to be honest, but not too often. So do I experience the liturgy as punctuating the times of my day? No, I don't because I don't live an enclosed life. If I were more disciplined, more like I'd want to be, then I'd be better about organizing my day around the Liturgy of the Hours."

A similar experience is described by Fr. Leo, a young Franciscan priest who is currently a doctoral student in religious studies. Like Fr. Charlie, he compares his liturgical schedule to a monastic schedule and expresses regret at the lack of liturgical regularity: "I tend to do daily prayer and the Office of Readings at irregular times . . . so the Hours do not evenly layer my day the way they would if I were a cloistered monastic." Fr. Leo finds, however, that his practice of praying the Hours, even if it occurs at irregular times, still has a profound effect on his sense of time: "I notice the way they affect my sense of time most acutely when I skip it for a couple of days [for example, when visiting family], because then I feel very distant from my life of prayer. . . . If I skip the office for a couple days, I find myself physically tired, and I physically miss it." This suggests that the recitation of the Liturgy of the Hours has been deeply internalized by Fr. Leo, so that even though he regularly shifts the daily time of the Hours, he feels a physical loss when the practice is absent; it affects his sense of time.

A tension between a spiritual internalization of prayer on the one hand and a casual attitude toward the scheduling of the liturgy on the other is also indicated by Fr. Charlie. He speaks of an intense spiritual awareness that he occasionally experiences during prayer: "I'm conscious of a larger, praying body, praying these psalms that day, in this reality, that's also connected to the whole concrete history stretching back to the author of the Psalms." Yet, he clarifies, "That's in my best moments. In my worst moments, I gallop through them, because it's an obligation I have to get over with, because I have other things to do." Here, two very different approaches to daily prayer are evidenced, operative within the same person, as he struggles to incorporate spiritual contemplation and the prayer of the Liturgy of the Hours into the secular time frame of a professional schedule.

The spiritual awareness that Fr. Charlie expresses in this statement points to a profound liturgical experience. He feels that he participates in a communal liturgical body that's greater than his individual self, and greater than his religious community, mystically incorporating a universal community. This community, in his experience, is continuous through time, into ancient history. He elaborates on this, drawing a connection between all people who pray the same text within the Liturgy of the Hours each day and a universal spiritual communion: "We're all on the same page, so to speak, that day. So there's an actual event happening that day where people are praying the same psalm. There's that level, then there's a higher level of the Church as a whole . . . a larger liturgical subject. I do feel a connection with those who have gone before and those who are still around."

While Fr. Charlie feels an identification with the past through the prayer of the Liturgy of the Hours, Fr. Leo feels an identification with the past through the history of his religious order: "One reality for me, as a member of a religious order with a long history like the Franciscans, is I feel that identity helps to close the gap between my present and Scripture. Because, in between the life of the Lord and the other events described in Scripture—there's obviously a couple thousand years intervening—but about eight hundred years of that intervening time is Franciscan history. So that sense of a very fraternal and very proximate connection with the history of my own community is something that helps collapse the distance to salvation history somewhat."

When he uses the phrase "collapse the distance to salvation history," Fr. Leo expresses a experience of time contracting. He experiences this through identifying with the history of his religious order, and this identification is akin to identifying with the religious narrative through liturgy. In both cases, the participation in a community and series of practices allows one to feel that an ancient narrative becomes alive and present in one's life. For Fr. Leo, these two contexts are woven together, and it is in this intermingling of liturgical practice and religious community that he feels a sense of identification with the ancient past.

Fr. Leo speaks of feeling an identification with the ancient past through the liturgical practice of praying for the dead, which is a specific part of the liturgical practice of the Franciscan order and involves praying for deceased friars in the community. "Specifically, that [identification with history] comes through in our practice of praying for the dead. . . . In terms of the way the prayer life of the Liturgy of the Hours connects me to time, it is primarily with that injunction to pray for the dead." This practice of praying for the dead connects him to the personal history of his community and also to ancient history, which for him connects back to the biblical narrative and to the life, passion, and resurrection of Jesus Christ.

When asked if he feels identified with the past to the extent that it becomes part of the present moment, he immediately replies in the affirmative but then struggles to explain how exactly he experiences it: "I'm thinking about how to articulate the connection, because I know that the connection is there, and how is that connection established? I experience that the past is projected forward into the present rather than me being vaulted back into the past. . . . The direction of closure is that the past is coming toward the present and not the other way around. I have very little to do with first-century Palestine or with thirteenth-century Assisi but in the experience of prayer, first-century Palestine and thirteenth-century Assisi have a lot to do with me."

While Fr. Leo expresses a distinct sense of connection with the ancient past, he does not experience a similar sense of connection with the eschatological future. When asked if eschatological anticipation is something he consciously thinks about or experiences in liturgy, he acknowledges a discrepancy between his cognitive theological thought and his lived liturgical experience: "Obviously, my instinct is to answer this like a theologian, and the theologian in me has to say "yes.". . . I do have those fleeting moments of what I could call eschatological anticipation, but if I were to speak very personally, very phenomenologically, how do I sense that with any sort of regularity? I don't. . . . Obviously, I know that the language is there in the liturgy. . . . Can I say that I really experience them that tangibly? It's rare."

He has a firm belief in the content of the eschatological future but rarely experiences a sense of reality and presence comparable to the feeling he has when meditating on the past: "Even though I just said that I don't have a very conscious sense of anticipation of the "the end," I will say that my understanding of what the end is—and this understanding is not purely intellectual, it's born of prayer—is the resurrection of the dead, when all of creation will be transformed. . . . And that's what I'm waiting for, but I can't say that I anticipate it in the sense that it might be coming soon. It feels like a reality that's very distant. It is a reality that's very real, but I don't experience it as being as proximate as much as I wish it would be.

Fr. Charlie also finds the eschatological future to be distant from his thoughts. It serves as a source of hope for him, but he rarely meditates on it consciously: "The final end of the narrative, I guess I don't really pay that much attention to it, apart from knowing that it's there, and it's a cause of hope and of joy. I don't put my mind to actively thinking of what it would be like too often. It's a horizon or something, it's the end point, but I don't meditate on what it would be like too much."

Although Fr. Charlie considers the eschatological future to be located on a horizon too distant to contemplate directly, he does experience a sense of the future reaching back into the present moment during liturgy. He feels that the past, present, and future come together in liturgy, and he clarifies that it's not due to any cognitive activity or any specific text but simply because it is prayer: "It's because it's prayer. It's not because the text directs me toward thinking of anamnesis, but because I'm praying, then God is somehow working in me, and of course everything comes together. Past, present, future, the communion of saints, are somehow inserted in that mystery. I'm not separated from the people who went before me, nor the future, which somehow is being worked out."

Fr. Charlie feels that the past and future of the religious narrative are so inseparable from the present reality that he finds that the term "religious narrative" is unsuited to his experience: "That's why I don't connect too much with the term "narrative," because it has a beginning and an end and someone who tells it." He finds the content of faith to be a part of each present moment: "I guess I don't really think of it as narrative, as such. It's more immediate and present and actual. Present in my existential situation in life, basically."

When asked if he ever has the sense during liturgy that the past, present, and future are intertwined in the present reality, he consents that he experiences it often: "I say that expresses pretty accurately what I would feel a lot of the time celebrating Mass or the Liturgy of the Hours, that all things come together, future, past, present." They are inseparable parts of his experience of time during liturgy, and he reflects, "I can't separate myself out from the past or the future."

The sense of the interpenetration of past, present, and future during liturgical performance is an experience that feels very familiar to another Jesuit, Fr. Frank. An older priest who works in formation with young Jesuits, Fr. Frank readily speaks of his thoughts of the eschatological future and finds that meditation on these topics is a regular part of his liturgical experience. The theological concept that the past, present, and future are brought into one through Jesus Christ is, for Fr. Frank, not just an idea; he experiences it in prayer and in liturgical ritual.[6]

Fr. Frank understands this unification of the past, present, and future in Jesus Christ to extend to all people unified by the divine mystery: "Jesus is being born in Bethlehem now. Jesus is dying on the cross now. He is experiencing all of this now, just as he did in history. And when we make contact with him, we are there. . . . Christ is the one who is, he was, and he is to come. . . . Insofar as we are one with him . . . all time becomes one. All time becomes now."

This concept of the unification of time in Jesus Christ is not simply conceptual; in liturgical performance, Fr. Frank experiences it. Giving an example of a tangible symbol that he uses to mark this experience, he explains, "When I celebrate Mass I take my watch off, and that's a symbolic statement . . . that we have left ordinary time, and that we are now in cosmic time, or the time of the spirit." He refers to this cosmic time as eternity; he then clarifies that he does not see eternity as an absence of time but a fullness of time: "I see eternity as a valuing of time, an enrichment of time, a giving meaning to time. That's why I don't think of eternity as being something that comes after time. . . . Eternity is now. It's the nowness of all time."

The interweaving of the past, present, and future is a fundamental aspect of Fr. Frank's daily liturgical experience and is central to the way he thinks about time, life, and liturgy. Identifying his own experience of temporal interpenetration, he exclaims, "I love the way the liturgy pulls together the past and the future into a present

[6] The work of Hans Urs von Balthasar and Jean Danielou on this notion is explored in chapter 7.

experience." With excitement, he exclaims, "It's real. It's real, it's not just an idea. It's like in quantum physics, it's like time folding into itself."

Part 3

The Experience of Time
in Jewish Liturgy

Chapter 5

Time in Jewish Thought

Judaism is a religion of time aiming at the sanctification of time. . . .
Judaism teaches us to be attached to holiness in time, to be attached to
sacred events, to learn how to consecrate sanctuaries that emerge from
the magnificent stream of a year.

—Abraham Joshua Heschel[1]

THE CENTRALITY OF TIME IN BIBLICAL JUDAISM

Judaism's engagement with memory and the consciousness of time is one of the defining characteristics of the tradition, as evidenced by the celebration of memorial holy seasons and days and the liturgical marking of appointed hours. The centrality of time to Judaism is expressed succinctly by Abraham Joshua Heschel in his work *God in Search of Man: A Philosophy of Judaism*: "Judaism is a religion of history, a religion of time. The God of Israel was not found primarily in the facts of nature. He spoke through events in history. While the deities of other peoples were associated with places or things, the God of the prophets was the God of events: the Redeemer from slavery, the Revealer of the Torah, manifesting Himself in events of history rather than in things or places."[2]

This understanding of God's action in history is introduced in scriptural texts which establish the significance of marking specific

---

[1] Abraham Joshua Heschel, *The Sabbath: Its Meaning for Modern Man* (New York: Farrar, Straus and Giroux, 2005), 8.
[2] Abraham Joshua Heschel, *God in Search of Man: A Philosophy of Judaism* (New York: Noonday Press, 1955), 200.

times and of the element of time itself. The concept of time first appears in the opening of Genesis, when God's creation of light is immediately followed by the division of light from darkness, creating the distinction between day and night (Gen 1:3-5). This is followed by the creation of light-producing cosmic bodies: "God said, 'Let there be lights in the expanse of the sky to separate day from night; they shall serve as signs for the set times—the days and the years'" (Gen 1:14). Here, on the fourth day, the main purpose of the creation of light is not to shed light but to mark time. In this passage, the marking of time through the distinction between day and night is presented as more significant than the fundamental need to see the physical world by the light of day.

The significance of marking and remembering time is repeatedly emphasized throughout the first five books of the Hebrew Bible. In the Passover narrative, the instructions for the ritual meal and slaughter of the lamb whose blood saves the Israelites from the loss of each firstborn son begins with these words: "This month shall mark for you the beginning on the months; it shall be the first of the month of the year for you" (Exod 12:2). In the same chapter, the instruction for the observation of the seven days of Passover begins with another injunction to mark and remember time: "This day shall be a day of remembrance for you. You shall celebrate it as a festival to the LORD; throughout your generations you shall observe it as a perpetual ordinance" (Exod 12:14). The marking of time is again commanded by God at Mount Sinai, including the pivotal command to observe the Sabbath: "Remember the Sabbath day, and keep it holy. For six days you shall labor and do all your work. But the seventh day is a Sabbath to the LORD your God; you shall not do any work—you, your son or your daughter, your male or female slave, your livestock, or the alien resident in your towns. For in six days the LORD made heaven and earth, the sea, and all that is in them, but rested the seventh day; therefore the LORD blessed the Sabbath day and consecrated it" (Exod 20:8-11).

The twenty-third chapter of Leviticus outlines in detail the holy days that must be observed through the year, repeating the phrase *mo'adei Adonai*, "fixed times of the LORD" or "set times of the LORD," throughout the chapter. "Speak to the Israelite people and say unto them: These are My fixed times, the fixed times of the

LORD, which you shall proclaim as sacred occasions" (Lev 23:2). "These are the set times of the LORD, the sacred occasions, which you shall celebrate each at its appointed time" (Lev 23:4). "Those are the set times of the LORD that you shall celebrate as sacred occasions" (Lev 23:37).[3]

The Hebrew Bible treats time as a system established by God and given to humanity with the injunction to honor the gift through marking and observing time as instructed. This drive to measure and observe the passing of time reflects an understanding of time as historical and comprised of a past, present, and future rather than an endlessly recurring cycle. This is seen in the scriptural passages listed above, which command the commemoration of specific times in relation to the historical progression portrayed by the events in the biblical narrative in which God intervenes in history, within time.

In the biblical vision, time progresses ever forward and does not rest in an eternal present. This biblical understanding of time set the foundations for later developments in Jewish thought and introduced a temporal orientation that was eventually adopted by Christianity and Islam as well.[4] In *The Jewish Experience of Time*, Eliezer Schweid proposes that this innovation in the understanding of time was part of biblical Judaism's move to separate itself from pagan views: "For pagan Myth, the past and the future view of the cycle become identical as a perpetual now. The past is a future that may recur, and the future is a past that is about to recur, just as the present has already been and shall be. Contrary to Myth, historical time is an undertaking of memory and hope. Historical time begins with a memory of a one-time past, which has happened never to return and comes full circle in a hope of a one-time unprecedented future."[5]

The move to differentiate Judaism from the pagan traditions from which it arose is also tied in with the development of the

---

[3] New Jewish Publication Society translation.

[4] Yosef Hayim Yerushalmi, *Zakhor: Jewish History and Jewish Memory* (Seattle: University of Washington Press, 1982), 8.

[5] Eliezer Schweid, *The Jewish Experience of Time: Philosophical Dimensions of the Jewish High Holy Days*, trans. Amnon Hadary (Northvale, NJ: Jason Aronson, Inc., 2000), 17.

seven-day week. The practice of observing a week comprised of seven days divorced the week from the lunar cycle. Sociologist Eviatar Zerubavel argues that this created a unit of time that, in its disjunction from celestial cycles, spoke of God's transcendence through the element of time. "The rise of the Sabbath . . . within Judaism coincided with the withdrawal from worshipping the celestial bodies. . . . In other words, the disassociation of the week from a natural cycle such as the waxing and waning of the moon can be seen as part of a general movement toward introducing a supernatural deity. . . . Accordingly, the day dedicated to this God was to be regarded as part of a divine temporal pattern that transcends even nature itself."[6]

For ancient Judaism, the development of the notion of historical or linear time organized by the seven-day week also entailed another shift: time was no longer an element to be escaped but was welcomed as the medium of God's interaction with humanity. The life of faith entailed not a transcendence of time but an immersion into time.

CYCLICAL AND HISTORICAL TIME

In his essay "Counting Time," Rabbi Joseph B. Soloveitchik, a leading voice in twentieth-century American Orthodox Judaism, identifies the act of counting as an intrinsic part of Jewish life: "The Jew counts. He counts days, weeks, years, and shemittot—sabbatical years. He counts six days of every week and then celebrates the Sabbath. He counts forty-nine days as well as seven weeks during the omer period and concludes his count with the observance of Shavu'ot. He counts seven years and keeps shemittah. He counts forty-nine years and seven shemittot and then proclaims the yovel, the jubilee year."[7] Yet what is it precisely that one counts? In this passage, one counts days, weeks, years, and multiples of years.

[6] Eviatar Zerubavel, The Seven Day Circle: The History and Meaning of the Week (Chicago: University of Chicago Press, 1989), 11.

[7] Joseph B. Soloveitchik, Festival of Freedom: Essays on Pesah and the Haggadah, ed. Joel B. Wolowesky and Reuven Ziegler (Jersey City, NJ: Ktav Publishing House, 2006), 173.

The passage is about the counting of time, but more specifically, it is about the counting of the kind of time that is marked by the cycles of cosmic bodies. It is cyclical time, and its daily, monthly, and yearly cycles are observable in nature. Soloveitchik does not, however, suggest that this is the only type of time that is counted. Rather, this cyclical time is connected to historical time, which is not marked by cycles but by the narratives of the past, present, and future. Historical time exists as memory and as anticipation; it is not evident in cosmic cycles or the passage of seasons but is held within the consciousness through the idea of the past, present, and future. Soloveitchik proposes that the process of counting also engages historical time and encompasses notions of the past and the future:

> When one counts, one ushers in a mathematical series, a continuum. Kant remarked that at any position in which you find yourself while counting, you have to be aware of two things: the preceding positions and those that follow (*Critique of Pure Reason* [1781], Introduction, sec. V). For instance, when we count the thirty-third day of the omer, we ipso facto state that this position was preceded by thirty-two previous positions. At the same time, we know that thirty-three is not the last station; from here we will move on to additional positions. In other words, any act of counting embraces retrospection as well as anticipation.[8]

This passage demonstrates that the act of counting cyclical time involves the awareness of historical time as well. Counting, which in this context refers to the counting involved in maintaining liturgical celebrations, requires an awareness of the past and future. The process of counting the cyclical time required for maintaining liturgical schedules also touches on the awareness of the past and the future through memory and anticipation. The practice of liturgical remembrance and anticipation, experiencing the past and future of the historical religious narrative, occurs within the context of counting cyclical time. This notion of the intertwining of cyclical and historical time is also discussed by Rabbi Jonathan Sacks in an essay bearing the same title as Soloveitchik's: "Counting Time."

[8] Ibid., 177–78.

If we look at the festivals of the Bible—Pesach [Passover], Shavuot and Sukkot— we see that each has a dual logic. On the one hand, they belong to cyclical time. They celebrate seasons of the year— Pesach is the festival of spring, Shavuot of first fruits, and Sukkot of the autumn harvest. However, they also belong to covenantal/linear/historical time. They commemorate historic events. Pesach celebrates the exodus from Egypt, Shavuot the giving of the Torah, and Sukkot the forty years of wandering in the wilderness. It follows that the counting of the Omer also has two temporal dimensions. On the one hand, it belongs to cyclical time. The forty-nine days represent the period of the grain harvest, the time during which farmers had most to thank G-d for—for "bringing forth bread from the ground." Thus understood, each day of the counting is a separate religious act: "Blessed be the Lord day by day." Each day brought forth its own blessing in the form of new grain, and each therefore called for its own act of thanksgiving. This is time as Hillel and R. Hai Gaon understood it. "Count off fifty days"—each of which is a command in itself, unaffected by the days that came before or those that will come after. But the Omer is also part of historical time. It represents the journey from Egypt to Sinai, from exodus to revelation.[9]

Let us return now to Soloveitchik's essay of the same name, in which he makes a claim that brings us directly to the thesis argued in the present study: "In consequence, the Jew is aware experientially of the past and committed to the future, which is a reality to him. To exist as a Jew means to be at the juncture of past and future, of that which is no longer real and that which is not yet real. Our mission is to live in both dimensions. This experiential merger of past and future, of recollection and anticipation, is symbolized by the process of counting."[10] Here, Soloveitchik proposes that the past and the future experientially merge in liturgical counting. The liturgical meeting of cyclical daily time and historical consciousness becomes a launching point for the transformed experience of

[9] Jonathan Sacks, "Counting Time," in *Shabuot Reader: Torah Readings and The Book of Ruth with Laws and Commentaries*, ed. Nathan M. Dweck (New York: Tebah Educational Series, 2008), 20–21.

[10] Soloveitchik, *Festival of Freedom*, 177.

time, in which the past, present, and future merge in the experience of the liturgical participant.

HISTORY AND MEMORY IN RABBINIC THOUGHT

With the development of rabbinic Judaism, the biblical foundation was reinterpreted and its meanings rewritten. The observation
of time became more systematized as rabbinic literature further
codified the marking of time through copious discussions of the
precise time for prayer. An example of this systematization is
found in the opening passage of the Mishnah, which discusses the
issue of the time at which the Shema may be recited in the evening.

> From what time may one recite the Shema in the evening? From the
> time that the priests enter [their houses] in order to eat their *terumah*
> until the end of the first watch. These are the words of Rabbi Eliezer.
> The sages say: Until midnight. R. Gamaliel says: Until the dawn
> comes up. Once it happened that his sons came home [late] from a
> wedding feast and they said to him: We have not yet recited the
> [evening] Shema. He said to them: If the dawn has not yet come up
> you are still bound to recite. And not in respect to this alone did they
> so decide, but wherever the sages say "until midnight," the mitzvah
> may be performed until the dawn comes up. The burning of the fat
> and the pieces may be performed till dawn. Similarly, all [the offer-
> ings] that are to be eaten within one day may lawfully be consumed
> till the coming up of the dawn. Why then did the sages say "until
> midnight"? In order to keep a man far from transgression.[11]

The discussion is continued in the second mishnah, now addressing the time of the morning Shema: "From what time may one recite
the Shema in the morning? From the time that one can distinguish
between blue and white. R. Eliezer says: Between blue and green.
And he has time to finish until sunrise. R. Joshua says: Until the
third hour of the day, for such is the custom of kings, to rise at the
third hour. If one recites the Shema later he loses nothing, being like
one who reads in the Torah."[12] These passages serve as an illustration

---

[11] *The Babylonian Talmud*, trans. Isidore Epstein (London: Soncino Press,
1948), Berachot 1.1.

[12] *Babylonian Talmud*, Berachot 1.2.

of the extent to which the determination of precise windows of time is a matter of great concern to the rabbinic mind. The passages assign a sizable significance to time; the process through which they measure time gives order and meaning to the cycles of daily time, connecting the times to ritual norms exemplified through reference to the ancient Temple liturgy as well as to natural time.[13]

The systematization of time within rabbinic tradition involves not only the determination of appropriate times for prayer, which addresses cyclical time, but also the categorization of eons of historical time. Rabbinic tradition categorizes time into three eons, not measured by years, but by phases in the divine plan. The first eon is the time when the Temple stood in Jerusalem; the second eon is *hazeman hazeh*, or *haolam hazeh*, the present time, and it includes all time from the destruction of the Temple through the present time and into the future until the coming of the messiah. The third eon is the time of the messiah and redemption and is called *haolam haba*, the time to come, or *yemot hamashiach*, the days of the messiah.[14] Rabbinic literature contains very little explicit reflection on the circumstances of the time in which it was written, which may be an indication of the devaluation of the eon of the present time. The literature is oriented toward the time to come, and the present time is significant primarily as a ground for working out the details of commandments and obligations, the observance of which will allow the time to come to eventually arrive.[15]

---

[13] In Tractate Berachot, the Babylonian Talmud discusses the phrase "*et ratzon*," literally "a pleasing time" or "an acceptable time," which has taken on the meaning of an auspicious time for prayer: "What is the meaning of the verse: But as for me, let my prayer be made unto Thee, O Lord, in an acceptable time? When is the time acceptable? When the congregation prays" (*Babylonian Talmud*, Berachot 8a). The verse discussed here is Psalm 69:13, and in its Talmudic context, the phrase "*et ratzon*" from this verse has taken on its current meaning as an ideal time for prayer.

[14] Lawrence A. Hoffman, *Beyond the Text: A Holistic Approach to Liturgy* (Bloomington, IN: Indiana University Press, 1989), 82. The last two terms differ subtly in that the former tends to refer to a future state beyond time whereas the latter often involves the notion of a specific messianic time.

[15] Ibid., 83. Likewise, Hoffman has noticed that the various medieval commentaries on the Passover Haggadah are for the most part unconcerned with

In his 1982 publication, *Zakhor: Jewish History and Jewish Memory*, Yosef Hayim Yersushalmi explores rabbinic Judaism's preoccupation with memory and discusses its relative disinterest in history. Differentiating between memory and the discipline of history, Yerushalmi observes that "Israel is told only that it must be a kingdom of priests and a holy people; nowhere is it suggested that it become a nation of historians. Memory is, by its nature, selective, and the demand that Israel remember is no exception."[16]

Memory tends to lend uneven weight to the events of history, creating a criteria of historical significance that does not necessarily value every event equally. In religious memory, God's intervention in history becomes the primary measurement of historical significance and determines the weight attributed to particular times.[17] For the rabbinic mind, the Bible reveals the events of past history, but more importantly, it reveals the pattern of history as a whole.[18] This pattern, as perceived by rabbinic tradition, does not measure by strict chronology but by the events of divine intervention. The holistic pattern of religiously envisioned history thus provides an interpretive framework that allows the narrative of the Bible to be seen within a cohesive pattern of history.

Privileging memory over history, this rabbinic understanding of time differs from the biblical precedent. Yerushalmi contrasts the biblical style of historical writing with the rabbinic license to creatively warp history. Although biblical history is rooted in myth and memory, located far from the modern academic discipline of history, it has none of the playful pushing and pulling of time exhibited in rabbinic literature.

---

their contemporary context and with the historical process in general. They tend to ignore history, because although Passover is focused on the recollection of a past time, it does not concern history as such but rather "the metahistorical pattern of history." Ibid., 105. For the rabbinic mind, "God had established a grand plan in which history as we moderns know it is incidental." Hoffman supports this claim by citing a rabbinic principle which indicates a nonchronological understanding: "*Ein mukdam ume'uchar batorah*," translated as "the events of Torah do not follow chronological succession." Ibid., 82–83.

[16] Yerushalmi, *Zakhor*, 10.

[17] Ibid., 10–11.

[18] Ibid., 21.

Unlike the biblical writers the rabbis seem to play with time as though with an accordion, expanding and collapsing it at will. Where historical specificity is a hallmark of the biblical narratives, here that acute biblical sense of time and place often gives way to rampant and seemingly unselfconscious anachronism. In the world of aggadah Adam can instruct his son Seth in the Torah, Shem and Eber establish a house of study, the patriarchs institute the three daily prayer-services of the normative Jewish liturgy, Og King of Bashan is present at Isaac's circumcision, and Noah prophesies the translation of the Bible into Greek.[19]

Yerushalmi's observations are echoed and developed by Michael Signer, who explains in his introduction to *Memory and History in Christianity and Judaism* that the two are not entirely complementary. "Historical thinking provides a critical approach to the past, which puts issues of memory grounded in the authority of divine revelation seriously at risk."[20] He observes that historical thinking is a modern phenomenon, foreign to the rabbinic worldview. It is primarily an academic activity, with its origin in secular institutions. As such, modern historical thinking tends to view the past through a very different lens than that used by the rabbinic mind.[21]

Yerushalmi identifies the type of memory operative in rabbinic thought as a communal activity rather than an individual experience. He uses the work of sociologist Maurice Halbwachs, who ar-

[19] Ibid., 17.

[20] Michael A. Signer, "Memory and History in the Jewish and Christian Traditions," in *Memory and History in Christianity and Judaism*, ed. Michael A. Signer (Notre Dame, IN: University of Notre Dame Press, 2001), ix.

[21] Ibid., x. In the same volume, contemporary biblical scholar Marc Brettler also notes that memory occupies a more central place than history within rabbinic thought. He argues that the rabbis were not primarily concerned with history *per se* but with history as interpreted by memory. Rabbinic thought was "largely agnostic toward the real past" and did not focus on "history in the sense of the past for its own sake." Rather, it was concerned with history for the sake of its religious significance, which is communicated through religious memory. Marc Brettler, "Memory in Ancient Israel," in *Memory and History in Christianity and Judaism*, ed. Michael A. Signer (Notre Dame, IN: University of Notre Dame Press, 2001), 6; 2.

gued that "collective memory is not a metaphor but a social reality transmitted and sustained through the conscious efforts and institutions of the group" to construct an understanding of the nature of memory as something developed through communal structures of tradition.[22] The notion of memory operative in the present study refers to communal rather than individual memory, and attendant to the concept of communal memory is the notion of a communal sense of time, for memory requires a consciousness of time. The religious community that shares a sense of memory also, then, experiences a communal sense of time.

The rabbinic tradition communicates a communally experienced sense of time, shaped by the contours of religious tradition. In this vision, time is understood in relation to the remembered past and the anticipated future, which each influence the present. Within the worldview evoked by the rabbinic tradition, therefore, a communal experience of time, shaped by the communal memory and anticipation inherent in the tradition, arises.

MESSIANIC HOPE

The Jewish engagement with memory is not entirely focused on the past, for the narrative of God's saving action in the past also functions as an indication of future promise.[23] The notion of the

---

[22] Yerushalmi, *Zakhor*, xv. See Maurice Halbwachs, *On Collective Memory* (Chicago: University of Chicago Press, 1992). See also Adin Steinsaltz, *A Guide to Jewish Prayer* (New York: Schocken Books, 2000), 16. Steinsaltz notes the communal nature of Jewish prayer: "When a congregation is deeply absorbed in prayer, a new entity is created—no longer a collection of individuals, but a *Kahal Kadosh* ('Holy Congregation'), praying in unison. Each worshipper then becomes part of a greater unity, drawing strength from the other worshippers, and giving a part of himself in return. Whether consciously or unconsciously, a new set of experiences is created through these interrelated communal components."

[23] As Kenneth Seeskin observes, the orientation toward the future is embedded in the opening line of the Hebrew Bible. "Even the most casual reader," he writes, "cannot fail to notice that the Hebrew Bible is future oriented. Without any sort of prelude or introduction, it opens with the words 'In the beginning,' which, on any reasonable interpretation, implies that it is legitimate to ask

future encompasses not only the future that is expected to unfold chronologically with the passing of years but also the vision of an eschatological future. This future-oriented dimension of religious memory, referred to throughout this study as "eschatological memory," is concretized in Judaism in the visions of a messianic future as conceived in tradition and in the religious imagination.

The messianic temporal question—that is, the question concerning the time when the messiah will come—addresses both the temporal designation of the messianic redemption and the quality of the time. The designation of the time is undetermined in Jewish tradition; accompanying this issue is a more subtle argument concerning the qualities that this time will bear. A rabbinic discussion that addresses the latter portrays the coming of the messiah in successive stages. In this story, Rabbi Hiyya and Rabbi Simeon are walking before dawn and witness the sun beginning to rise from below the horizon. Rabbi Hiyya observes, "So too is Israel's redemption; at first it will be only very slightly visible, then it will shine forth more brightly, and only afterwards will it break forth in all of its glory."[24] This image indicates a slow progression of the redemptive process, in which a gradual introduction is followed by an eventual fullness of redemption. Other strands of messianic thought, however, oppose this image of a slow inauguration and envision the messiah coming suddenly, without warning.

Messianism involves elements of both time and space, for while its primary focus is the anticipation of redemption in a future time, this temporality is connected to the place of Jerusalem. The messianic hope in the rebuilding of the Temple and the creation of an independent state are tied to the geographical place of Jerusalem and the surrounding land of Israel. The messianic vision refers to a time and a place, which suggests that messianic thought envisions the dimensions of time—the past, present, and future—as a multi-

---

about the middle and end." Kenneth Seeskin, *Jewish Messianic Thoughts in an Age of Despair* (New York: Cambridge University Press, 2012), 5.

[24] "Song of Songs Rabbah," 6.25. Transcribed in Gershom Scholem, "Toward an Understanding of the Messianic Idea in Judaism," in *The Messianic Idea in Judaism*, trans. Michael A. Meyer (New York: Schocken, 1971), 10–11.

dimensional phenomenon, for in the messianic imagination, the future is both temporal and spatial.

The embeddedness of time and space in the religious imagination reflects the interpenetration of temporal dimensions in Jewish thought. Just as time is inseparable from space, the present time cannot be conceptualized without the notion of the past and the future. In the understanding of time formed by rabbinic tradition, the dimensions of time, shaped by communal memory and by the religious narrative, cease to be simply sequential. They begin to interpenetrate, as the past is experienced in the present, and the future envisioned through eschatological anticipation.

Human behavior, specifically the completion of righteous deeds, is generally considered to have the capacity to hasten redemption, as suggested by the midrash from Exodus Rabbah: "If Israel would repent even for a single day, they would be instantly redeemed and the Son of David would instantly come, for it says (Ps. 95:7): *Today* if you listen to His voice."[25] This implies a certain flexibility of time; i.e., if human action can hasten the messianic redemption, then the duration of time is capable of being shortened by deeds or, conversely, lengthened by sin. This notion implies that the span of time is, to a certain degree, placed in human hands and made malleable by human action.[26]

The relationship between messianic hope and the notion of the flexibility of time is also suggested by Gershom Scholem's assertion that the messianic idea is the site of the interconnection of the restorative and utopian impulses in rabbinic Judaism. In *The Messianic Idea in Judaism,* Scholem identifies three main forces at work in rabbinic Judaism: conservative, restorative, and utopian. The conservative impulse seeks to preserve the existing condition and to protect it against the threat of change. This impulse does not play a

---

[25] Exodus Rabbah, 25.16. Transcribed in Scholem, "Toward an Understanding of the Messianic Idea in Judaism," 11.

[26] This idea has been taken up by Franz Rosenzweig, who claims in *The Star of Redemption* that prayer hastens the future, allowing time to be contracted. Franz Rosenzweig, *The Star of Redemption,* trans. William W. Hallo (Notre Dame, IN: University of Notre Dame Press, 1985), 289.

part in messianism, however. Rather, messianism arises out of an interaction between the restorative impulse, which seeks to return to an ideal past condition, and the utopian impulse, which is entirely forward looking. Scholem writes, "Both tendencies are deeply intertwined and yet at the same time of a contradictory nature; the messianic idea crystallizes only out of the two of them together."[27] According to Scholem, messianic hope expresses the impulse to return to an ideal past as well as the impulse to enter into an ideal future. With the meeting of the two impulses in messianism, the past and the future are knit together in the religious imagination. The anticipated redemption is located in both the future and the past; it is an eschatological memory.

In the religious imagination, the anticipation of the messianic future is both eschatological and memorial, and the narratives of the past, present, and future merge. The narratives of biblical and post-biblical tradition do not remain lost in the past but impact the understanding of the present and the expectation of the future. The anticipated redemption is not just a conceptual idea remaining continually out of reach, but as Soloveitchik claims, it must be experienced in the present: "At the same time, Judaism requires of us to pre-experience the not-yet-real that will become real at some point in time. . . . The future is a reality before it manages to arrive. In tense expectation and anticipation, I pre-experience the future, I live it, I am involved in it and am very close to its events."[28]

The notion that the future is a reality that must be experienced in the present parallels the injunction so present in Jewish texts and traditions to continually remember the past, letting it shape the understanding of the present. This crucial role of religious experience in the memory of the past and the anticipation of the future leads us into the next chapter, which explores how memory, hope, and the notion of time are performed in liturgy.

---

[27] Scholem, "Toward an Understanding of the Messianic Idea in Judaism," 3.
[28] Soloveitchik, *Festival of Freedom: Essays on Pesah and the Haggadah*, 176–77.

Chapter 6

Memory and Anticipation in Jewish Liturgy

To exist as a Jew means to be at the juncture of past and future, of that which is no longer real and that which is not yet real. Our mission is to live in both dimensions.

—Rabbi Joseph B. Soloveitchik[1]

MEMORY IN THE LITURGICAL CALENDAR

In Jewish liturgy, memory and hope do not remain abstract but are contextualized and performed.[2] Liturgy functions as a performance of memory in which the act of memory is given a physical and enacted form beyond its intellectual abstraction. Liturgical performance is an experiential encounter with the fundamental elements of Judaism; Jewish visions of history and time are enacted in liturgy and engaged through ritual acts of memory and hope. This is concretized in the Jewish liturgical calendar, which performs the essential function of linking the memorialized narratives and the content of hope to the calendar. Through the codification of the observance of religious memory at specific times throughout the year, the liturgical calendar gives a temporal body to the memorialized narratives. It allows the narratives to inhabit the

---

[1] Joseph B. Soloveitchik, *Festival of Freedom: Essays on Pesah and the Haggadah,* ed. Joel B. Wolowesky and Reuven Ziegler (Jersey City, NJ: Ktav Publishing House, 2006), 177.

[2] Of the many expressions of Judaism, this chapter addresses contemporary traditional Judaism, using the Ashkenazi liturgy.

liturgical community and be performed in conjunction with the liturgical marking of time.

The development of rabbinic liturgy reflects, among other things, the history of the Jewish people's struggle to maintain and develop a distinct identity and ritual life after the destruction of the Second Temple. Faced with the task of developing a way to continue liturgical practice without the daily Temple sacrifices, the rabbis of the first century produced a systemization of daily prayer in place of the daily sacrifice, partially integrating the Temple liturgical system into rabbinic liturgy.[3] Rabbinic prayer, therefore, is an expression of memory: it commemorates the Temple that once stood at the center of Jewish liturgical life, and it constructs a memorial association with the biblical narrative of the patriarchs.[4]

The holidays of the rabbinic Jewish liturgical calendar all involve elements of historical memory: Passover is a commemoration of the exodus from Egypt, and the celebration of the holiday involves the participation of the individual in a communal reactualization of the past. Through participation in the seder and the recitation of the Haggadah, each person "remembers" the exodus in a ritual act that transcends the basic recollection of past events. As the Haggadah details, every person is obligated to see himself or herself as one who personally was set free from Egypt. The act of memory becomes a virtual experience of the past, ritually made present in the communal celebration. Shavuot celebrates the revelation of the Torah at Mount Sinai; Tish'ah b'Av mourns the destruction of the Temple; Sukkot commemorates the time in the wilderness; Hanukkah commemorates the Maccabean victory; and Purim recalls the Esther narrative, commemorating the victory over those who attempted to destroy the Jewish people.

---

[3] Ruth Langer, *To Worship God Properly: Tensions between Liturgical Custom and Halakhah in Judaism* (Cincinnati, OH: Hebrew Union College Press, 1998), 10.

[4] Although the daily prayers were mandated by rabbinic authority, the rabbis trace the roots of the three prayer times to Scripture, linking *Shacharit* to Abraham's prayer, *Mincha* to Isaac's, and *Maariv* to Jacob's, rooting the daily prayers deeply in mythological and biblical memory. *Babylonian Talmud*, Berachot 26b.

In the spring and summer, the Jewish calendar contains an extended season of memorial holidays, or "memory season," beginning with Shabbat Zakhor through Shavuot and then picking up again in the season surrounding Tish'ah b'Av.[5] Shabbat Zakhor, the Shabbat that falls immediately before Purim, begins the memory season with the reading of Deuteronomy 25:17-19: "Remember what Amalek did to you on your journey out of Egypt, how he attacked you on the way, when you were faint and weary, and struck down all who lagged behind you; he did not fear God. Therefore when the LORD your God has given you rest from all your enemies on every hand, in the land that the LORD your God is giving you as an inheritance to possess, you shall blot out the remembrance of Amalek from under heaven; do not forget."

The appeal to memory within this passage prepares the liturgical community for the commandment to eliminate Amalek, also through an act of memory, on Purim.[6] As Yehuda Kurtzer notes in *Shuva: The Future of the Jewish Past*, this introduces a complicated commandment of memory, for one must remember to forget: "On Shabbat Zakhor we fulfill the biblical mandate to remember the treachery of the people of Amalek by publically reciting aloud from the Torah the very obligation to remember; we do not so much remember the event itself as the obligations that emerge from its memory. How then do we remember Amalek? We remember Amalek by recommitting ourselves to the somewhat paradoxical command to not forget to eliminate the memory."[7]

Exactly one month after Purim comes the memorial holiday of Passover, and between Passover and Shavuot, during the biblical "omer," is a period of mourning in remembrance of the slain students of Rabbi Akiva, to which in more recent years has been added the new memorial holidays of Yom HaShoah, the day of

---

[5] Yehuda Kurtzer, *Shuva: The Future of the Jewish Past* (Waltham, MA: Brandeis University Press, 2012), 4.

[6] On Purim, the narrative of the war with Amalek is read in Exodus 17:8-16. Haman is understood to be a descendent of Amalek, and Purim is thus seen to be a victory over those who sought to destroy the Jewish people.

[7] Kutzer, *Shuva*, 4–5.

Holocaust remembrance, and Yom HaZikaron, the memorial for Israel's fallen soldiers. These modern memorial days introduce a new type of memorial, with a new way of remembering, based in historical commemoration rather than the creative identification with an ancient or mythical past.[8] Despite this distinction, these holidays join a liturgical memorial season comprised of a series of holidays based in the liturgical performance of communal memory.

SHABBAT AND THE EXPERIENCE OF TIME

The building block of the Jewish liturgical calendar, Shabbat is a celebration and performance of Jewish communal memory. In the celebration of Shabbat, the three temporal elements of the past, present, and future are symbolized by the concepts of creation, revelation, and redemption.[9] It is a remembrance of God's act of creation in six days and his rest on the seventh. It recalls the gift of manna after the exodus from Egypt, which was given for only six days out of every seven, requiring the Israelites to divide the days

---

[8] Kurtzer notes that very different concepts of memory are operative in the traditional and modern holidays: "Memory means two completely different and even opposing things. The remembering that characterizes Purim and Passover is malleable and playful: we remember Amalek by playing out its treachery at other times in Jewish history and even our own; we remember the exodus by trying to relive it—not by traveling through time but by privileging the centrality of its message of liberation in our own time. But the commanding memory of the Holocaust in our present climate, in and out of Yom Ha-Shoah, is precisely the opposite—it is a memory that fears forgetting, a memory for which the passing of time and the loss of precision seem ominous and fearful, a memory that has generated the cataloging of testimonials and the furious documentation of experiences lest the eyewitnesses themselves depart and take with them our memories. Is this really memory?" Ibid., 6–7.

[9] These three temporal elements are evoked in the *Kedushat haYom*, which replaces the thirteen middle benedictions of the Amidah on Shabbat. A different introduction to the blessing is recited during *Maariv*, *Shacharit*, and *Mincha*, and each blessing relates to the three temporal elements which can also be identified with creation, revelation, and redemption. The *Kedushat haYom* for *Maariv* speaks of creation; the *Shacharit* blessing speaks of the revelation at Mount Sinai and the present time; and the *Mincha* blessing speaks of joy, associated with redemption.

into weeks and to observe the seventh day as a day of rest from its harvest. Shabbat is also a memorial of the revelation at Mount Sinai, through which the commandment to observe the Sabbath was made explicit.[10] Finally, Shabbat is also a celebration of redemption and is traditionally believed to provide a taste of the world to come. As both a memorial of the past and an anticipation of the world to come, the celebration of Shabbat practices the "eschatological memory" that has been discussed throughout this book. In this way, Shabbat is a commemoration of historical time; that is, of events, whether mythical or historical in the modern sense, which are thought to have occurred along a chronological continuum. Yet this historical time is situated within a celebration of cyclical time, on the seventh day of each week. The cyclical holiday of Shabbat thus connects historical time to cyclical time, celebrating primordial history within a weekly cycle.

Mishnah Tamid suggests the anticipatory function of Shabbat in its commentary on the heading of Psalm 92, which reads "A psalm. A Song for Sabbath Day" (Ps 92:1). The mishnaic text comments, "A psalm, a song for the time to come, for the day that will be all Sabbath and rest for everlasting life."[11] Jon D. Levenson elaborates on this passage in his book *Sinai and Zion*, in which he attributes to Shabbat a proleptic function: "In this Mishnah [m. Tam. 7:4], the Sabbath is seen as a proleptic glimpse of the eternal life of the coming age. In other words, eternal life is not simply ordinary life prolonged indefinitely, like the life of Tennyson's Tithonus, but differs from it qualitatively. And the quality of eternal life the Jew can experience even now in the form of the Sabbath. Those who observe

---

[10] This memorial character is expressed succinctly in the Kiddush for Shabbat evening: "Blessed are You, Lord our God, King of the Universe, who has made us holy through his commandments, who has favored us, and in love and favor gave us His holy Sabbath as a heritage, a remembrance of the work of creation. It is the first among the holy days of assembly, a remembrance of the exodus from Egypt." Jonathan Sacks, ed., *The Koren Siddur* (Jerusalem: Koren Publishers, 2009), 382.

[11] *The Babylonian Talmud*, trans. Isidore Epstein (London: Soncino Press, 1948), Mishnah Tamid, 7.4.

the Sabbath experience an earnest of the coming redemption. They climb the cosmic mountain weekly."[12]

The Mishnah suggests that the celebration of Shabbat goes beyond the *anticipation* of the eschatological future; it allows an *experience* of it. The celebration of Shabbat is proleptic, he claims, in that it offers an opportunity to experientially transverse the boundaries of the present moment. He notes that the possibility of a proleptic taste of the world to come is supported by Maimonides, who understands the present world and world-to-come to exist simultaneously. In the Mishneh Torah, *Laws of Teshuvah*, 8:8, Maimonides writes, "That which the rabbis called 'the world-to-come' was not called thus because it is not in existence now, and this world is perishing, and so the world-to-come will follow it. Rather, it is in existence now, as the Bible says, 'which you have made,' etc."[13] This passage alludes to an interpenetration of the eschatological future and the present, which may be experienced through Shabbat.

While the observance of Shabbat is both memorial and proleptic, virtually collapsing time, it also requires an ongoing practice of timekeeping, marking every seven-day period. This can be challenging in situations in which the regular pattern of life is disrupted; a Talmudic discussion of this issue points to the significance of the practice of counting days: "R. Huna said: If one is travelling on a road or in the wilderness and does not know when it is the Sabbath, he must count six days and observe one."[14] This passage declares that a person is obligated to continue to measure time by counting off days, even if the day one ultimately designates for rest does not correlate with the calendrically determined Shabbat. This suggests that the consciousness of time is crucial, for even when the absolute date of Shabbat cannot be definitively determined, the process of counting the passage of days must continue. If the awareness of time, practiced through the counting of days, is indeed a central part of the commandment to

[12] Jon D. Levenson, *Sinai and Zion: An Entry into the Jewish Bible* (San Francisco: HarperOne, 1985), 183–84.

[13] Ibid., 183.

[14] *Babylonian Talmud*, Shabbath 69b.

observe Shabbat as a day of rest, then the observance of Shabbat is also the observance of time-consciousness.[15]

Shabbat invites a heightened awareness of the present moment, as well as a contemplation of the mythical past of the biblical narrative and the anticipated redemption of the future. With the consciousness of time comes an engagement with the past and future, creating the experience of a multidimensional, transtemporal present moment. This is alluded to in Abraham Joshua Heschel's *The Sabbath*, which addresses the memorial and eschatological transtemporal nature of Shabbat: "The difference between the Sabbath and all other days is not to be noticed in the physical structure of things, in this spatial dimension. Things do not change on that day. There is only a difference in the dimension of time, in the relation of the universe to God. The Sabbath preceded creation and the Sabbath completed creation; it is all of the spirit that the world can bear."[16]

Heschel claims that although the physical structure of the world does not change on Shabbat, the dimension of time changes. His assertion that this change in time is located "in the relation of the universe to God" suggests that the dimension of time is found in that relationship. This points to how liturgical performance can change the experience of time: if the dimension of time lies in the relationship of the world to God, then the performance of liturgy, which directly addresses that relationship, has the capacity to transform the way that this dimension of time is experienced.

THE JEWISH DAILY SERVICES

While studies of the role of time within Jewish liturgy largely focus on the arrangement of liturgical festivals across the seasons, the Jewish daily services are the site of another crucial intersection

---

[15] In rabbinic Judaism and in modern Hebrew, the days of the week do not have independent names but are referred to by counting the days, beginning with Sunday. This demonstrates the way that the awareness of Shabbat shapes the perception of all the days of the week.

[16] Abraham Joshua Heschel, *The Sabbath: Its Meaning for Modern Man* (New York: Farrar, Straus and Giroux, 2005), 21.

between Jewish liturgy and time. The three services of *Shacharit*, *Mincha*, and *Maariv*, recited in the morning, afternoon, and evening, respectively, give a liturgical shape to each day as they punctuate the passage of the hours of the day with prayer.

The calculation of the times at which the daily services should be prayed is regularly, precisely recalculated in relation to the available daylight hours. Hours are measured in proportion to the length of the day, and so a proportional hour, a *sha'ah zmanit*, is one-twelfth of the daylight hours.[17] Each *sha'ah zmanit* is thus longer in the summer and shorter in the winter. The obligation to pray three times a day during specific time frames contributes to the heightening of time awareness, particularly when the length of the hours continually shifts, for the liturgical participant must always remain aware of the shifting parameters of the hours. Furthermore, as the length of the hours is stretched or shortened, the experience of time shifts proportionately.[18] Through this system, the dimensions of each hour shift throughout the liturgical calendar. Although this was a standard measurement of time in its origins, its use today intensifies the sense that liturgical time is unique, operating in a mode different from that of secular historical time and highlighting the liturgical shaping of time.

Perhaps reflecting the Talmudic preference for textual studies and textual argumentation over theological reflection, however, most liturgical commentaries give scant attention to the way that the services affect the consciousness of time and focus instead on historical and textual concerns.[19] Studies that address the role of time and memory in Jewish liturgy, with few exceptions, address the time within which liturgy is performed rather than the liturgies within which time is performed. This is exemplified in classic twentieth-

---

[17] See Maimonides's commentary to Mishnah Berakhot 1.5.

[18] This system of timekeeping, based on the flexible hours of daylight, was for the most part the norm in the premodern world before the development of modern clocks, as discussed in chapter 1.

[19] The inclination toward textual and historical approaches to liturgical studies, while prevalent in studies of Christian liturgy, is even more characteristic of studies of Jewish liturgy.

century siddur commentaries such as those of Elie Munk and B. S. Jacobson, which primarily address the relationship of the liturgical texts to other rabbinic and scriptural passages and discuss issues such as textual variation and historical origin.[20] They address historical and textual issues but rarely address issues that are distinctly theological or concerned with the text in its liturgical performance.

The preference for textual and historical concerns in siddur commentaries is so ingrained that little attention is given to the life the texts take on in performance. The performed, experiential aspects of the text as prayer are not central concerns, even when the commentaries address liturgical texts that are directly evocative of experiential elements such as the ritually marked passing of time. This can be seen in the commentaries that these collections offer on the text of the *Yotzer*, the first blessing of the Shema during the service of *Shacharit*. This blessing is replete with allusions to time, particularly to cyclical time. This is reflected in the title by which it is commonly referred, *Yotzer*, which is the first word of the line "who forms light and creates darkness." Despite the rich allusions to time in this prayer, however, the commentaries do not address any aspect of the experience of time in prayer. This tendency is also displayed within the genre of contemporary, more spiritually oriented siddur commentaries. While commentaries in both the classic and contemporary genres provide thorough examination of the textual content of the prayers, their focus remains within the text rather than on aspects of the life the texts take on in liturgical performance.[21]

---

[20] Dr. Elie Munk, *Daily Prayers* and *Sabbath and Festival Prayers*, vols. 1 and 2 of *The World of Prayer* (New York: Feldheim, Inc., 1961); B. S. Jacobson, *Meditations on the Siddur: Studies in the Essential Problems and Ideas of Jewish Worship*, trans. Leonard Oschry (Tel Aviv: Sinai, 1978); B. S. Jacobson, *The Weekday Siddur: An Exposition and Analysis of Its Structure, Contents, Language, and Ideas*, trans. Leonard Oschry (Tel Aviv: Sinai, 1978); B. S. Jacobson, *The Sabbath Service: An Exposition and Analysis of Its Structure, Contents, Language, and Ideas*, trans. Leonard Oschry (Tel Aviv: Sinai, 1981). Jacobson published three additional volumes that have not been translated.

[21] E.g., Lawrence A. Hoffman, ed., *My People's Prayer Book: Shabbat Morning*, vol. 10 (Woodstock, VT: Jewish Lights Publishing, 2007); Lawrence A. Hoffman,

Because the siddur is an ordering of prayer that is intended not just to be read as a literary segment but to be recited in a given order and at a specific time in conjunction with other prayers, any individual component of a prayer service does not reveal its full theological content when read alone. The various components must be interpreted within the context of their liturgical setting, for they are not literary excerpts that stand alone but are a part of a greater body whose form is best revealed as a liturgical whole. This is addressed by Reuven Kimelman, whose work is an exception to the norm within scholarship on the siddur, offering a theological reflection on the siddur that takes into account the role of the text in its performed liturgical setting. Kimelman's work is based in the liturgical texts yet also sees beyond the texts as texts and considers the dimensions that these texts take on in their performed, ritual contexts. To paraphrase Hoffman, he is concerned not only with "texts qua texts" but also with "texts qua prayer."[22]

In "The Literary Structure of the Amidah and the Rhetoric of Redemption," Kimelman argues that the Amidah is a sustained prayer for redemption; furthermore, he notes that this role arises in its liturgical setting in which it interacts with the Shema. The Amidah and the Shema share a particular relationship in which the memorialization of the past in the Shema is joined to the anticipation of the future in the Amidah; Kimelman claims that together they become a template for a vision of the eschatological future.

As a liturgical text, the Amidah is made more theologically potent by its liturgical recitation, as its theological weight does not reside entirely within its written form. The Amidah is recited three times each day, with an additional two repetitions in public prayer; each recitation insists that God will bring redemption. And so, three times a day the person who recites this series of blessings reaffirms with the breath and the voice that God is the redeemer of

---

ed., *My People's Prayer Book: The Sh'ma and Its Blessings*, vol. 1 (Woodstock, VT: Jewish Lights Publishing, 1997); Meir Zlotowitz and Sheah Brander, eds., *The Complete ArtScroll Siddur: Weekday/Sabbath/Festival*, 2nd ed. (Brooklyn, NY: Mesorah Publications, 1986).

   [22] Lawrence A. Hoffman, *Beyond the Text: A Holistic Approach to Liturgy* (Bloomington, IN: Indiana University Press, 1989), 6.

Israel. This theological content is then developed through its relationship to the other components of liturgy which, according to Kimelman, together form a liturgical expression of redemption from the conjunction of the memory of past redemption and the hope for future redemption.

When the Amidah is understood through its relationship to the Shema, it provides a liturgical expression of the anticipation of redemption. The memory of the past redemption becomes the theological foundation upon which the hope for future redemption rests. In the understanding of time suggested by the liturgical order, created through the conjoining of the various liturgical elements, the memory of the past informs the vision of the future. In this way, the past, present, and future are interrelated in the special quality of time created through the liturgy.

This liturgical quality of time, oriented toward both the past and the redemptive future, creates a unique liturgical present in which "joining in the chorus of past redemption, the worshipper finds him/herself praying for, if not actually announcing, the future redemption. The present is only where the memory of past redemption flowers into the expectation of future redemption."[23] The liturgical performance of the text expresses the past redemption and the promise of the future redemption. At the same time, the act of its recitation creates a liturgical present in which the past reaches to meet the future.

LITURGICAL MEMORY IN THE PASSOVER HAGGADAH

The celebration of Passover engages memory through liturgical celebration, refiguring the experience of time through the enactment of the religious narrative. The recitation of the Haggadah, the

[23] Reuven Kimelman, "The Literary Structure of the Amidah and the Rhetoric of Redemption," in *The Echoes of Many Texts: Reflection on Jewish and Christian Traditions, Essays in Honor of Lou H. Silberman*, ed. William G. Dever and J. Edward Wright (Atlanta: Scholars Press, 1997), 129. See also Reuven Kimelman, "The Messiah of the Amidah: A Study in Comparative Messianism," *Journal of Biblical Literature* 116, no.2 (1997): 313–24; Reuven Kimelman, "The Shema and Its Rhetoric: The Case for the Shema Being More than Creation, Revelation, and Redemption," *Journal of Jewish Thought and Philosophy* 2 (1992): 111–56.

liturgical text of the seder, invites participants to relive the memory of the exodus as if it were occurring in the present. As an act of ritual memory, its recitation heightens time-consciousness, while loosening the distinction between past, present and future. The following discussion traces the way that the Haggadah initiates an intensification of time-consciousness, contracting time through ritual memory, and then explores a similar temporal dynamic within Tish'ah b'Av.

The seder is an active, participatory remembrance of the paradigmatic events of the exodus from Egypt. It offers a way of participating in the journey out of Egypt and experiencing the transition from slavery to freedom. The text of the Haggadah provides the forum in which the remembrance is to occur; its recitation is an event that requires active, creative engagement. Central to the Haggadah is the obligation to remember the exodus from Egypt, and this obligation is made explicit in a portion of the *maggid*, or storytelling, section of the Haggadah:

> In every generation a person is obligated to regard himself as if he had come out of Egypt, as it is said: "You shall tell your child on that day, it is because of this that the Lord did for me when I left Egypt" (Ex. 13:8). The Holy One, blessed be He, redeemed not only our ancestors from Egypt, but He redeemed also us with him, as it is said: "It was us that He brought out from there, so that He might bring us to give us the land that He swore to our ancestors."[24]

Despite the centrality of this obligation, the terminology available for describing the act of remembrance offers an incomplete picture, as terms such as "memory," "reenactment," and "memorial" tend to lead to an image of a simple recollection of a past event which emphasizes a distinction between the history and the present. The ideal recitation of the Haggadah, however, requires that distinction to blur. The Haggadah does not chronicle history,

---

[24] Joseph B. Soloveitchik, *The Seder Night: An Exalted Evening: The Passover Haggadah*, ed. Menachem Genak (New York: Orthodox Union Press, 2009), 101. This is a citation of the Haggadah text, which is an elaboration of the dictate as it is expressed in Mishnah Pesachim 10.

nor does it simply reenact the past; its concern it not with the modern concept of historical time but with the sacred myth which reveals a religiously shaped pattern of history.[25]

The Passover obligation to see oneself as one who had personally come out of Egypt is not a simple obligation to perform, because it involves an inner participation that cannot be achieved through actions alone. Rabbi Joseph B. Soloveitchik comments on the elements of the seder that require a particular inner state. He writes, "However, *Be-khol dor va-dor* [in every generation] . . . [is a mitzvah] of an emotion, a state of mind. It is the involvement of a modern person who nevertheless lives within ancient events—a very complicated *mitzvah*."[26] Soloveitchik speaks of an inner involvement that is both intellectual and emotional and relates it to the condition of straddling times, so to speak. The participant not only lives in the contemporary time but also, symbolically, dwells in ancient, mythical time.

The recitation of the Haggadah collapses the boundaries between the past and the present; it also casts light on the transition from the present time to the future time. The future, epitomized in the Haggadah by the messianic vision of the complete ingathering of all the exiles to Israel, is invoked through the well-known line that came to conclude the formal part of the seder, "*l'shana ha'ba'a biyerusha-layim!*" ("next year in Jerusalem!"). This line comes at the close of the *Nirtzah*, the concluding prayer of the Haggadah, and is recited immediately after a petition to God to "soon lead offshoots of the stock You have planted, redeemed to Zion, rejoicing in song."[27] Placed at the end of the seder, it emphasizes the eschatological

[25] Marc Michael Epstein identifies a form of temporal interpenetration in the images of the illuminated manuscript known as the Birds' Head Haggadah: "In the Birds' Head Haggadah, the Passover seder is presented as a metahistorical topos that predates, parallels, and indeed rivals the metahistoricity of the mass. Certain scenes in the narrative sequence seem to be deliberately designed to be read asynchronically in order to create an indigenously Jewish species of temporal interpenetrability." Marc Michael Epstein, *The Medieval Haggadah: Art, Narrative, and Religious Imagination* (New Haven, CT: Yale University Press, 2011), 105.

[26] Soloveitchik, *The Seder Night*, 102.

[27] Ibid., 159.

orientation of the meal, concluding the celebration with a gesture toward the future.

Although it is most explicit in this closing line, the anticipation of the time of redemption is present throughout the Haggadah. In one such case, the *maggid* recalls a conversation between the rabbis regarding Deuteronomy 16:3, "That you may remember the day when you left Egypt all the days of your life," in which they dispute the meaning of "all the days of your life." Rabbi Elazar cites Ben Zoma's interpretation, claiming that the inclusion of the word "all" refers to nights as well as days, but the final word is given to the rabbis who clarify that "the days of your life" refer to the time of this life, whereas "*all* the days of your life" implies a continuation into the messianic future.[28] This decision extends the act of memory into the messianic future and insists that the past must be brought into the eschatological future through the act of memory.

In addition to this eschatological allusion, a number of passages in the Haggadah contain references to the time of redemption. This can be seen in the text of *Ha Lachma Anya* (the bread of affliction), recited during the *maggid* portion of the seder, which proclaims, "This year we are still here, next year in the land of Israel. This year [we are] slaves; next year we will be free people."[29] Images of the future redemption in the Holy City continue to arise throughout the Haggadah, as seen in the prayer at the second cup of wine, which includes a petition to God to allow future holidays to be celebrated in God's rebuilt city.[30] This prayer connects the celebration of liturgical festivals to the anticipated redemption, perceiving the hoped-for future in terms of the liturgical calendar.

[28] Ibid., 43. The Haggadah refers here to the discussion of the third passage of the Shema in Mishnah Berachot 1.5.

[29] Ibid., 27. The anticipation of redemption also appears in the standard grace after the meal incorporated into the seder, which on festive days is preceded by a recitation of Psalm 126, the psalm of messianic hope that begins "When the Lord restores the fortunes of Zion, we see it as in a dream."

[30] The petition to celebrate future holidays in the rebuilt Jerusalem is disputed in Mishnah Pesachim 10, and its inclusion in the Haggadah reinforces the eschatological orientation of the latter text.

The recitation of the Haggadah traces the deliverance from Egypt as a history, but it also virtually collapses history by bringing the past into the present and relating the present to the future. Historical chronology is not the guiding rule; Passover performs a narrative based on collective memory and identification rather than historical documentation. In the Haggadah, the boundary between the historical chronology of the exodus narrative and its mythical transtemporal significance seems to become permeable, blurring the distinction between the past, present, and future.

THE LITURGICAL PERFORMANCE OF MEMORY IN TISH'AH B'AV

The liturgical act of memory characteristic of the celebration of Passover occurs in a similar form during Tish'ah b'Av. Both transcend the static recollection of events of the past and allow the community to engage in an activity that perceptually draws the past into the present while looking toward the future.[31] The meaning of Tish'ah b'Av, the commemoration of the destruction of the First and Second Temples and subsequent disasters, has been reflected on in great depth in a series of lectures given by Soloveitchik between the years of 1970 and 1984 and collected in a volume titled *The Lord Is Righteous in All His Ways: Reflections on the Tish'ah be-Av Kinot*. In these lectures, Soloveitchik makes frequent recourse to the specific type of memory that Tish'ah b'Av requires. Here, he notes its relationship to the memory required for the celebration of Passover:

> To celebrate the Passover, the holiday of redemption and liberation, we must reexperience it, relive it, redramatize it, and restage it. This is true not only with regard to Passover. Tish'ah be-Av is also based upon this principle. It is not easy to observe Tish'ah be-Av. Sitting on the floor is very easy, of course. But Tish'ah be-Av means much more than that. . . . Tish'ah be-Av is for us a complete reexperiencing of the *hurban*. *Yahadut* [Judaism] demands that we feel a historical proximity or closeness to the events that are ancient in terms of the

[31] Tish'ah b'Av is the annual liturgical commemoration of the destruction of the First and Second Temples, and subsequent disasters.

calendar, if one counts the number of years. But historically we must be close, very close.[32]

The communal, liturgical memory of Tish'ah b'Av changes the perception of the span of history, for it allows the very distant past to feel as if it were in the present: "And, in fact, through the mourning we observe on Tish'ah be-Av we *do* remember the *hurban Beit ha-Mikdash*. It is remarkable how we remember an event that occurred so many years ago. It is now more than nineteen hundred years and we still remember. And not only do we observe the laws of Tish'ah be-Av, we actually feel sadness."[33] Soloveitchik explains how the great distance of the past event collapses in the perception of the person who mourns the destruction of the Temple, making the event have the clarity of a recent event. In the following line, he takes another step, not only noting how recent the event seems to the memory, but also claiming that the event indeed is occurring in the present day, metaphorically: "On Tish'ah be-Av we mourn for the *Beit ha-Mikdash* that was *just burned*, not for the *Beit ha-Mikdash* that was destroyed and burned over nineteen hundred years ago. Oh, no! The *Beit ha-Mikdash* that was burned just recently, and is still burning, is very real for us."[34]

This identification with the past is aided by the ascetic practices required on Tish'ah b'Av. It is one of the few days of fasting within the Jewish calendar. Eating and drinking are prohibited; in addition, a number of other ascetic practices are prescribed, including abstention from washing, sexual relations, the wearing of leather shoes, and the wearing of fine clothing.[35] These traditions bring the liturgical performance of mourning into the body, allowing the despair to be felt physically and facilitating identification with the narrative of the past.

---

[32] Joseph B. Soloveitchik, *The Lord Is Righteous in All His Ways: Reflections on the Tish'ah be-Av Kinot*, ed. Jacob J. Schacter (Jersey City, NJ: Ktav Publishing House, 2006), 72.

[33] Ibid., 25.

[34] Ibid.

[35] Adin Steinsaltz, *A Guide to Jewish Prayer* (New York: Schocken Books, 2000), 230.

Soloveitchik observes that Tish'ah b'Av is not only memorial but also eschatological, acting as a day of mourning as well as a day of hope:

> The mourning of Tish'ah be-Av is important not simply to elicit thoughts of the past but also to evoke thoughts of the future. Tish'ah be-Av is guided by the principle of *bi'at melekh ha-mashiah*, the coming of the Messiah. The reason this day of *avelut* [mourning] has been observed for so long is that it is both a day of *hurban* [destruction of the Temple] and a day of *nehamah* [hope]. For half the day there is *hurban*, despair, terrible despair, and for the next half, not terrible despair but, on the contrary, a note of hope, of courage, of consolation. And the hope, or *nehamah*, is focused on the belief in the coming of the Messiah. We say to each other, "Never mind what has happened, the future will be different." The faith in *bi'at melekh ha-mashiah* is the very essence of the *avelut* of Tish'ah be-Av, because its *avelut* is not pure *avelut*. It is *avelut* plus *nehamah*. Tish'ah be-Av is an expression of the catastrophe that occurred in the past, and it is also about the glory that will take place in the future.[36]

The conjunction of ritual memory and eschatological hope within the celebrations of both Passover and Tish'ah b'Av engenders a transformation in the experience of time. Both liturgical observances allow the various dimensions of time to all be experienced in a performance of transtemporality that blurs the distinctions between the past, present, and future. During Passover, the eras of time from the exodus from slavery through the present time and into the anticipated messianic future interpenetrate into one liturgical present. Likewise, on Tish'ah b'Av, the memory of the destruction of the Second Temple, which also remembers the destruction of the First Temple, becomes one with the present. The present, in turn, anticipates the eschatological future. The perception of chronological time becomes synthesized with the perception of ancient time, and the liturgical participants experience the memorialized narrative as a "continual present" in the liturgical transformation of time.

[36] Soloveitchik, *The Lord Is Righteous in All His Ways*, 61.

THE CONSCIOUSNESS OF TIME

The idea that time is performed in liturgy rests on the notion that time is given shape through subjective experience. While the cosmic cycles that determine the passage of day and night and the change of seasons continue regularly, the subjective experience of time is in a state of continual flux; this grants ritual performance the capacity to alter the experience of time. Eliezer Schweid points to this phenomenon in *The Jewish Experience of Time: Philosophical Dimensions of the Jewish Holy Days*:

> Ostensibly the transitions from day to night, the waxing and waning of the moon, and the change of seasons are givens over which man has no control. But this is not so. The meaning attached to these cosmic events can completely alter the sense of existing in time. The various orientations that cultures possess have shaped vastly different time frames. Take, for instance, the consensual observation of the transition from day to night. One can measure a 24-hour period beginning at sunset, or one can measure it from dawn onward. The factual data remain unchanged but there is a definite difference in the significance of the event for the person who experiences it.[37]

This speaks to the way that one's experience of time is determined by one's perspective. While the external markers of time remain consistent, the experience of time shifts based on the vantage point of the observer. This is reminiscent of the theory of the relativity of time, discussed in chapter 1, which holds that time cannot be objectively measured, for its measurement is inescapably relative to the position of the observer. Similarly, the experience of even the most fundamental markers of time—day and night—is determined by one's position, whether that position be physical, as in the case of the scientific theory, or theoretical, as in the case of a religiously formed notion of the nature of time.

The spiritual significance of the consciousness of time is explored by Soloveitchik, whose treatment of the category of subjec-

---

[37] Eliezer Schweid, *The Jewish Experience of Time: Philosophical Dimensions of the Jewish High Holy Days*, trans. Amnon Hadary (Northvale, NJ: Jason Aronson, Inc., 2000), 7.

tive experience is unique, particularly within Orthodox thought. Soloveitchik promotes an active engagement with time in which the consciousness of time is comprised of a creative interaction of memory and hope.

> While everything exists in time, only the human being is capable of experiencing time. God endowed man with time awareness, the ability to sense and feel time and the existential stream of selfhood. Unfortunately, not every human being takes advantage of the unique human endowment to experience time—to live time rather than to live in time. Many human beings float with the tide of time because there is no alternative to it. Time is an all-powerful, irresistible force. This time awareness or experience has three basic component parts. First, retrospection: without memory, there is no time. Second, the time experience includes exploration or close examination of things yet unborn and events not yet in existence. This means the anticipatory experience of events not yet in being. Third is appreciation or evaluation of the present moment as one's most precious possession.[38]

This passage makes a number of points relevant to the current discussion. Soloveitchik's claim that time awareness is a gift from God implies that it was given for a purpose and intended for use in a righteous life. He then breaks down the gift of time awareness into three components. First, he cites the necessary role of memory in the awareness of time, echoing the rabbinic preference for memory over historical thinking. Second, he points to the equal necessity of the anticipation of the future, which supports the claim made throughout this book that the experience of time is shaped by the past and the future. Third, he observes that the appreciation of the present is invaluable. This last point suggests that simply living in time is enough; the awareness of the present moment, shaped by the past and the future, is the key to a full human experience.

---

[38] Joseph B. Soloveitchik, *Festival of Freedom: Essays on Pesah and the Haggadah*, ed. Joel B. Wolowesky and Reuven Ziegler (Jersey City, NJ: Ktav Publishing House, 2006), 39.

The consciousness of time for Soloveitchik is a passage to freedom. Referring to the haste with which the Jews departed from Egypt in the Passover narrative, he declares: "It refers to our acquisition of time-consciousness—the Exodus can happen now, and may not happen later. This sense of time was the shibboleth of our ancestors when they left Egypt. The first commandment they were given in Egypt, marking the commencement of their liberation, was to mark time: 'This month shall be to you the beginning of months' (Ex. 12:2). *Bi-vehilu yaza'nu mi-Mizrayim (we departed from Egypt in haste)*—we have gained the consciousness of time, and hence we are free."[39] Soloveitchik makes a bold statement about the intrinsic importance of the consciousness of time, equating it with freedom. Further emphasizing his claim, he reiterates: "The basic criterion which distinguishes free man from slave is the kind of relationship each has with time and its experience. Freedom is identical with a rich, colorful, creative time-consciousness. Bondage is identical with passive intuition and reception of an empty, formal time-stream."[40]

The consciousness of time allows liturgical performance to shape the experienced dimensions of time. This concept also lies behind Yerushalmi's observation that rabbinic thought plays with time as an accordion player pulls and pushes the bellows of his instrument.[41] Both point to the interactive, creative nature of time awareness in Jewish thought and liturgical practice.

This brings into focus the flexibility and vibrancy of the consciousness of time in Jewish liturgical experience, in which time is

[39] Ibid., 42. Here, Soloveitchik addresses an unnamed commentary in which Maimonides claims that the haste with which the Jews left Egypt is of great importance. The line he quotes in Hebrew is found in the Sephardi Haggadah texts of Maimonides's tradition but not in Soloveitchik's own Ashkenazi tradition. The essay "Slavery and Freedom," in which this discussion is found, consists of a combination of a lecture titled "The Philosophy of Avadim Hayinu," material from an undated manuscript titled "Avadim Hayinu," and the texts of *shi 'urim* delivered March 16, 1969; May 18, 1970; and March 23, 1977.

[40] Joseph B. Soloveitchik, "Sacred and Profane: Kodesh and Chol in World Perspectives," *Gesher* 3, no. 1 (June 1966): 16.

[41] Yosef Hayim Yerushalmi, *Zakhor: Jewish History and Jewish Memory* (Seattle: University of Washington Press, 1982), 17.

subjectively determined through an active, performed engagement of memory and hope. The liturgical experience of time is shaped not by an unrelenting and inflexible sequential passage of time but by the contours of religious memory, continually reworked in each person's liturgical experience. In the religious imagination, time is flexible and an aspect of freedom.

This book takes up Soloveitchik's equation of the consciousness of time with freedom and builds on it by proposing that the religiously shaped consciousness of time offers a freedom *of* time as well. The freedom of time lies in the liberation of the experience of time from the constraints of chronological sequence and from the temporal condition by which the present perpetually recedes into the past, never to return. The consciousness of time allows the present to be infused with the past and the future and its boundaries to be opened into a transformed liturgical present.

PERFORMING MEMORY AND ANTICIPATION

These chapters have demonstrated that memory, as a central activity and unifying theme in Jewish thought and practice, is not primarily an intellectual process; memory is performed. As memory is contextualized in liturgical performance, it becomes more than just an idea. In liturgical performance, memory becomes a situation.[42]

The performed nature of Jewish memory is suggested by Yerushalmi, who argues that memory in Judaism is not just an intellectual

---

[42] The presence of this notion of performed memory in rabbinic thought, as well as in biblical literature, is noted by Marc Brettler, who writes that the Bavli recognizes that "biblical remembering should not be conceived of as an abstract activity, but as one intimately connected to performance." Brettler sees the roots of this performative form of memory in the Hebrew Bible, in the use of *zkr*, the root of the word denoting remembrance. He notes that the word is used in the Hebrew Bible not as an expression of purely abstract, cognitive memory but in relation to ritual performance. In the biblical context, as well as in rabbinic literature, memory is not a free-standing idea but is embodied in action. Marc Brettler, "Memory in Ancient Israel," in *Memory and History in Christianity and Judaism*, ed. Michael A. Signer (Notre Dame, IN: University of Notre Dame Press, 2001), 5.

abstraction but an activity that involves self-identification with the memorialized event. "For whatever memories were unleashed by the commemorative rituals and liturgies were surely not a matter of intellection, but of evocation and identification. There are sufficient clues to indicate that what was suddenly drawn up from the past was not a series of facts to be contemplated at a distance, but a series of situations into which one could somehow be existentially drawn."[43]

In liturgy, memory is something that one lives and breathes. The liturgical participant puts on memory, so to speak, and becomes clothed in memory. Yet memory is not only external clothing, resting on the participant through the utterance of words and the fulfillment of actions. It also becomes internalized as one is "existentially drawn" into it, to borrow Yerushalmi's words. This activity performs the transformation of time. One enters into the past, within the present, through the liturgical performance of memory. Similarly, one enters the future through hope. The performance of memory and hope constitutes a virtual, perceptual reshaping of time.

Heschel expresses a similar concept in his chapter "A Religion of Time," in *God in Search of Man: A Philosophy of Judaism*. Here Heschel considers how one must enter history and continue the lives of the patriarchs:

> The term "God of Abraham, Isaac, and Jacob" is semantically different from a term such as "the God of truth, goodness, and beauty." Abraham, Isaac, and Jacob do not signify ideas, principles, or abstract values. Nor do they stand for teachers or thinkers, and the term is not to be understood like that of "the God of Kant, Hegel, and Schelling." Abraham, Isaac, and Jacob are not principles to be comprehended but lives to be continued. The life of him who joins the covenant of Abraham continues the life of Abraham. For the present is not apart from the past. "Abraham is still standing before God" (Gen. 18:22). Abraham endures forever. We are Abraham, Isaac, Jacob.[44]

[43] Yerushalmi, *Zakhor*, 44.
[44] Abraham Joshua Heschel, *God in Search of Man: A Philosophy of Judaism* (New York: Noonday Press, 1955), 201.

Heschel implies that the divine name "God of Abraham, Isaac, and Jacob" entails an obligation to place oneself in the past through an active engagement of memory. The name suggests a religious truth that is not just conceptual but must be performed. This is also evident in the work of Soloveitchik, who sees prayer as identification with the communally remembered past: "The Jew who prays sees himself as integrated with those who have carried the burden over the generations, as connected to the past and the future like a link in one long chain. Awareness of historical continuity, strong faith in the messianic, eschatological destiny of the nation, and the experience of attachment to the generations assure the praying person that God will not reject him."[45]

For Soloveitchik, prayer is decidedly anamnetic, although he does not use this precise term.[46] Prayer involves not just an intellectual recollection of the past but the process of experiencing the past within the present: "We not only know our history, we also live it. The latter experience is, to us, not knowledge of the past, a mere narrative about events that took place once upon a time, but repetition: re-experiencing and reliving those events."[47]

Moving a step further, Soloveitchik sees prayer as the act of entering the past:

> In prayer, we experience the presence of God; we stand near and commune with Him. In reading the *Shema*, by contrast, we enter the presence of those persons who walked with Him, we stand in their shadow. . . . The first principle—accepting the Yoke of Heaven—on this reading, asserts itself in this analysis, in an act of self-identification with the history and destiny of our people, in the experience of oneness of ages and events, the merger of the multi-dimensional time-feeling into one focal point, a point that is, *eo ipso*, the center of my own self. It asserts itself in the pouring of the individual stream of existence into the mighty sea swept by the

[45] Rabbi Joseph B. Soloveitchik, *Worship of the Heart: Essays on Jewish Prayer*, ed. Shalom Carmy (New York: Toras HoRav Foundation, 2003), 155.

[46] The term "anamnetic" is used more frequently in reference to Christian liturgy.

[47] Soloveitchik, *Festival of Freedom*, 176.

hurricane of historic occurrence, enveloped in the mists of past and future, meeting with the thought, longing and will of a world physically long gone yet metaphysically still living, great and awesome.[48]

In this passage, prayer allows the individual to enter into history and to identify with the mythical past. Through prayer, one identifies with the past and also with the anticipated future, which Soloveitchik refers to as the "destiny" of the Jewish people. This creates a "multidimensional time-feeling" within the present moment, which sounds very much like the notion of temporal interpenetration thematic to the present study.

Soloveitchik's claim that the present and the past merge within the act of prayer bears resemblance to a theory introduced by Franz Rosenzweig.[49] While for Soloveitchik, prayer lets the past enter the present and the present enter the past, for Rosenzweig, prayer reaches into the future. Rosenzweig describes this in *The Star of Redemption*: "Into the darkness of the future, prayer casts a beam of light which reaches the farthest corners with its last off-shoots, while it illuminates the nearest point for the suppliant at the place of its first impact."[50]

The metaphorical quality of Rosenzweig's language leaves its meaning unspecified and its implications unclear. In the context of the introduction to part 3 of *The Star of Redemption*, however, titled "On the Possibility of Entreating the Kingdom," Rosenzweig clearly claims that prayer is capable of entering into the domain of the future. In this passage, prayer acts as a light illuminating the future, and in the following passage, he makes an even bolder claim: "It [prayer] must hasten the future, must turn eternity into the nighest, the Today. Such anticipation of the future into the moment would have to be a true conversion of eternity into a

---

[48] Soloveitchik, *Worship of the Heart*, 112.

[49] Rosenzweig's thought is located outside the mainstream of Jewish thought, unlike Soloveitchik, who represents American Orthodox Jewish thought.

[50] Franz Rosenzweig, *The Star of Redemption*, trans. William W. Hallo (Notre Dame, IN: University of Notre Dame Press, 1985), 272.

Today."[51] Here, Rosenzweig makes an astonishing statement. He claims that prayer must speed the arrival of the future. The term "future" here denotes the eschatological, redeemed world to come, which for Rosenzweig is equated with eternity. He claims that this capacity of prayer draws the future into the present, essentially merging the two, which he refers to as the "conversion of eternity" into the present. This concept is explained in more depth in a passage found a few pages later in *The Star of Redemption*:

> It [the week] is meant to regulate the service of the earth, the work of "culture," rhythmically, and thus to mirror, in miniature, the eternal, in which beginning and end come together, by means of the ever repeated present, the imperishable by means of the Today. . . . As law of cultivation laid down by man the week is the earthly analogy of the eternal, but it is more than this: as law of the cult laid down by God it attracts the eternal into the Today, not just by analogy but in reality. . . . By virtue of the week, the day too, and the year too, become human hours, temporal abodes into which the eternal is invited. The cycles of the cultic prayer are repeated every day, every week, every year, and in this repetition faith turns the moment into an "hour," it prepares time to accept eternity, and eternity, by finding acceptance in time, itself becomes—like time.[52]

Rosenzweig sees the act of timekeeping, practiced through the maintenance of the week, to be a virtue that invites the eternal into the present. He makes the bold claim that the repetition of liturgical cycles is efficacious in shifting the nature of time, for through "repetition faith turns the moment into an 'hour.'" Furthermore, Rosenzweig understands this to occur not simply as an analogy but in reality. While he does not clearly explicate this claim, it is clear that he is convinced of the potency of prayer in transforming time.

For Rosenzweig and for Soloveitchik, prayer creates a connection between earthly, chronological time and a mythical, redeemed temporality or state beyond chronology. For Rosenzweig, the latter

[51] Ibid., 289.
[52] Ibid., 291–92.

is equated with eternity. While Soloveitchik focuses mainly on the engagement of time-consciousness, rather than on a state beyond time, he also notes that the transcendence of chronological time achieved by prayer touches on the infinite. "Both prayer and prophecy," he writes, "are basically dialogues between finitude and infinity."[53] Prayer communicates between the present and eternity, connecting time with that which is beyond time.

[53] Soloveitchik, *Worship of the Heart*, 10.

Part 4

The Experience of Time
in Christian Liturgy

Chapter 7

Time in Christian Thought

*Then I saw a new heaven and a new earth; for the first heaven and the
first earth had passed away, and the sea was no more.*

—Revelation 21:1

THE EIGHTH DAY

Christian thought understands the work of Jesus Christ to have
radically transformed time. The redemption of the world, which is
both already completed and yet to occur, is believed to infuse time
with a taste of eternity. In some theologies, time is such an intrinsic
component of the work of Jesus Christ that it is envisioned to be
encased within the Christian mystery.[1] This chapter investigates
the complex shape of time in Christian thought; it is neither solely
linear nor cyclical and is experienced through the liturgical performance of memory and hope. Surveying theological conceptions of
time that are thoroughly christological, i.e., that understand time
through the narrative of Christ's life, death, and resurrection, it
gleans from the Christian theological tradition theories that contribute to the transformation of the experience of time in liturgical
performance.

In the process of defining the Christian celebration of the Sabbath in contrast to the Jewish Sabbath in the first few centuries of
Christianity, patristic theologians connected the day with the eschaton and referred to Sunday as a symbol of the eschatological
eighth day. The Christian concept of the eighth day symbolized the

---

[1] Jean Daniélou, *The Lord of History* (Chicago: H. Regnery, 1958), 24.

beginning of a new world. It connected the eighth day to the first day of creation as a new creation that followed the memorial of God's rest on the seventh day.[2] While used as means of distancing Sunday from the Jewish Sabbath, the notion of the eighth day also borrowed from the Jewish apocalyptic notion of a cosmic week of seven thousand years, in which each day is one thousand years.[3] The eighth day, then, acted as a symbol of the eighth millennium, envisioned as an eschatological reality beyond the completion of all time.[4]

In the tension between the cycles of natural time and the shaping of time through the narrative of divine intervention, the eighth day symbolized the transcendence of time. The eighth day was seen to overflow the boundaries of the seven-day week and to overcome sequential time.[5] The concept of the eighth day addressed the tension between natural time and the time indicated through the salvation narrative by allowing the latter a victory over the former. In this theological tradition, sequential time is burst open by the eschatological age, and time is transformed and transcended.

This tension between cyclical time and the time frame of salvation history was heightened as the Christian theological tradition

[2] This is seen in the fourth-century writings of St. Basil, who saw the first day of creation in the Genesis narrative to contain all history within itself, linked to the eighth day. See Mario Baghos, "St. Basil's Eschatological Vision: Aspects of the Recapitulation of History and the 'Eighth Day,'" *Phronema* 25 (2010): 85–103; St. Basil the Great, *Exegetical Homilies*, The Fathers of the Church Series, trans. Agnes Clare Way (Washington, DC: The Catholic University of America Press, 2003); St. Basil the Great, *On the Holy Spirit*, Popular Patristics Series, trans. David Anderson (Crestwood, NY: St. Vladimir's Seminary Press, 2001).

[3] See Epistle of Barnabas, chapter 15.

[4] Alexander Schmemann, *Introduction to Liturgical Theology*, trans. Asheleigh E. Moorhouse (Crestwood, NY: St. Vladimir's Seminary Press, 1966), 77. Schmemann describes the early Christian theology of the eighth day as a supersession of the Jewish Sabbath, in which "the week and its final unit—the sabbath—appear as signs of this fallen world, of the old aeon, of that which must be overcome with the advent of the Lord's Day." The current study rejects this supersessionist reading of Judaism.

[5] Ibid., 77.

developed around the life and death of the person of Jesus Christ. While the tradition inherited the biblical foundation in which time is formed by the influence of both cosmic bodies and divine intervention, a particularly Christian understanding of time arose in relation to the belief in the divine incarnation of Jesus Christ. Born fully human, his life was shaped by the natural passing of time, and yet through his passion and resurrection, he is believed to have transcended time entirely, breaking through the bounds of death and time, as this chapter will discuss. This dual temporal nature in Jesus Christ is also reflected in the liturgical calendar, incorporating both the cosmic cycles of time and the nature-transcending narrative of his life, death, and resurrection. The Christian understanding of time is thus in tension, embracing both the natural cycles of time and a theological understanding of time shaped by the acts of divine intervention and epitomized by the time-transforming act of Jesus Christ's crucifixion and resurrection.

Christian thought maintains that the salvation of the world was accomplished by Jesus Christ on the cross. Yet time continues as it always has, and sin and suffering remain. The promises of the past are, in a sense, yet to come; yet in another sense, they are already fulfilled. Faith holds that salvation was indeed achieved, and yet the world still awaits final fulfillment through the Second Coming. The world is already but not yet fulfilled. The Christian vision of time, therefore, is hardly simple. The past and the future are present; the pivotal event on the cross is perpetual and present in all time. The salvation brought by Jesus Christ has been completed yet is still incomplete. Christian thought dwells between the times, where the past, present, and future meet.

REMEMBERING TIME

One of the earliest and most well-known theological studies of time is found in Saint Augustine's autobiographical narrative *Confessions*. Grappling with the concept of time, Augustine searches for a way to reconcile the multiple layers of contrast and incompatibility he observes between the natural world, the human mind, the scriptural narrative, and the nature of God. Pondering the distinction between the temporal flux he observes in nature and the unchangeable eternality he attributes to God, he divides time and God into two distinct categories: "There was therefore no time when you had not made something, because you made time itself. No times are coeternal with you since you are permanent. If they were permanent, they would not be times."[6] He sees a metaphysical distinction between time and eternity in which time concerns the mundane progression of events within the material, finite world. Eternity, on the other hand, falls nowhere along the continuum of time but exists beyond time. It is an ideal state of an unchanging order, united with God. Augustine's thought follows in the footsteps of the Greek philosophical tradition's understanding of time and change as contrary to the unchanging character of eternity and the transcendent. Reflecting Neoplatonic metaphysics, Augustine saw only the unchangeable to be true and anything that is subject to time to be less true. The polarization of time and eternity, present in Augustine's work as well as in Greek classical philosophy, sees eternity as a higher state and time as the condition of the flawed world.

Augustine asserts the dissimilarity between time and eternity, and yet he also expresses bewilderment over the concept of time and acknowledges his inability to discern its nature: "What is time? Who can explain this easily and briefly? Who can comprehend this even in thought so as to articulate the answer in words? Yet what do we speak of, in our familiar everyday conversation, more than of time? We surely know what we mean when we speak of it. We also know what is meant when we hear someone else talking about it. What then is time? Provided that no one asks me, I know. If I want to explain it to an inquirer, I do not know."[7]

Augustine's preoccupation with time in *Confessions* at first glance seems to be motivated simply by philosophical curiosity, but it is rooted in a religiously motivated question. In the context of his autobiography on religious conversion, his preoccupation with time reflects the religious narrative and worldview which he adopts as

---

[6] Augustine, *Confessions*, trans. Henry Chadwick (Oxford: Oxford University Press, 1992), 11.14.17.
[7] Ibid.

his own through the course of his entrance into faith. Contemplating God's creation of time, Augustine attempts to reconcile the biblical narrative with scientific theories of time. When he hears "from a learned man that the movements of sun, moon, and stars in themselves constitute time," he "could not agree." In his response to this scientific theory, he cites Genesis 1:14, claiming "There are stars and heavenly luminaries to be 'for signs and for times, and for days and for years.'"[8] Disturbed by the notion that the cosmic bodies are a part of the condition of temporality and change, he argues for their permanence, established biblically as signs installed by God to direct our measurement of time.

Although Augustine's biblically informed vision of the creation of time rests on the notion of a foundational primordial time as presented in Scripture, his philosophical questions about time revolve around issues of the psychological perception of time. He ponders the inability to experience anything but the present moment which constantly slips away. This brings us to the main contribution of Augustine's work on time to the thesis argued here. For Augustine, the past and the future exist only interiorly and are experienced within the mind through memory and hope: "What is by now evident and clear is that neither future nor past exists, and it is inexact language to speak of three times—past, present, and future. Perhaps it would be exact to say: there are three times, a present of things past, a present of things present, a present of things to come. In the soul there are these three aspects of time, and I do not see them anywhere else. The present considering the past is the memory, the present considering the present is immediate awareness, the present considering the future is expectation."[9]

While the past and the future do in some sense exist for Augustine, they do so only in the mind, in memory and anticipation, and are experienced as three types of the present, for only the present exists to the senses. Through the activities of memory and anticipation, the past and the future come alive in the present. So, for

[8] Ibid., 11.23.29.
[9] Ibid., 11.19.25.

Augustine, the past and the future exist through internal, subjective experience within the present.[10]

Although Augustine understands the past to exist only in the mind, he paradoxically also sees it as a foundational reality of the biblical narrative. There is a disjunction between Augustine's fidelity to the notion of the creation of time in the Genesis narrative and his observation that the past exists only within the mind. When he refers to the creation narrative, he speaks as if God's creation of time exists as a historical truth, independent of the mind, and yet he also ponders how the past and the future have no similarly independent existence. On the one hand, the biblically narrated past stands as a solid foundation to the unfolding of time. On the other hand, the highly memorial and eschatological elements of Christian faith exist in the mind as memory and anticipation. These two types of time are held in tension within the Christian vision of time, and as this chapter will discuss, this tension is heightened by understandings of the time-transforming salvific work of Jesus Christ.

Augustine's phenomenological approach to the experience of time, through which he claims that the past, present, and future are not times as such but various experiences within the present, informs this study of memory and anticipation in liturgy. While liturgical performance seems to play with the past and future, it is not the past and future as such that are at play but rather the *experience* of the past and future. Augustine's assertion of the subjective, experiential nature of time in which the past and future are elements of the present sheds light on the way that liturgical performance is capable of shifting the experience of time, for it is this complex temporal landscape that is experienced in liturgical performance.

THE CHRISTOLOGICAL SHAPE OF TIME

In *The Lord of History*, Jean Daniélou claims that Christian faith stands on the belief that an event—the life, death, and resurrection

---

[10] In a sense, his reflection on the relation of the past and future to the experience of the present anticipates modern physicists' theories of time, in which time is relative to the observer, as discussed in chapter 1 of the current study.

of Jesus Christ—has changed the world forever. He argues that time is an essential element of faith; built on the memory of Christ, Christianity cannot be separated from the significance of the past, present, and future.

Daniélou identifies two attributes of the Christian vision of time. The first is the concept that time has a beginning and an end. Progress occurs within time which is shaped by divine intervention from beginning to end. The finitude of history, in this vision, is defined by the return of Jesus Christ, at which point time will be completed.[11] Second, he claims that there is nothing beyond Christianity: "Christianity is itself the term of development: Christ professedly comes 'late in time,' and inaugurates the stage that will not pass away. So there is nothing beyond Christianity."[12] In Daniélou's thought, time is not only a crucial medium of divine action but is also defined by that action. In other words, his vision of time is so entirely christological that he believes that the Christian mystery is not contained within time; rather, time is contained within the Christian mystery.

According to Daniélou, secular history points to and reveals the pattern of salvation history. Yet secular history is only an introduction and is encompassed by the far greater realm of sacred history. He elaborates: "But on the other hand, history falls within Christianity: all secular history is included in sacred history, as a part, a prolegomenon, a preparatory introduction. Profane history covers the whole period of this world's existence, but Christianity is essentially the next world itself, present here and now in mystery."[13] Daniélou claims here that while all time is contained within Christianity, sacred time is broader and deeper than secular time, for it is not contained to this world. He understands time to be so utterly shaped by Christianity that it does not exist outside of it; time is an aspect of Christ rather than Christ a person within the aspect of time.

The notion that "history falls within Christianity" is not shared by all theologians, and while it expresses aspects of Christian

[11] Daniélou, *The Lord of History*, 7.
[12] Ibid., 7.
[13] Ibid., 24.

thought on the nature of time and history, it does not reflect a fundamental Christian belief. The paradox of time and redemption arising from the paschal mystery, however, has been a central theological issue since the time of the earliest Christian writings.

According to Christian thought, Jesus Christ redeemed the world from the cross, and in doing so, brought the world to fulfillment. Thus, time has already been fulfilled through Jesus Christ and, in a sense, already taken up into eternity. Yet, a tension remains between this completion of time and the ongoing continuity of time, commonly referred to as the paradox of "already-not-yet." This tension is addressed in depth in Hans Urs von Balthasar's work on time which explores the conceptual problems that arise from the paradox. He proposes a way to understand the apparent contradiction of the fulfilled yet unfulfilled state of redemption, examining the nature of time through a christological lens. Balthasar finds in the Christian theological tradition a way to understand how Jesus Christ's act on the cross transforms time itself.

Balthasar sees Jesus Christ's work to be so complete that time becomes christocentric. And yet, what has been so radically changed in a qualitative way remains quantitatively the same, i.e., time goes on appearing to be the same as always. He writes that the essential quality of time is transformed, "without for this reason causing a dissolution of the quantitative substratum which must unconsciously accompany it."[14]

Balthasar sees the tension between eternality and temporality to exist within the person of Jesus Christ. In the incarnation, he is made flesh in a fully human, fully temporal body without in any way comprising his eternality. Despite Balthasar's claim that the temporality and eternality of Jesus Christ are without contradiction, the relationship between the elements is not easily understood. This relationship between temporality and eternity is seen in his mission which is on a cosmic scale but achieved within the finite bounds of his incarnation. Although his salvific work reaches

---

[14] Hans Urs Von Balthasar, *The Glory of the Lord: A Theological Aesthetics*, vol. 7, *Theology: The New Covenant*, trans. Brian McNeil (San Francisco: Ignatius Press, 1989), 164.

back to the beginning of time and forward to the end of time and thus transcends it, it is achieved through his temporality. Yet, despite this cosmic, time-transcending salvific action, the world seems to continue undisturbed. Jesus Christ is believed to have brought about a salvific completion of all time through his crucifixion, resurrection, and ascension, but even after this, time continues as always.

This points to an irresolvable gap between prophecy and fulfillment; Balthasar offers a few theories that attempt to resolve this temporal inconsistency and then offers his own: "Against such unsatisfactory attempts at compromise, the more difficult hypothesis seems theologically required: one that attributes to Jesus as it were a double temporal horizon, because, in accordance with his mission, he must in the time of his own finite existence complete what has to be done with the 'world' as a whole (and that includes its temporal future) so that he attains the end of time in the fullest truth with his death and his Resurrection."[15]

This proposal offers a type of both/and model, and the two horizons allow for the coexistence of the "already" and the "not yet," i.e., the completion of all time as predicted and the seeming continuity of earthly time. It exchanges the notion of the "delay" of imminent expectation, replacing it with a vision of time in which the expectation continues in the Church while its fulfillment has already been achieved. With this understanding, there is no reason to speculate on reasons for the supposed delay of the imminent expectation; the completion of time has in truth already been accomplished. Within the double horizon model, Jesus Christ's salvific activity on a cosmic scale is accompanied by the reality of chronological continuity and the ongoing normalcy of earthly chronological time. Time does indeed appear to continue in an undisturbed manner after the resurrection, but as this passage suggests, a fundamental soteriological transformation has occurred: time continues as it had before, but it is now a transformed "time of salvation."

[15] Ibid., 171.

Time has been completed through Jesus Christ's bearing of sin and descent into death, but the temporal reality within which this has occurred is incommensurate with our own. Balthasar writes that it is "objectively impossible and theologically false to allot this endless end a place in the 'chronology of salvation history,' and to situate in a temporal succession the radical change of the Resurrection."[16] In other words, according to Balthasar, it is futile to attempt to identify the events of salvation history as points of time in a chronological timeline.

In Balthasar's work, time is a gift from God and is entirely real. Time has been broken open by divine intervention and taken up into the time of Jesus Christ, but it has not been obliterated in the process of being transformed. Balthasar writes, "In fact, the eternal is present in this human life and in each of its moments, in a manner never realized before or afterwards, not as what is timelessly valid (the 'idea'), but as that which occurs here and now."[17] The kingdom of God is eternal, but it is not an abstract concept of timelessness. It "occurs here and now"; its presence is active, and its action is in this very time.[18]

Implicit in Balthasar's work is the notion that time is inherent in the work of God and is an aspect of divine communication. The essential goodness of time is seen in contrast to the idea of hell, which Balthasar claims lacks the element of time. Citing the work of his theological partner Adrienne von Speyr, he echoes "Hell is timeless."[19] The timelessness of hell "is definitive and affords no

---

[16] Ibid., 172.

[17] Ibid., 167.

[18] This is reminiscent of the "realized eschatology" that C. H. Dodd identifies within the gospels. Dodd claims that "for the New Testament writers in general, the eschaton has entered history; the hidden rule of God has been revealed; the Age to Come has come. The Gospel of primitive Christianity is a Gospel of realized eschatology." C. H. Dodd, *The Apostolic Preaching and Its Developments* (London: Hodder and Stoughton, 1936), 210. This is evident most clearly in the Gospel of John, which portrays eternal life as existing experientially in the present.

[19] Hans Urs Von Balthasar, *Theo-Logic: Theological Logical Theory*, vol. 2, *Truth of God*, trans. Adrian J. Walker (San Francisco: Ignatius Press, 2004), 348. Adrienne

prospect of escape on any side," as opposed to the freedom granted by living in time and in a time that has been transformed by Jesus Christ.[20] Without time there is no past and future and hence no memory or hope.

Balthasar's theology of time speaks to two issues of direct relevance to the thesis argued here. First he addresses the paradox of the Christian vision of time, which is held in the tension of the "already-not-yet." This paradox points to the complexity of time in Christian thought; time is not simply linear but is doubled or folded and, paradoxically, fulfilled and not yet fulfilled. This sheds light on the unique shape of time in Christian thought, which allows the past, present, and future to coexist in Christ's double temporal horizon.

Second, Balthasar's work on the veracity, dignity, and God-givenness of time suggests the extent to which Christian thought values the element of time. To perform the essentials of faith, liturgy must perform our embeddedness in earthly time. That is, Christian liturgy performs the mystery of the eschatological fulfillment of time in Christ and also celebrates the ongoing cycles of earthly time. It engages both the memorial and eschatological sweep of religiously envisioned time and the experience of daily time.

A similar theological position is taken by Russian Orthodox theologian Alexander Schmemann, who argues that time is the element within which God acts. According to Schmemann, time is not opposed to eternity but a part of it. Unlike the other theologians discussed in this chapter, however, Schmemann's work contemplates the nature of Christian time specifically as it is formed through liturgy. He brings us closer to the main argument of this study by directly claiming that Christian liturgy participates in the transformation of time.

In stressing the thoroughly eschatological nature of the Church, Schmemann clarifies that time is not rejected from this eschatological

---

von Speyr was a Swiss medical doctor, theologian, and mystic who worked closely with Balthasar and whose mystical visions inspired his work.

[20] Ibid., 348.

character. He explains that eschatology does not entail a renunciation of time, as evidenced by the celebration of the Sabbath, which
observes the weekly cycle of time. "The eschatology of the new
Christian cult does not mean the renunciation of time. There would
have been no need for a fixed day (*statu die*) in a "wholly world-
renouncing" cult, it could be celebrated on any day and at any
hour."[21]

While the celebration of the Sabbath in Christianity witnesses the
sanctity of time, the eschatological quality of time is not restricted
to one day. Schmemann argues that the eschatological quality of
time is present at all times in the celebration of the Eucharist,
which transcends the normal sequence of time, even as it is celebrated within time. He holds that the Eucharist "is joined with
time in order that time itself might become the time of the Church,
the time of salvation."[22] Here Schmemann makes the claim that the
Eucharist participates in time for the purpose of transforming time.
In other words, he proposes that the liturgy invites ordinary time
to be taken up and transformed into a special quality of time.

Schmemann names this special time as the "time of the Church,
the time of salvation," referring to the quality of time brought
about through divine, transformative action; namely, for Christian
theologians, the redemptive act on the cross. Time is taken up into
the eschatological nature of the Church, lifted from the monoto-
nous chronology of profane time into sacred time. Time is neither
excluded from the eschatological Church nor allowed to rule it
with the weight of a purely linear chronology. The eschatological
Church is temporal, but this temporality has been transformed
from the ordinary to the extraordinary.

This transformation, through which time participates in an eschatological reality, constitutes for Schmemann the sanctification of
time. He understands the interaction of chronological time and the
eschaton to lead to the fulfillment of time. In his own words, "It is
precisely this fulfillment of time by the 'Eschaton,' by that which
overcomes time and is above it and bears witness to its finitude

[21] Schmemann, *Introduction to Liturgical Theology*, 80.
[22] Ibid.

and limitedness, which constitutes the sanctification of time."[23] Time is not rejected as something less than eternity but is transformed and taken up into eternity.

For Schmemann, the eschatology of the Church is not world renouncing. Rather, it is an affirmation of the reality of the eschatological future, which is proleptically experienced in liturgy. He writes, "This is a conquest of time not in the sense of rendering it empty and valueless, but rather in the sense of creating the possibility of being made partakers of or participants in the 'coming aeon,' in the fullness, joy and peace that is found in the Holy Spirit, while still living in 'this world.'"[24] Like Balthasar, Schmemann insists that the Christian vision of time involves the embrace of time as a redemptive element; it acknowledges the sanctity of time that is transformed through Jesus Christ and experienced through liturgy.

ESCHATOLOGICAL MEMORY

The Christian vision of time incorporates both the memorialized past and the anticipated future; both influence the understanding of the present. Comprising a web supporting the Christian vision of time, memory and hope are each constituted of elements of the other: hope is memorial and memory is eschatological.

Louis-Marie Chauvet discusses the eschatological quality of memory in *Symbol and Sacrament*, observing that "in the recalling—the anamnesis—of the *second* coming of the Lord Jesus, as well as of his death and resurrection, the Christian memory is eschatological: it is memory of the future."[25] The promise of a second coming in the future is a "remembered promise"; it is based in memory, and that memory holds the future promise within it. Chauvet draws a connection between eschatology and history and advocates a positive evaluation of time, proposing that "eschatology

---

[23] Ibid.

[24] Ibid., 73.

[25] Louis-Marie Chauvet, *Symbol and Sacrament: A Sacramental Reinterpretation of Christian Existence*, trans. Patrick Madigan and Madeleine Beaumont (Collegeville, MN: Liturgical Press, 1995), 239.

requires present history as the very place of the eschaton's possibility. To devalue history is also and necessarily to devalue eschatology. The eschatological dimension of the Christian cult thus implies a return to the historic-prophetic dimension of the Jewish cult whose heir it is."[26] Here Chauvet points to the link between anticipation and memory. The anticipated eschatological future is based on the remembered biblical narrative through the "historic-prophetic dimension" established in the Hebrew Bible, which sets a precedent of the pattern of divine promise and fulfillment. The eschatological nature of Christianity is not solely rooted in the future; eschatological hope is validated by, and thrives on, the past and present as well.[27]

In the Christian understanding of time and salvation history, the past not only has a causal effect on later events but can also be present in them. Salvation history is not merely a series of events locked in the past, never to return, but is relevant and present in all times, for in the anamnesis of salvation history, the past becomes present. Citing the twelfth-century monk St. Bernard of Clairvaux, Joseph Ratzinger considers this dynamic of the interpenetration of past and future to be made possible through Jesus Christ: "The real interior act, though it does not exist without the exterior, transcends time, but since it comes from time, time can again and again be brought into it. This is how we can become contemporary with the past events of salvation. St. Bernard of Clairvaux has this in mind when he says that the true *semel* ('once') bears within itself the *semper* ('always'). What is perpetual takes place in what

---

[26] Ibid., 240.

[27] Liam Bergin makes a similar observation regarding the anamnetic and eschatological qualities of the sacraments: "Christian sacraments are commemorative, demonstrative and prognostic actions: they recall the saving actions completed by the passion of Christ; they make this saving reality present in the community that celebrates; and they look forward in hope to their fulfillment in heaven. Past, present and future dimensions coalesce in the ritual action." Liam Bergin, "Between Memory and Promise: Sacramental Theology since Vatican II," in *Faith, Word and Culture*, ed. Liam Bergin (Dublin: The Columbia Press, 2004), 91.

happened only once."[28] Ratzinger claims that the act on the cross reaches from time to timelessness, allowing the past to be a present reality. This notion displays a radical departure from the secular understanding of time, in which events of the past may *influence* later events but cannot be said to be actually *present* in them. According to Ratzinger, the paschal mystery participates in all time, perpetually, and this is because in Christ's work, "time is drawn into what reaches beyond time."[29]

For each of the theologians discussed in this chapter, time participates in eternity and is already infused with the eschatological future. This makes a significant impact on the experience of time in liturgical performance, as the eschatological state in which liturgy stakes its hope is seen as existing proleptically within the present time. The minutes and hours marked by liturgical celebrations are related to eternity and already partake in the eschatological redemption. With this understanding of the porousness between time and eternity, as well as between the boundaries of the past, present, and future, the liturgical experience of time is transformed.

[28] Joseph Ratzinger, *The Spirit of the Liturgy* (San Francisco: Ignatius Press, 2000), 56.
[29] Ibid., 56.

Chapter 8

The Sanctification of Time
Memory and Anticipation
in the Liturgy of the Hours

The Hours of the Work of God are not simply intermittent periods in the course of cosmic time (in Greek chronos). They are periods which, through celebration of the liturgy, take on the special character of moments in the history of salvation (kairoi), moments when God permits us to encounter him.

—Directory for the Celebration of the Work of God[1]

ANAMNETIC AND PROLEPTIC QUALITIES
OF THE LITURGY OF THE HOURS

Christian liturgy is by nature memorial. It is, in essence, a recollection of the life, death, and resurrection of Jesus Christ, but it is more than simply a memorial: in recalling the paschal mystery, it draws it into the present, actualizing the mystery in the experience of the Church. Christian liturgy is thus anamnetic, as Robert Taft, SJ, observes: "Remembrance, anamnesis, is also at the heart of all ritual celebration, for celebrations are celebrations *of* something: through symbol and gesture and text we render present—proclaim—once again the reality we feast."[2]

---

[1] *The Monastic Hours: Directory for the Celebration of the Work of God and Directive Norms for the Monastic Liturgy of the Hours*, ed. Anne M. Field (Collegeville, MN: Liturgical Press, 2001), 27.

[2] Robert Taft, *The Liturgy of the Hours in East and West* (Collegeville, MN: Liturgical Press, 1993), 358.

Christian liturgy is both—and indeed, simultaneously—anamnetic and eschatological. As Aidan Kavanagh notes, "Liturgy has an eschatological dimension throughout, even when its surface structures may seem to be concerned overtly with a historical commemoration."[3] Liturgy presents a vision of time in which the present contains the past as an active, actualized reality; at the same time, it is also traditionally believed to provide a proleptic taste of the eschatological future.[4] This proleptic quality is claimed explicitly in *Sacrosanctum Concilium*, the Second Vatican Council's Constitution on the Sacred Liturgy, which declares that liturgy offers a foretaste of heaven: "In the earthly liturgy we take part in a foretaste of that heavenly liturgy which is celebrated in the holy city of Jerusalem toward which we journey as pilgrims."[5]

While the anamnetic and proleptic qualities of liturgy are most readily observable in the Eucharist, both are also present in the Liturgy of the Hours. The latter also celebrates the salvation inaugurated through Jesus Christ and recreates the mystery, not in an act of mimicry, but through rendering it into the present reality.[6] The eschatological nature of the Liturgy of the Hours is described by Taft: "Hence the Liturgy of the Hours, like all Christian liturgy, is an eschatological proclamation of the salvation received in Christ, and a glorification and thanksgiving to God for that gift. In this original and primitive sense the Liturgy of the Hours—indeed, all liturgy— is beyond time."[7] Echoing *Sacrosanctum Concilium*, the notion that

---

[3] Aidan Kavanagh, *On Liturgical Theology: The Hale Memorial Lectures of Seabury-Western Theological Seminary* (New York: Pueblo Publishing Company, 1984), 142.

[4] See Maxime Gimenez, "La liturgie et le temps," *Irenikon* 4 (1980): 473–82. Gimenez argues that liturgy, as a temporal activity, is an expression of eschatological hope, allowing the symbolic structure of the biblical week of creation to be mystically experienced in anticipation of the consummation of all time.

[5] All citations from the Second Vatican Council are taken from *Vatican Council II: The Basic Sixteen Documents; Constitutions, Decrees, Declarations*, trans. Austin Flannery (Collegeville, MN: Liturgical Press, 2014).

[6] Stanislaus Campbell, "Liturgy of the Hours," in *The New Dictionary of Sacramental Worship*, ed. Peter E. Fink (Collegeville, MN: Liturgical Press, 1990), 574.

[7] Taft, *Liturgy of the Hours in East and West*, 359.

the liturgy offers a foretaste of heaven is again claimed by the *General Instruction on the Liturgy of the Hours*, which attributes the proleptic function of liturgy specifically to the Liturgy of the Hours.[8]

The Liturgy of the Hours is a contemporary evolution of the early forms of the prayer of the hours. In one of the earliest forms, dating to the third century, the Office was comprised of a daily morning and evening prayer, with additional private prayer at the third, sixth, and ninth hours and during the night.[9] Evidence of daily gatherings for public liturgical prayer begins in the fourth century, however, when the Church experienced a flowering of liturgical life due in part to political peace under Constantine.[10] The liturgical developments of the fourth century included the distinction between two main forms of the prayer of the hours: communal prayer assembled around priests or a bishop, commonly called the cathedral office, and the prayer of ascetics and monks, commonly called the monastic office.[11] The cathedral prayer was a public prayer that used psalms and hymns that corresponded to the hour of the day. The monastic prayer, originating with ascetics of Egypt, was more contemplative and less ritualized, consisting of psalms and other scriptural passages, with little relation to the time of day during which they were recited. The cathedral and monastic offices became intermingled in various developments of the daily Office, and later developments in both the East and the West are primarily based on a mixture of these two traditions.[12]

---

[8] Citations from the General Instruction on the Liturgy of the Hours (hereafter GILH) are from *General Instruction on the Liturgy of the Hours* (Collegeville, MN: Liturgical Press, 1975).

[9] Juan Mateos, "The Origins of the Divine Office," *Worship* 41 (1967): 477–85.

[10] Taft notes that while most scholars agree with the general outline given by Mateos, the origins of vigils, lauds, and prime remain undetermined. Robert F. Taft, "*Quaestiones Disputatae* in the History of the Liturgy of the Hours: The Origins of Nocturnes, Matins, Prime," *Worship* 58, no. 2 (1984): 130–31.

[11] Campbell, "Liturgy of the Hours," 564. Mateos, however, divides these fourth-century forms into three main forms: a monastic office, a cathedral office, and an office containing elements of both of the others.

[12] John F. Baldovin, "Christian Worship to the Reformation," in *The Making of Jewish and Christian Worship*, ed. Paul F. Bradshaw and Lawrence A. Hoffman (Notre Dame, IN: University of Notre Dame Press, 1991), 171–72.

The Liturgy of the Hours today serves as the primary Catholic liturgical setting of the psalms, in which the entire biblical book of Psalms is recited in its entirety in one-week or four-week cycles, in the monastic and cathedral offices, respectively. The monastic office maintains the early tradition of completing the psalms every week, while the contemporary cathedral office, introduced with the reforms of Vatican II, completes the psalms in a four week cycle.

Prayed regularly through the course of the day and night, the Liturgy of the Hours celebrates time. Whereas the feasts of the liturgical calendar celebrate specific points in time and follow the narrative flow of the liturgical year, the Liturgy of the Hours marks the passing of hours in each day. It marks time, but it does so in a celebration that connects mundane time to the Christian vision of the eschatological completion of time. The Liturgy of the Hours remembers and anticipates the historical arc of the salvation narrative, from primordial beginning to eschatological ending, within the context of the daily cycle of the passing hours.

The *Directory for the Celebration of the Work of God*, an official document that serves as one of the preliminary texts of the *Theasaurus Liturgiae Horarum Monasticae*, declares the Liturgy of the Hours to be a celebration of the past, present, and future of salvation history. It claims that the liturgy, which it calls the Work of God, "embraces the mystery of salvation in its totality," including the "announcement of salvation," "its fulfillment in Christ," and "the prolongation of this fulfillment in the Church until it attains its plenitude at the end of time."[13] When put together, these elements point to the full scope of salvation history from the past, through the present, and into the future. The "announcement of salvation" refers to the biblical past in the narratives of the Hebrew Bible; "its fulfillment in Christ" refers to the narratives of the New Testament; "the prolongation of this fulfillment in the Church" refers to the present time (i.e., the "present" defined as the time stretching from the ascension to the Parousia); and the "plenitude at the end of time" points toward the eschatological future.

---

[13] *The Monastic Hours: Directory for the Celebration of the Work of God and Directive Norms for the Monastic Liturgy of the Hours*, 29.

The *General Instruction on the Liturgy of the Hours* considers the memorial and anticipatory characteristics of the Liturgy of the Hours to proceed from the same functions in the Eucharist. It states, "The Liturgy of the Hours extends to the various hours of the day the praise and thanksgiving, the memorial of the mysteries of salvation, the entreaties, and the foretaste of heavenly glory which are to be found in the Eucharistic mystery" (GILH 12). This text focuses on the interaction between the Eucharist and the Liturgy of the Hours, expressing the latter's function in extending the anamnetic and proleptic aspects of the eucharistic mystery throughout the hours of the day. While paragraph 12 focuses on the transmission of the central mystery of Christian liturgy in the Liturgy of the Hours, however, it does not address qualities held by the Liturgy of the Hours itself.

Paragraph 16 takes this important step, claiming that the Church's "song of praise is a foretaste of that heavenly praise which resounds unceasingly before the throne of God and the Lamb" (GILH 16). While according to paragraph 12, the Liturgy of the Hours acts to transmit the memorial and anticipatory attributes of the Eucharistic mystery, in paragraph 16, the Liturgy of the Hours does not simply transmit the foretaste of heaven found in the Eucharist; it *is* a foretaste of heavenly praise. Rather than simply transmitting memory and anticipation, it offers itself as a proleptic experience. This supports the argument presented in this book that liturgical performance, and particularly the celebration of the Liturgy of the Hours, transforms the way that time is experienced. If the celebration of the Liturgy of the Hours is understood as a foretaste of heaven, then its performance offers a proleptic experience of the eschatological future, transforming the experience of the present into an experience of the future.

THE SANCTIFICATION OF TIME

The *General Instruction on the Liturgy of the Hours* claims that the purpose of the Liturgy of the Hours is to "sanctify the day" (GILH 11). The document clarifies that this purpose is the specific duty and gift of the Liturgy of the Hours, setting it apart from other liturgies, for "Compared with other liturgical actions, the particular characteristic which ancient tradition has attached to the Liturgy of the Hours is that it should consecrate the course of day and night" (GILH 10). The designation of this purpose raises the question of the precise meaning of the sanctification of time. The notion that time needs to be consecrated or sanctified suggests that natural time is profane or lacking in grace, but Christian thought teaches otherwise.

This question has been addressed in various ways; Dom Gregory Dix's 1945 publication of *The Shape of the Liturgy* offered an answer that made a great impact but has since been widely rejected. Dix understood the sanctification of time to refer to an engagement with mundane time, that is, the profane time marked by the passing of hours. The capacity of the Liturgy of the Hours to sanctify time, therefore, means that it is concerned with mundane time. Dix posits the Liturgy of the Hours in distinction from the Eucharist, claiming that the former is a liturgy of mundane time while the latter is eschatological.[14] In this formulation, the sanctification of time is situated in distinction from eschatological hope, and the relationship of the Liturgy of the Hours to time is nothing more than a celebration of profane chronological time in distinction from the eschatological focus and proleptic function of the Eucharist. Dix's claim, however, fails to account for the anamnetic and proleptic nature of all Christian liturgy, and it misinterprets and undervalues the complex transformative relationship with time held by the Liturgy of the Hours.

Dix's theory has been implicitly rejected by the documents of Vatican II, specifically by the attribution in the *General Instruction on the Liturgy of the Hours* of an eschatological proleptic function to the Liturgy of the Hours (GILH 12). In addition, Dix's theory is directly and forcefully countered in a number of contemporary studies of the Liturgy of the Hours, including Robert Taft's *The Liturgy of the Hours in East and West* and Thomas Talley's essay "History and Eschatology in the Primitive Pascha," which reject the dichotomy between the eschatological character of the Eucharist and the linkage of the Liturgy of the Hours with profane, mundane time.[15]

---

[14] Dom Gregory Dix, *The Shape of the Liturgy* (London: Dacre Press, 1975), 319–32.

[15] Taft, *Liturgy of the Hours in East and West*, 331; Thomas Talley, "History and Eschatology in the Primitive Pascha," *Worship* 47 (1973): 212; see also Campbell, "Liturgy of the Hours," 575.

The phrase "the sanctification of time" can be misinterpreted to suggest that the Liturgy of the Hours effects a change in secular time. The sanctification of time, however, does not consecrate and transform secular time into sacred time but creates an experience of time which communicates the divine mystery. It is not, as Dix claims, a sanctification of the profane element of time but a participation in and means of union with the sacred. In this way, the function of Liturgy of the Hours in sanctifying time is not opposed to the eschatological orientation of the Eucharist but participates in it.

CONSECRATING THE COURSE OF DAY AND NIGHT

The connection of the offices of the early Liturgy of the Hours to the hours of the day and night was systematized and made authoritative in the fifth-century Rule of Benedict. The liturgical code that early monastic communities in the Benedictine tradition observed is formulated in chapters 8 to 20 of the Rule, which provide detailed instruction for the liturgical practices, particularly the Liturgy of the Hours. The sixteenth chapter of the Rule explains the cycle of eight daily offices, seven in the day and one at night, and cites verses of Psalm 119 as rationale for the eight offices.

> The Prophet says: *Seven times a day I have praised you* (Ps 118 [119]: 164). We will fulfill this sacred number of seven if we satisfy our obligations of service at Lauds, Prime, Terce, Sext, None, Vespers and Compline, for it was of these hours during the day that he said: *Seven times a day I have praised you* (Ps 118 [119]: 164). Concerning Vigils, the same Prophet says: *At midnight I arose to give you praise* (Ps 118 [119]: 62). Therefore, we should *praise* our Creator *for his just judgments* at these times: Lauds, Prime, Terce, Sext, None, Vespers and Compline; and *let us arise at night to give* him *praise* (Ps 118 [119]: 164, 62).[16]

The Rule of St. Benedict here uses a textual excerpt from the Psalms to justify the tradition of praying the psalms throughout the course of the day and night. The justification for this perhaps

---

[16] *Rule of St. Benedict 1980*, ed. Timothy Fry (Collegeville, MN: Liturgical Press, 1981), chapter 16.

reflects a liturgical life already highly theologically shaped by the recitation of the psalms in which the texts of the psalms so infuse the life of the community that the logic for praying the psalms comes from the psalms themselves. The *General Instruction on the Liturgy of the Hours*, however, also notes that the early church fathers found the Liturgy of the Hours to be indicated or foreshadowed in the Acts of the Apostles, as well: "Peter went to the housetop at about the sixth hour to pray (Acts 10:9)" (GILH 1).

The correlation between particular times of day and particular offices is acknowledged in the *General Instruction on the Liturgy of the Hours*, which states, "Because the purpose of the Office is to sanctify the day and all human activity, the traditional sequence of the Hours has been so restored that, as far as possible, they may be genuinely related to the time of the day at which they are prayed" (GILH 11). This passage draws a causal connection between the sanctification of time and the offices being "genuinely related" to the times at which they are prayed. This causal connection suggests that a genuine relationship between the offices and their particular times is somehow conducive to the sanctification of time.

Connections between theological themes and the times of day that the liturgy is prayed have been made since the early centuries of Christianity. The morning prayer is often associated with the symbolization of the rising sun as Christ as introduced in Zechariah's prophecy in Luke 1:78-79: "By the tender mercy of our God, the dawn from on high will break upon us, to give light to those who sit in darkness and in the shadow of death, to guide our feet into the way of peace." This symbol was attached to the morning prayer by St. Clement of Alexandria, St. Cyprian, and St. Clement of Rome, each of whom saw the morning prayer to be significantly connected to the christological symbol of the time of day in which it is prayed.[17]

Similarly, the time of evening prayer recalls the passion of Jesus Christ. Psalm 141 has been adopted as an evening psalm across

[17] A. G. Martimort, "The Liturgy of the Hours," in *The Liturgy and Time*, ed. A. G. Martimort, I. H. Dalmais, and P. Jounel, trans. Matthew J. O'Connell (Collegeville, MN: Liturgical Press, 1986), 259–60.

many forms of the office, and the christological interpretation of the psalm as a foreshadowing of the paschal sacrifice of Christ—"Let my prayer be counted as incense before you, and the lifting up of my hands as an evening sacrifice" (Ps 141:2)—attributes a memorial of the passion of Jesus Christ to the particular time of the evening. An eschatological association is also attached to the evening prayer, in which the darkness, according to St. Cyprian, awakens a longing for the return of the light, symbolic of the return of Christ.[18]

The monastic office of Compline includes requests for protection during the night, beginning with the ancient hymn *"Te Lucis Ante Terminum,"* which begins "Before we reach the close of day, creator of the world, we pray, that in your mercy you will keep a guard around us while we sleep." (*Te lucis ante terminum, rerum Creator, poscimus ut pro tua clementia sis praesul et custodia.*) These requests for protection, including verses such as "we know not the hour," and "death comes like a thief in the night," appeal to eschatological anticipation, recalling "the cosmic theme of those at vigil joining their voices to those of the angels and all creation in praise of God, as in the Benedicite of Daniel, while all the world sleeps."[19]

The attributions of theological meanings to the times of day during which the offices are prayed is significant for a number of reasons. First, it reveals an attempt to understand the passing of time and the cosmic cycles of day and night to be related to the salvation narrative. This is, in essence, a form of the sanctification of time. The celebration of the offices at particular times of day connects the times of day and night to a theologically charged set of symbols and meanings, linking time with the divine as it is understood through the narratives of Scripture and tradition.

The connection of elements of the salvation narrative to the times of day during which the Office is prayed draws the attention of those who perform it to the element of time. It acts, in effect, as a meditation on time. The Liturgy of the Hours, prayed at set times of day and night, harnesses the mind to the experience of time and to the idea of time. Once the attention is in this way drawn into a temporal focus, it finds that time no longer seems to be what it once was. The morning

[18] Ibid., 264.
[19] Taft, *Liturgy of the Hours in East and West*, 357.

is not only the beginning of the day but also a sign of Christ, symbolized by the rising sun. The evening is not only the end of the daylight but also a remembrance of the passion of Christ. The darkness becomes a time to nightly reenter a state of existential fear from which the praying community calls out for protection and summons hope in the promise of eschatological redemption.

The praying of the Liturgy of the Hours at set times changes not time itself but the experience of time. The words of the prayers become more than that which is communicated by the basic content of the psalms, hymns, readings, and antiphons. They become a declaration of eschatological hope and a performance of the memory of salvation history. They invite the liturgical community into a present moment unlike others, into a liturgical present that resembles the shape of salvation history: it is the shape of memory and the shape of hope. In this way, in the words of the *General Instruction on the Liturgy of the Hours*, "The Liturgy of the Hours sanctifies time" (GILH 11).

LITURGICAL TIMEKEEPING

In monastic settings where the Liturgy of the Hours are prayed daily in their full form, time is experienced through the liturgy, as the hours of each day are divided into short segments punctuated by the offices. The daily passing of time is experienced and measured in relation to the schedule of the Liturgy of the Hours. The hours of the morning are experienced less as measured hours of sixty minutes and more as the stretches of time between the offices—the time between Matins and Prime, between Prime and Lauds, and between Lauds and Terce. The passing of time, day to day and hour to hour, becomes defined by liturgy. The community experiences time through liturgy, and reality is experienced according to the patterns of liturgical practice.

In the early years of monasticism, timekeeping was determined not by a steady progression of minutes but by the ebb and flow of daylight throughout the seasons.[20] A full day—what would today

---

[20] Nathan Mitchell, "The Liturgical Code in the Rule of St. Benedict," in *Rule of St. Benedict 1980*, ed. Timothy Fry (Collegeville, MN: Liturgical Press, 1981), 409.

be called a twenty-four-hour time period—was divided into two parts, day and night, marked by the sunrise and the sunset. Each of these two parts was then divided into twelve segments called *horae*, or hours. This division of time is attested from the time of Alexander the Great and was later adopted by the Church.[21] The practice of scheduling the liturgy according to this measurement of time fits with the narratives of the New Testament, in which time is measured as the third, sixth, and ninth hours, as well as sunrise and sunset, indicating twelve *horae* of daytime divided into four equal parts.[22] Despite the fact that the length of the daylight and the nighttime darkness varies across the seasons of the year, twelve equally spaced hours were maintained in each day. The daytime hours were thus longer segments of time in the summer and shorter segments in the winter.

As can be seen in the liturgical code in the Rule of Benedict (chapters 8 through 20, which give detailed instructions on the early prayer of the hours and indicate the appropriate times of prayer according to this system), St. Benedict used this system of time computation.[23] For monastic communities, this meant that the number of liturgical offices in the day and night remained stable while the actual minutes and hours remained always in flux. In this ancient system of time computation, time was fluid. It expanded and contracted, and the stable unit of measurement was not the unit of sixty minutes but the number of *horae* in the day. The fluctuating length of liturgical hours, therefore, became the normative measurement of time in the monastic community.

In monastic settings, the Liturgy of the Hours shapes the dimensions of the hours of the day as they are squeezed or stretched to fit the contours of the liturgy. The period of time between liturgical

[21] Gerard Dohrn-van Rossum, *History of the Hour: Clocks and Modern Temporal Orders*, trans. Thomas Dunlap (Chicago: University of Chicago Press, 1996), 18.

[22] Ibid., 29.

[23] Discussions of specific times and hours permeate the Rule. In the context of what is a very brief document, the word "hour" or "hours" occurs forty-nine times and the word "time" or "times" occurs fifty-two times.

offices is experienced according to the arrangement of the offices throughout the day rather than by the number of minutes or hours. For instance, in a monastery, the stretch of available work time in the afternoon is likely to be measured by the space between the offices of None and Vespers. In other words, although the time may be three and one-half hours, it is experienced through its liturgical parameters. In monastic life, the experience of the passing of time from day through night is formed by the liturgy, and the experience of time becomes thoroughly liturgical.

THE LITURGICAL PRESENT

In *The Spirit of the Liturgy*, Joseph Ratzinger claims, "The immediate event—the liturgy—makes sense and has a meaning for our lives only because it contains the other two dimensions. Past, present, and future interpenetrate and touch upon eternity."[24] In these two short sentences, Ratzinger makes three bold claims. The first states that liturgy has meaning for us *because* of its interplay with time. The role of the past and the future in liturgy is not an interesting addition to an activity which is coherent and meaningful without it; the past and the future make liturgy meaningful. Second, he suggests that liturgy does not merely evoke or enact the past and the future but *contains* the two elements. Third, he claims that the three temporal elements interpenetrate each other; in this fusion, they encounter eternity.

Taking care that his claims are not dismissed as merely metaphorical, Ratzinger stresses the veracity of liturgy's participation in the past and the future: "Becoming contemporary with the Pasch of Christ in the liturgy of the Church is also, in fact, an anthropological reality. The celebration is not just a rite, not just a liturgical 'game.' It is meant to be indeed a *logikelatreia*, the 'logicizing' of my existence, my interior contemporaneity with the self-giving of Christ."[25]

Ratzinger clarifies that liturgy, while indeed a performance, is not an artificial reenactment. It actualizes a transformation through

[24] Joseph Ratzinger, *The Spirit of the Liturgy* (San Francisco: Ignatius Press, 2000), 60.
[25] Ibid., 58.

which the central event to Christian faith—the redemption wrought through Christ's act on the cross—is made contemporaneous with the present. He emphasizes the objective nature of this phenomenon, but in doing so, he does not reject its significance for the individual. He writes of an "interior contemporaneity" in which the union with the paschal mystery occurs subjectively, bringing about an interior transformation of the individual as well as of the liturgical community.

This mystical, temporal identification with the paschal mystery is also associated with the celebration of the Liturgy of the Hours, as Patrick Regan observes: "In the liturgy of the hours and the cycles of the year, the Spirit brings the time of the world to perfection by making the fullness of time present within it. Thus the Christian is delivered from the tyranny of linear time as well as the boredom of cyclical time and is free simply to be a gift which God has given in the day that God has made."[26] Here, Regan claims that in the Liturgy of the Hours, the "fullness of time" becomes present within time. This occurs in the communal experience of time as perceived by the community of faith, as well as in individual experience, as the individual becomes freed from the "tyranny of linear time" and released into the fullness of time.

This discussion requires a clarification of what is meant by the "fullness of time." It is different from linear time and from cyclical time; the phrase is often used to refer to an eschatological quality of time, or redeemed time. For this clarification, we turn to Alexander Schmemann's concept of the eschatological transparency of liturgical time. When Schmemann speaks of liturgical time as being "eschatologically transparent," he refers to a quality of time in which God is continually acting.

> Morning, evening, day, the sabbath, feast days—all these have an "eschatological" significance, as reminders of the ultimate and great "Day of the Lord" which is coming in time. This is the liturgy of time; but not natural or cyclical time, not that time which is, so to

---

[26] Patrick Regan, "Pneumatological and Eschatological Aspects of Liturgical Celebration," *Worship* 51, no. 4 (1977): 349.

speak, "immanent" in the world, determining and containing it within its own self-sufficient, cyclical rhythm. It is that time that is "eschatologically transparent," time within which and over which the living God of Abraham, Isaac, and Jacob is constantly acting, and which discovers its real meaning in the Kingdom of Yahweh, "the Kingdom of all ages."[27]

According to Schmemann, time becomes eschatologically transparent through its relationship to the redeemed eschatological future. He writes that liturgy is a reminder of the eschaton, but in addition, it also partakes in the eschaton, finding its meaning in the future kingdom. For Schmemann, as for Ratzinger and Regan, liturgy does not only refer to the past and future but also participates in them.

Through this understanding, the boundaries between the past, present, and future become porous, as each category melds with the others. In Schmemann's words, "The event which is 'actualized' in the Eucharist is an event of the past when viewed within the categories of time, but by virtue of its eschatological, determining, completing significance it is also an event which is taking place eternally."[28] The categories are distinct only through a secular, linear understanding of time, whereas the theological vision sees their boundaries to be indeterminate, as each overflows into the other.

Schmemann's most bold statement on the relationship between liturgy and time is found in his posthumously published article "Liturgy and Eschatology": "The unique—I repeat, unique—function of worship in the life of the Church and in theology is to convey a sense of this eschatological reality; and what eschatology does is to hold together things which otherwise are broken up and treated as separate events occurring at different points in a time sequence."[29]

[27] Alexander Schmemann, *Introduction to Liturgical Theology*, trans. Asheleigh E. Moorhouse (Crestwood, NY: St. Vladimir's Seminary Press, 1966), 71.

[28] Ibid., 72.

[29] Alexander Schmemann, "Liturgy and Eschatology," *Sobornost* 7, no. 1 (1985): 10.

Whereas secular time exists along a linear continuum in which the past is always gone, the present is always slipping into the past, and the future is unreachable, eschatology erases these distinctions and limitations. It allows the past, present, and future to exist in a unity, each giving meaning to the other. Eschatologically transparent time, therefore, is a quality of time that has been transformed through liturgy into the unified form of eschatological time. It is this unified sense of time that characterizes the liturgical present and that allows the liturgical community to "remember the future" through the liturgical performance of "eschatological memory." For, in liturgical performance, memory and eschatological anticipation link together the disparate fragments of temporality into a unity, creating a unique liturgical present which is eschatologically—and anamnetically—transparent.

Part 5

Performing Time

Chapter 9

The Liturgical Transformation of Time
Ritual, Repetition, and Flow

Joining in the chorus of past redemption, the worshipper finds him/ herself praying for, if not actually announcing, the future redemption. The present is only where the memory of past redemption flowers into the expectation of future redemption.

—Reuven Kimelman[1]

Liturgy helps the waiting for redemption by making itself into a form of mediation between time and eternity.

—Steven Kepnes[2]

THE LANGUAGE OF RITUAL

Liturgy is neither a corpus of literature nor a school of thought— it is a performed act. It is ritual and is comprised of actions set apart from other actions, distinguished from the mundane. While there are many understandings of what constitutes ritual, Victor Turner summarizes a general anthropological definition of ritual: "Many anthropologists define 'ritual' as prescribed formal behavior for occasions not given over to technological routine, having

---

[1] Reuven Kimelman, "The Shema and its Rhetoric: The Case for the Shema Being More than Creation, Revelation, and Redemption," *Journal of Jewish Thought and Philosophy* 2, no. 1 (1993): 129.

[2] Steven Kepnes, *Jewish Liturgical Reasoning* (New York: Oxford University Press, 2007), 120.

reference to beliefs in invisible beings or powers regarded as the first and final causes of all effects."[3]

Ritual theorist Ronald Grimes finds this definition limited, however, and criticizes the connection between ritual and religious belief. Grimes argues that ritual is not by necessity related to religious belief; in *Ritual Criticism*, he chooses to list numerous qualities of ritual rather than offer a specific definition. He identifies the following qualities as "indicators that begin to appear when action moves in the direction of ritual":

- performed, embodied, enacted, gestural (not merely thought or said)
- formalized, elevated, stylized, differentiated (not ordinary, unadorned, or undifferentiated)
- repetitive, redundant, rhythmic (not singular or once-for-all)
- collective, institutionalized, consensual (not personal or private)
- patterned, invariant, standardized, stereotyped, ordered, rehearsed (not improvised, idiosyncratic, or spontaneous)
- traditional, archaic, primordial (not invented or recent)
- valued highly or ultimately, deeply felt, sentiment-laden, meaningful, serious (not trivial or shallow)
- condensed, multilayered (not obvious; requiring interpretation)
- symbolic, referential (not merely technological or primarily means-end oriented)
- perfected, idealized, pure, ideal (not conflictual or subject to criticism and failure)
- dramatic, ludic [i.e., playlike] (not primarily discursive or explanatory; not without special framing or boundaries)
- paradigmatic (not ineffectual in modeling either other rites or nonritualized action)

[3] Victor Turner, "Ritual, Tribal and Catholic," *Worship* 50 (1976): 504.

- mystical, transcendent, religious, cosmic (not secular or merely empirical)
- adaptive, functional (not obsessional, neurotic, dysfunctional)
- conscious, deliberate (not unconscious or preconscious)[4]

A number of the diverse qualities listed by Grimes point to the unique "language" in which ritual "speaks." Grimes indicates that rituals are performed and embodied rather than thought or said and are dramatic rather than discursive. The language of ritual is of another order than that of discursive thought; its content is more likely to be performed than explicitly proposed through cognitive means. Propositional languages often play a role in ritual, but ritual itself is a performance that operates in a mode separate from that of discursive thought. It operates not in the mode of the cognitive but rather in the mode of the symbolic.

In *Symbol and Sacrament*, Louis-Marie Chauvet expands on the differences between the cognitive mode and the symbolic mode, which he identifies as the mode of the metaphysical and the mode of language. Chauvet's categories are rooted in Catholic thought, reflecting on the tradition of Scholastic metaphysical theology as well as the Catholic concept of sacramentality, yet they are pertinent to our discussion of modes of theological "language" in Christian and Jewish contexts alike. Launching his criticism of Scholastic categories of thought in the book's opening chapter, Chauvet discusses the radical difference between the two modes.

> [The metaphysical] is a *methodological* concept which we give our-
> selves, a concept showing a *tendency* or an attracting pole character-
> istic of Western thought since the Greeks; this attraction is
> characterized as the "foundational way of thinking" and therefore
> as the very impossibility of taking as the point of departure for
> thought the very distance between discourse and reality. This is to
> say, we suppose another possible tendency or attracting pole for
> thought, starting from and remaining within this disparity: this

[4] Ronald. L. Grimes, *Ritual Criticism: Case Studies in Its Practice, Essays on Its Theory* (Columbia, SC: University of South Carolina Press, 1990), 13–14.

second way is that of language, or of the symbolic. We must specify here—it is all-important—that what we have just presented roughly as a tendency or a pole of attraction opposed to that of the metaphysical, proves to be not simply the reverse model of the metaphysical, therefore placed on the same ground, but in fact another *epistemological terrain* for our thinking activity.[5]

When Chauvet writes that the symbolic mode exists on an entirely different epistemological terrain, he highlights the uniqueness of the mode and of ritual itself. For Chauvet, rituals do not belong to the cognitive order, which he refers to as the order of "-logy," as in the word "theology." Rather, rituals belong to the practical order, characterized by words ending in "urgy," such as "liturgy." Belonging to the practical order, rituals operate at a level different from that of the discursive mode of theology.[6] Rituals do not explain; rather, they invite an *experience* of their context.

LITURGICAL LIMINALITY

Central to ritual studies is the idea that rituals function as agents of transformation within social groups. Setting the foundation for modern ritual studies in the early twentieth century, Emile Durkheim concluded that rituals function in two main ways: (1) they differentiate between the sacred and profane; (2) they integrate those involved in the rites into a sense of solidarity.[7] The capacity of rituals to forge a sense of solidarity was developed further by Arnold van Gennep in his theory of the three main stages in rites of passage: separation, margin, and aggregation.[8]

---

[5] Louis-Marie Chauvet, *Symbol and Sacrament: A Sacramental Reinterpretation of Christian Existence*, trans. Patrick Madigan and Madeleine Beaumont (Collegeville, MN: Liturgical Press, 1995), 9.

[6] Ibid., 324.

[7] Emile Durkheim, *Elementary Forms of the Religious Life*, trans. J. W. Swain (New York: Free Press, 1965).

[8] Arnold van Gennep, *The Rites of Passage*, trans. Monika B. Vizedom and Gabrielle L. Caffee (University of Chicago Press, 2011). First published as *Les Rites de Passage* (Paris: Nourry, 1909).

Victor Turner developed these three stages in more depth in his theory of social drama and through his work on the stage of liminality (from the Latin "*limen*" or "threshold"), which he put in place of Gennep's stage of margin.[9] He characterized the liminal stage as one of flux and transition in which status and identity become uncertain. After the separation into a ritual state, followed by the procession through the liminal state, ritual participants emerge back into the social group in a transformed state in the phase referred to as aggregation. In this state, a new place within the community is experienced, characterized as *communitas*.

The particular characteristics of liminality are multiple and elusive, as Turner observes: "The attributes of liminality or of liminal personae ('threshold people') are necessarily ambiguous, since this condition and these persons elude or slip through the network of classifications that normally locate states and positions in cultural space."[10] Liminality functions as the ground for fluidity and transformation in ritual, lending ritual the capacity to forge communal understandings of reality through the process of deconstructing existing concepts of mundane normalcy.

Turner writes, "Since [ritual] communicates the deepest values, it has a paradigmatic function; ritual can anticipate change as well as inscribe order in the minds and hearts of participants."[11] This instillation of order and of a communal vision of reality is also achieved by liturgical rituals.[12] Within the liturgical context, the social drama sequence unfolds as participants gather together from an initial stage of nonliturgical normalcy and transition into the stage of separation. Here, liturgical participants enter a time and

[9] Victor Turner, *The Ritual Process: Structure and Anti-Structure* (New York: Aldine Publishing Company, 1969).

[10] Ibid., 95.

[11] Turner, "Ritual, Tribal and Catholic," 506.

[12] Turner understands ritual to have inherently religious elements, and although he primarily applies his theory to rituals that are not explicitly religious, he does acknowledge the liturgical applications of his work. He applies his theory of social drama specifically to Roman Catholic liturgy in his essay "Ritual, Tribal and Catholic," in which he argues for the benefits of the traditional preconciliar form of the Catholic Mass.

space removed from the regular pace of daily life. They set aside the normal patterns of behavior and take on the prescribed behavior of liturgical tradition. Through elements such as ritual speech, song, gesture, and meditation, the participants enter a liminal time and place. In the stage of liminality, the liturgical community understands itself to be engaged in an encounter with God, and in this liturgical encounter with the transcendent, the usual parameters of reality shift. The subjectivity of the participant, clothed now in ritual and tradition, addresses the transcendent and enters into a unique mode of being. The regular order of life is transformed into a liturgical mode, and the horizon of reality is theologically understood to be open toward the transcendent. Thus, in liturgy, participants traverse from an initial conception of reality through a liturgical place of liminality and into a new sense of reality. Finally, in the stage of aggregation, the participants return in a renewed state from the liturgical to the postliturgical.[13]

Turner's use of the concept of liminality points to the means by which liturgy invites a plunge into a realm entirely different than that of daily life. In this realm, Turner suggests, the reformulation of the perception of reality involves a shift in the perception of time. In "Ritual, Tribal and Catholic," Turner speaks of a shift in the experience of time during liturgical performance. "When men and women enter the 'liminality,' the tract of sacred space-time, which is made available to them by such a traditional liturgy, they cease to be bounded by the secular structures of their own age and confront eternity which is equidistant from all ages."[14]

---

[13] The term "liturgy" is descended from the Greek word *leitourgia*, "the work of the people," taken over from polytheist liturgies. In Christian usage, while liturgy is the work of the people in praising God, the concept also suggests that the work might be done *on* or *for* the people, as well, as indicated by *Sacrosanctum Concilium*, paragraph 2, which defines liturgy as "that through which the work of our redemption is accomplished." In addition to the goal of offering praise to God, this study argues, liturgy also functions in the transformation of the community through the stages of separation, liminality, and aggregation.

[14] Turner, "Ritual, Tribal and Catholic," 524.

Turner observes that the stage of liminality is marked by a quality of "sacred space-time" in which the usual secular structures of time are opened to the encounter with eternity. The present study builds on this in the liturgical context, proposing that memory and anticipation are key factors in this transformation of the perception of time. The liturgical engagement with memory and eschatological anticipation leads to a perceived shift in the parameters of time, so that the present is experienced as thoroughly imbued with the past and the future. In this liturgical liminality, borrowing Turner's vision, the participants encounter eternity.

The insights of ritual studies make it clear that the individual experience of ritual is not merely individual. As developed in depth by Turner, ritual theory holds that rituals act to transform societies, bringing the participants into liminal experiences and then reintegrating them into the society in a new form. This same dynamic occurs in liturgical celebrations in which the participants enter a liminal state, and in this position, experience a fluidity in the perception of reality. In liturgical performance, even the most subjective liturgical experience is part of the communal experience of the tradition, and the perception of reality formulated through experience joins the layers of meaning in liturgy.

LITURGICAL REPETITION

The element of repetition significantly contributes to the capacity of liturgical performance to alter the sense of reality, and with it, the experience of time. This holds for repetition *of* the liturgy as well as repetition *within* the liturgy. A person who only rarely experiences a liturgy is unlikely to deeply absorb the theological-cultural-symbolic schema of the liturgy, i.e., the theological meanings, cultural function, and general symbolic world contained within the liturgy. With regular liturgical celebration, however, the theological-cultural-symbolic schema is more likely to be internalized.

When a ritual is practiced time and again, it allows the ritual participant to feel at ease and to proceed through the actions as if by intuition. The internalization of the actions of the liturgy facilitates the absorption of the liturgy's schema as well, which allows the symbolic content to penetrate more deeply. As the participant absorbs the theological-cultural-symbolic schema and experiences reality through the structures of this schema, an encounter occurs between the subjectivity of the participant and the religious tradition as transmitted through the liturgical schema.

Repetition also contributes to the transformation of the experience of time through repeated elements *within* the liturgy, as well as through repetition *of* the liturgy. A ritual that contains repetition within its structure, such as the repetition of words or actions, facilitates the internalization of the ritual's content in many ways. On a basic level, an element that is repeated takes on a greater significance. Its repetition draws attention and intensifies the significance of the content it communicates. Secondly, repetition facilitates the state of ritual ease as the participant relaxes into the rhythm of repetition. When the repeated elements are expected, the anticipation of the repetition allows it to seem natural, as if it were arising from the impulse of the ritual agent.

Finally, repetition in liturgy introduces an element of timekeeping as the repeated element punctuates the flow of time. A good example is in the recitation of particularly repetitive psalms, such as Psalm 136, in which a vast array of events in the Hebrew Bible is narrated, and yet each line of the psalm concludes with an identical phrase: "for his love endures forever." When this psalm is recited in a liturgical context, each repetition contributes to a regular rhythm, punctuating the passing of time like the ticking of a clock.[15] As the liturgical community repeats this line, the declaration that God's love "endures forever" marks the passing of time—as it is experi-

[15] In Jewish liturgy, Psalm 136 is known as the Great Hallel and is recited during *pesukei de-zimra* on Shabbat mornings and on festivals. It is also recited after the Lesser Hallel during the Passover Seder. In Catholic tradition, Psalm 136 is recited in the Benedictine Office every Wednesday during Vespers. In the Liturgy of the Hours, it occurs in the Saturday Week II Office of Readings; Monday Week IV Evening Prayer; Monday Week IV within Advent and Christmas Season Evening Prayer; Friday within the Octave of Easter Office of Readings; and Tuesday Week II during Lent and Easter Season Office of Readings. Maxwell E. Johnson, ed. *Benedictine Daily Prayer: A Short Breviary* (Collegeville, MN: Liturgical Press), 2005.

enced through the time of the psalm's recitation, measured by the rhythm of its poetry—with an evocation of eternality.

As repetition flows from one occurrence to the next, as if arising intuitively rather than imposed through liturgical structure, it allows the theological-cultural-symbolic schema of the liturgy to be internalized. Through the internalization of the ritual content, repetition thus functions in implanting meaning, as discussed by Chauvet: "Ritual's regular repetition has an initiatory effect of the greatest importance. Reiterating the same gestures and the same formulas in identical circumstances and following a fairly regular periodic rhythm, it implants the values of the group into the body of each member, in the end 'sticking to the skin' (for here also— here especially—everything is in the 'skin') so that the values appear completely 'natural.'"[16] Chauvet's observation that repetition "implants the values of the group" addresses the internalization of liturgical schema. Using the metaphor of skin, Chauvet demonstrates how ritual repetition allows the participants to be so immersed in the ritual that its values form an all-encompassing atmosphere, "sticking to the skin." The values, or the theological-cultural-symbolic schema, then seem to be entirely interior to the participants.

In the context of liturgy, the specific values internalized through repetition and the liturgical state of flow arise from the religious narrative. The values are transmitted through the liturgical schema, which performs the memory of the past and the anticipation of the future. When the liturgical participants internalize the schema, they become immersed in the experience of time. More specifically, they become immersed in an experience of time in which the boundaries of the past, present, and future are porous, as indicated by both Jewish and Christian tradition.

This immersion into a shifting temporal realm is expressed eloquently by an Orthodox Christian nun who writes of her experience of praying Vespers: "The repetitive rhythmic reiteration takes us up into the flow of tradition, out of the past into the present,

---

[16] Chauvet, *Symbol and Sacrament*, 340.

and out of the present in to the future. And, with this sense of time-lessness within time, we are naturally drawn into the awareness of the transcendent, into the incomprehensible no-time of God."[17] Through liturgical repetition, she writes, the liturgical community is enveloped by the flow of tradition. The narrative of tradition becomes the lens through which reality is experienced, as the mythical history of the religious narrative, from the primordial past to the eschatological future, is experienced through the liturgical present.

A similar experience is described by Fr. Frank, the Jesuit priest interviewed in chapter 4: "The rhythm of the recitation of the psalms, the regular meter of it, draws a person into a contemplative union. . . . I don't *think* about it as bringing the past and future, it's not a cognitive intellectual activity; it's an *experience* of regularity." Fr. Frank finds that the act of reciting the psalms in the Liturgy of the Hours places him in a meditative state in which he is not concerned with cognitive thought. Instead, through the rhythmic repetition of the liturgy, he experiences a sense of union, accompanied by an intuitive experience of transformed time.

In the context of Jewish liturgy, repetition functions in a similar way. David, the Orthodox Jewish scholar interviewed in chapter 3, discusses the effect of liturgical repetition on the sense of time: "[This world is] infinitely extensive, not only in the past, but in the future. Liturgy, with all the cyclicality and all the repetition and so forth, reinforces that feeling." He finds that the rhythmic, repetitive qualities of liturgical recitation attune him to a sense of the infinite reach of time.

The discussion up to this point has addressed repetition as a soothing, naturalizing experience, allowing the liturgical participant to intuitively identify with the repeated elements. Repetition, however, can also serve as a rupture, breaking apart the expected order; this too can affect the experience of time. Jacques Derrida identifies repetition with a rupture in structure: "The event I called a rupture . . . would have come about when the structurality of

---

[17] Sister Thekla, "The Service of Vespers: Prayers of the Day," *Library of Orthodox Thinking* 3 (1976): 6.

structure had to begin to be thought, that is to say, repeated, and this is why I said that this disruption was repetition in every sense of the word."[18] He proposes that repetition signals a rupture, in which the fact that a given system is structured is noticed and reflected on. When the form or center of a structure is identified, and then repeated, that center becomes transposed through repetition, and the structure is disrupted. For example, the numbers one through five are established within a sequential structure, and if a person counting that sequence repeats the number three, the structure is disrupted through repetition, and attention is drawn to the structurality of the structure.

A composition by the contemporary composer Philip Glass illustrates this well: In the musical composition "Einstein on the Beach," the choir sings the sequence of the numbers one through eight and repeats the sequence in fragments, first stopping at the number four, then repeating and stopping at the number six, and then repeating and stopping at the number eight. With some repetitions, certain numbers are left unsaid, and a silent pause is left in their place, which resonates with the anticipation of the missing number. As the sung numbers repeat cyclically, their repetition is disturbing; it creates a rupture in the expected flow of time and draws the listener into a relentless cycle of fragmented time. A rupture in structure translates into a rupture in the experience of time.

In the awareness of structure is an implicit awareness of regularity and of time. Structure and time are intimately linked; when one contemplates the existence of time, one struggles to concretize the abstract, to systematize what is experienced as a flow, and to envision the experience of the present moment within a sequential structure. In drawing attention to the structure, repetition plays with it and plays with time. Repetition, then, creates a rupture in the experience of time, comparable to the ritual stage of liminality. The rupture of repetition heightens the consciousness of time and

---

[18] Jacques Derrida, "Structure, Sign and Play in the Discourse of the Human Sciences," in *A Postmodern Reader*, ed. Joseph Natoli and Linda Hutcheon (New York: SUNY Press, 1993), 225.

creates a sense of time unique to the ritual in which the repetition is performed.

THE STATE OF FLOW

Flow theory, developed by psychologist Mihaly Csikszentmih-alyi in the 1970s, considers the effects of a state called "flow," in which seamless ease and fluency are experienced in the execution of tasks requiring skill and competency.[19] According to Csikszent-mihalyi, flow is a state in which actions seem to occur intuitively with no interference of hesitancy or anxiety. The characteristics of the state of flow are subjective and thus not easily observed or categorized definitively. Nevertheless, Csikszentmihalyi offers a list of traits of the state of flow:

- Intense and focused concentration on what one is doing in the present moment

- Merging of action and awareness

- Loss of reflective self-consciousness (i.e., loss of awareness of oneself as a social actor)

- A sense that one can control one's actions; that is, a sense that one can in principle deal with the situation because one knows how to respond to whatever happens next

- Distortion of temporal experience (typically, a sense that time has passed faster than normal)

- Experience of the activity as intrinsically rewarding, such that often the end goal is just an excuse for the process.[20]

Csikszentmihalyi studies the phenomenon of flow within a number of activities, mostly within the arts, science, and sports, but he does not apply the theory directly to liturgy. This application is

[19] Mihaly Csikszentmihalyi, *Flow: The Psychology of Optimal Experience* (New York: Harper and Row, 1990).
[20] Jeanne Nakamura and Mihaly Csikszentmihalyi, "The Concept of Flow," *Handbook of Positive Psychology* (2002): 89–105; 90.

made by Victor Turner, however, who uses the theory of flow in his argument for the benefits of maintaining a traditional liturgy. Turner's description of the state of flow suggests how the theory may be applied to the liturgical experience of time: "'Flow' is, for [Csikszentmihalyi], a state in which action follows action according to an internal logic which seems to need no conscious intervention on our part; we experience it as a unified flowing from one moment to the next, in which we feel in control of our actions, and in which there is little distinction between self and environment, between stimulus and response, or between past, present and future."[21] The characteristics of the state of flow involve a dissolution of boundaries, and as Turner observes, the dissolution of the distinction between the past, present, and future.

In the list offered by Csikszentmihalyi, the dissolution of boundaries is seen in a number of characteristics: the boundary between action and awareness is dissolved as the two merge, and the boundary between the self and the social group is forgotten as one loses self-consciousness and awareness of one's role as a social actor. Most significantly, Csikszentmihalyi claims that one of the boundaries dissolved in the state of flow is temporal, resulting in the distortion of temporal experience. In his work, the connection between ritual action and the distortion of the experience of time can be traced. In examples such as rock climbing or painting, the agents engage in patterns specific to the activity and indicated by the projected goal, whether the goal be the safe ascent of a rock wall or aesthetic creativity. In the process of engaging in these ritual actions, the agents immerse themselves so deeply into the activity that the connection between the self and the practice appears seamless. As the boundary between the self and the ritual dissolves, the agents lose awareness of the prescribed rules or limits of "regular" activity, including the sense of time. The more immersed one becomes in the activity, losing awareness of the distinction between the self and the activity, the greater the distortion of the experience of time.

---

[21] Turner, "Ritual, Tribal and Catholic," 520.

The subjective experience of liturgical performance has not been categorized as precisely as the experience of flow has by Csikszentmihalyi and others in his field, and the liturgical equivalent of flow remains largely unsystematized. Characteristics of liturgical experience that resemble those of flow are, however, discussed by some liturgical theologians. In the context of Christian prayer, a phenomenon similar to the total immersion obtained within the state of flow can occur in the recitation of the Liturgy of the Hours, which is rhythmic, repetitive, and poetic. In *Company of Voices: Daily Prayer and the People of God*, George Guiver establishes two categories of prayer, "stream prayer" and "prayer of careful concentration," based on the subjective state within each type of prayer. He identifies the Liturgy of the Hours as "stream prayer," likening the liturgy to a stream gradually and steadily wearing away the stones and banks. Stream prayer offers a panoramic view, while the latter is detail oriented.[22] According to this model, the celebration of the Liturgy of the Hours induces a meditative state in which the liturgical community becomes immersed in the religious narrative as expressed through the poetry of the liturgical office.

Patrick Regan, a Benedictine monk and former abbot of St. Joseph's Abbey who has dedicated a lifetime to the praying of the Liturgy of the Hours, also describes a liturgical state similar to flow and identifies the activity of the Holy Spirit in this state.

> The pneumatological aspect of ritual is above all qualitative and attitudinal. It is sensed in the wholeness, fullness and density of the entire celebration. It is evident when speech and gesture, movement and song are complete, fluid, rhythmic and concentrated not truncated, dangling, diffused and thin. This can happen only when those who celebrate transcend the dislocations of time, space and mind inherent in social structure, and enter the world of homology, the world of the Spirit, in which everything mutually indwells and points to everything else.[23]

[22] George Guiver, *Company of Voices: Daily Prayer and the People of God* (New York: Pueblo Publishing Company, 1988), 23.

[23] Patrick Regan, "Pneumatological and Eschatological Aspects of Liturgical Celebration," *Worship* 51, no. 4 (1977): 350.

The characteristics of this kind of liturgical experience closely resemble those identified by flow theory. In this passage, Regan offers a description of an aspect of liturgy marked by an uninterrupted flow, in which the boundaries of "normal" activity become porous. For Regan, this characterizes the "world of the Spirit," and is not caused by purely psychological factors. In this thoroughly theological explanation of a state of flow, the state requires the overcoming of "the dislocations of time, space and mind inherent in social structure."

In the context of Jewish prayer, a state of awareness similar to the state of flow can also be identified. Halakhic indications for prayer contribute to a careful regulation of the psychological state of a person engaged in prayer. This phenomenon is studied by Paul R. Bindler, who notes that "Jewish law seeks to deploy attention in circumscribed ways in order to produce the state of mind characteristic of prayer; that is, maximizing one's awareness of God by reducing extraneous stimuli which are not at particular times relevant to this awareness."[24] He continues, "Hence, incorporated into the body of Jewish law is the recognition that uncalibrated awareness of the external, physical world impedes the development of religious experience."[25] The awareness of external factors is regulated precisely to attain an ideal state for prayer: "Decreasing both environmental stimuli and physiological activation automatically focuses attention on mental imagery and verbal thoughts. To further reduce distracting, irrelevant ideation and to focus concentration on the content of prayer, Jewish law regulates a process of selective attention. Through this process concentration on prayer is refined, reinforced, and enhanced while extraneous thoughts are deemphasized and ignored, so that eventually awareness of them habituates."[26]

This halakhically mandated system contributes to a state of intense concentration in prayer, which is related to, yet distinct from,

[24] Paul Bindler, "Meditative Prayer and Rabbinic Perspectives on the Psychology of Consciousness: Environmental, Physiological, and Attentional Variables," *Journal of Psychology and Judaism* 4 (1980): 230.
[25] Ibid., 232.
[26] Ibid., 245.

the state of flow as identified by Csikszentmihalyi. The rabbinic guidelines for prayer establish a system to enhance concentration, but they do not specify a required interior quality or character of concentration. The internal quality of concentration, however, is described by Rabbi Joseph B. Soloveitchik in his discussion of a rabbinic concept termed *avodah she-ba-lev*, service or prayer of the heart. In a discussion on Maimondies's *Guide for the Perplexed*, Soloveitchik addresses the rabbinic regulations on attention, beginning with the parameters governing attention and focus and then continuing onto a discussion of the interior, mystical state that may be achieved in prayer.

> The Maimonidean idea of service of the heart is to be seen at two levels: the psychological and the mystical. From the psychological viewpoint, *avodah she-ba-lev* is identical with the state of mind which is called mono-ideism, the giving of attention to one idea exclusively. Our attention to the *mitzvah* is divorced from all other centers of interest and is focused upon a single subject. In other words, *avodah she-ba-lev* borders on total involvement with God and total separation from finite goods and values. It is a type of fixation, however voluntary, that borders on the anomalous, divine madness (*shiggayon*). . . . At a mystical level, *avodah she-ba-lev* is identical with communion, with closeness to God and the ecstatic act of perception of Him. *Devekut* [clinging to God, or the ecstatic state of communion with God] is the transcendence of finitude; it is the extension of the existential experience into the boundlessness of the beyond in the direction of the supreme Being.[27]

In this passage, an experiential state related to the state of flow can be observed. The person at prayer becomes deeply and exclusively focused on the activity of prayer, to the exclusion of awareness of his or her surroundings. When Soloveitchik refers to divine madness, he alludes to a transformation of consciousness, similar to the "loss of reflective self-consciousness" identified by Csikszentmihalyi. The state of *devekut*, the mystical ecstasy of clinging to God, is

---

[27] Joseph B. Soloveitchik, *Worship of the Heart: Essays on Jewish Prayer*, ed. Shalom Carmy, (New York: Toras HoRav Foundation, 2003), 23–24.

associated with the overcoming of finitude, which hearkens to Csikszentmihalyi's category of "distortion of temporal experience."

The associations between aspects of liturgical experience and the state of flow are multiple, yet a major distinction remains. In Jewish and Christian traditions, prayer is considered to be an act of communication with the transcendent God, whereas in the psychological state of flow, no communication with a transcendent element is assumed. The identification of similarities between liturgical experience and the state of flow, however, remains relevant, for it points to the ways in which liturgical performance can transform the experience of time.

Flow theory addresses a state experienced in activities requiring skill, and these activities involve sets of rules and specific actions similar to those of liturgy. In liturgy, the dissolution of the boundary between the self and the activity means that the normal rules by which one maintains the secular order of life are subsumed by the liturgical and theological rules. The theory of flow helps explain how liturgy invites a transformed sense of reality. The participant internalizes the ritual actions to such a degree that the norms governing the ritual become interiorly ingrained. In this process, the elements of the ritual become interiorized and projected onto the perception of reality. In liturgical ritual, the religious narrative and vision of reality act as an ideal order which is experienced in more fullness and dimensionality through the ritual performance.

This applies to the experience of time, as well. The secular structure of timekeeping indicates that time passes in evenly measured components as measured by clocks, neither speeding up nor slowing down. Past moments become more and more distant, and the future can never be reached. Yet, as the boundaries of the secular, nonritual order dissolve in liturgical ritual, so too does the rigidity of time. As time becomes internalized through liturgical performance, it transitions from being viewed as an external structure of regulation to being sensed as an interior experience. In this way, the liturgical community enters the interior domains of memory and hope, and in this interior meeting place, the past and the future are experienced within the present. In liturgical ritual, elements of repetition, embodiment, liminality, and flow come together to transport the participant into a unique state in which the experience of time witnesses a merging of the past, present, and future imagined by faith.

Chapter 10

Liturgy, Time, and Interreligious Learning

For a thousand years in your sight are like yesterday when it is past.
—Psalm 90:4

THE ATMOSPHERE OF TIME

We experience the world around us and our own existence through the element of time. All that we understand of ourselves and others we have found through the medium of time, and it is by time that our lives are bound, as a tenuous collection of years within the historical expanse of time that we imagine stretching before and after our brief lives.

The contemplation of the experience of time is thus also a meditation on our existence; our existential situation is, arguably, the central content on which faith meditates. The experience of time allows us to contemplate our temporality and transience in relation to notions of God's eternality, for the concept of the eternal requires the situation of temporality as its counterdefinition. If the contemplation of existence is at the root of theological reflection and religious practice in both Christianity and Judaism, then the experience of time is indeed a central part of faith.

Memory and hope in liturgy are inherently performative. The use of the term "performative" in this book generally differs from its use by J. L. Austin and others in the linguistic phenomenon of "performative utterances," in which statements are efficacious through their utterance, as words "do things."[1] Yet, at this point in the study we venture to consider another dimension of the performative nature of memory and hope and propose that they are performative not only in the most basic sense, i.e., as performed events, but also in a sense closer to that used by Austin. In the former sense, we see that they are enacted and embodied in liturgy, and the liturgical participant "does" memory and hope. In the latter sense, however, we now see that memory and hope also "do things," similar to the way that words "do things" in performative utterances. The performance of memory and hope draws the liturgical participant into a relationship with the past and the future, and even more, into an experiential *participation* in these temporal elements. In both Jewish and Christian liturgical performance, memory and hope integrate the past and future into the present.

The primary impetus of this book has been the identification of the experience of time as an essential element of religious identity and experience in Christianity and Judaism. It has demonstrated that the experience of time is intrinsic to the experience of faith and has illuminated the specifically liturgical implications of this. It has taken preliminary steps in mapping the experiential realm of time awareness in liturgical performance as communally shaped by the narratives and theologies of religious tradition and by the act of ritual performance.

JEWISH AND CHRISTIAN CONTOURS OF TIME

This book investigates the experience of time in both Christian and Jewish liturgical contexts, driven by the conviction that this is a significant point of convergence in Christian and Jewish religious experience that has been largely overlooked in scholarship to date. As discussed in the opening chapter, most work within Christian-Jewish comparative scholarship has addressed historical or sociological issues. This reflects, quite justifiably, the pressing concerns that the history of relations between Christians and Jews offers, for the history is fraught with tension, injustice, and violence. These

---

[1] J. L. Austin, *How to Do Things with Words* (Cambridge, MA: Harvard University Press, 1962).

174

studies are crucial to the project of reconciliation that still lies ahead of us. The body of comparative scholarship on Christianity and Judaism that addresses specifically religious or theological issues, rather than sociological, also tends toward studies of historical interaction. This reflects the closely intertwined histories of Jewish and Christian religious development and self-identification in what is often referred to as a "sibling" relationship.[2] This work, too, is crucial for the ongoing need for greater understanding of each tradition and in the self-understanding of each one in relationship to the other.[3]

---

[2] See Israel Jacob Yuval, *Two Nations in Your Womb: Perceptions of Jews and Christians in Late Antiquity and the Middle Ages* (Berkeley, CA: University of California Press, 2008), 10–12. Yuval discusses a Jewish typology dating from the early centuries of the Common Era that identified Judaea and Rome with the biblical brothers Jacob and Esau, respectively. When Rome became Christianized, this typology transitioned into symbolizing Judaism and Christianity. Yuval notes that in Christian tradition, however, Jacob was identified with Christianity, and Esau with Judaism.

[3] While the current study is primarily concerned with neither historical development nor sociological concerns, it does intend to help combat a dangerous ideology which is very present in Christian thought, i.e., the idea that Christianity has superseded Judaism by supplanting it with a new covenant and final truth, making null and void the promises of the old covenant. Inherent to Christian faith is the belief that Christ was incarnated in continuity with the Hebrew Scriptures, and that his incarnation, crucifixion, and resurrection introduced a new covenant. As Catholic teaching has made clear, however, most notably in *Nostra Aetate* (sec. 4), the covenant through Christ does not supersede or invalidate the covenant introduced at Mount Sinai between God and Israel. This supersessionist ideology often makes recourse to the seemingly benign Pauline image of the olive tree, of which Judaism is the roots and onto which Christians are grafted. This image, while established in Scripture and tradition, was developed in the early decades following the life of Christ, when the Christian movement was primarily a branch within the Jewish community. In the wake of the destruction of the Temple in Jerusalem, Christianity became a primarily Gentile religion, while Rabbinic Judaism developed into a codified system quite different from the Second Temple Judaism that preceded it. Accordingly, it is more fitting to envision the olive tree as two distinct and fully developed branches, representing Christianity and Rabbinic Judaism, growing out of the shared trunk of the religion of ancient Israel.

This book, however, has chosen to address a subject that is integral to both Christian and Jewish experience and yet rarely addressed academically. Comparative studies of Judaism and Christianity that examine ritual experience are rare, perhaps due to the difficulty in determining and interpreting the data. This book expands on current comparative scholarship of Judaism and Christianity, for although there are many studies on memory and hope in Christianity and Judaism, there is to my knowledge no comparative study of the two traditions that focuses on the *experience* of memory and hope in each.

The contribution of ritually enacted memory and hope to a liturgical transformation of the experience of time constitutes a shared ground in Christian and Jewish experience. Yet Christian and Jewish understandings of the nature of time and the trajectory of history are quite distinct. The distinction between the eschatological visions of Christianity and Judaism—i.e., between the anticipated return of Jesus Christ and the coming of the Jewish messiah—is often cited as the most significant divergence of temporal understandings. A site of greater disjunction, however, lies in their visions of the overall structure of time.

Christian theologians have long understood time to have been substantively changed through the passion of Jesus Christ. This is evident in the notion of the eighth day, in which the resurrection is seen to change the structure of time, proleptically inaugurating the eternal eon.[4] We also see this in Jean Daniélou's theology of Christ as the Lord of Time, within whom all time is contained.[5] Similarly, Hans Urs von Balthasar understands time to have been transformed by the redemption brought through Jesus Christ's passion and claims that the Christ event becomes "the source of history, the point whence the whole of history before and after Christ emanates: its center."[6]

---

[4] See Mario Baghos, "St. Basil's Eschatological Vision: Aspects of the Recapitulation of History and the 'Eighth Day,'" *Phronema* 25 (2010): 85–103; see also chapter 7 of the current study.

[5] Jean Daniélou, *The Lord of History* (Chicago: H. Regnery, 1958), 24.

[6] Hans Urs von Balthasar, *A Theology of History* (San Francisco: Ignatius Press, 1994), 18–19.

Christian thought tends toward an intensive spiritualization of time, in which time has been radically transformed through transcendental divine activity and the event on the cross transgresses all chronological boundaries. In Christian theologies of time, the element of time is lifted out of chronological sequence and reshaped into a form that is already redeemed, and yet that also holds the semblance of continuing chronology.[7] This reshaping of time is not simply a reflection of the tendency toward theological analogizing and poetics which does, in fact, characterize much Christian theology. Rather, the spiritualization of time in Christian thought reflects a specific and concrete element of Christian faith: it reflects the belief that the future has already been "met" through Jesus Christ. Fundamental to Christian faith is the notion that Jesus Christ, through his passion, death, and resurrection, saved and continues to save humanity throughout time. As the Alpha and Omega, Jesus Christ is believed to be the ultimate beginning and the ultimate ending. The Christian tendency toward the spiritualization and theological reshaping of time, therefore, reflects these understandings of the nature of Jesus Christ and time.

In contrast to the Christian theologies of time addressed in this book, which incorporate a theological reshaping of time, most Jewish notions of time are more grounded in chronological time and less radically reshaped, reflecting the Jewish conviction that the messiah has not yet come and has not transformed time. In Jewish thought, the crucial event understood to have transformed time is the creation narrative. Serving as the central event determining the shape of time, the creation narrative speaks of the beginning of the world and of the creation of time. Shabbat, as the memorial of creation, is also believed to mystically participate in the completion of time. The narrative of the exodus from Egypt also serves as a major

---

[7] This is also seen in the work of Joseph Ratzinger, who writes "In the Son, time co-exists with eternity. . . . In the Word incarnate, who remains man forever, the presence of eternity with time becomes bodily and concrete." Ratzinger envisions a transformation of time in which eternity and time operate together in the incarnation of Jesus Christ. See Joseph Ratzinger, *The Spirit of the Liturgy* (San Francisco: Ignatius Press, 2000), 92.

temporal foundation, symbolizing the transition from slavery to freedom and marking the revelation at Mount Sinai.[8]

These are each forms of a Jewish spiritualization of time, for the narratives serve as templates for a spiritual vision of time. While the memorialized past is reexperienced in liturgical performance and the eschatological future anticipated, Jewish thought maintains a vision of time that follows a generally chronological sequence. Religious memory stretches and condenses history through its selective patterns of memory, as Yosef Hayim Yerushalmi observes, but time remains essentially linear.[9]

The difference in the extent to which Christian and Jewish thought each reshapes the sequence of time may be due to at least two factors. The first involves the temporal placement of the events that are understood to be time transforming. Judaism situates the beginning of time in the memorialized creation narrative, and although the biblical-historical events that follow it are of utmost importance to Judaism, the events in themselves are not understood to transform time. The engagement of active, creative time-consciousness and memory can transform the sense of time in liturgical performance, as Rabbi Joseph B. Soloveitchik proposes, but time itself is not changed.[10]

Christian thought, on the other hand, understands the event on the cross to have transformed time; complicating this claim is the fact that the event occurred in the midst of a historical progression that was established before the event and continued after the event. Historical time preceded the event on the cross, and time has continued on, seemingly unchanged, since the event. Theologians, therefore, have developed ways of reconceptualizing the shape of time in relation to this event. Jesus Christ is seen as the

---

[8] The exodus narrative is central to the Jewish narrative and serves as a primary source of religious memory, but it is understood to mark a *transition* in time rather than to *transform* time.

[9] Yosef Hayim Yerushalmi, *Zakhor: Jewish History and Jewish Memory* (Seattle: University of Washington Press, 1982), 16–17.

[10] See the discussion of Soloveitchik's theory of time-consciousness in chapter 6 of the current study.

Lord of History; his incarnation is understood to stand at the center of time, and all time before and after the crucifixion is contained within him.[11] This means that time can no longer be seen as purely linear but is multidimensional, folded, and complex.

The second factor contributing to the difference in Jewish and Christian shapes of time involves the orientations of Jewish and Christian thought toward memory and hope. Judaism and Christianity both maintain a dual focus on the memorialized past and the eschatological future, but each exhibits a distinctive tendency to focus on one side. Collective memory serves as an anchor of Jewish thought and practice, and Christian theology is heavily eschatological. Yet, despite their general inclinations to one side, Jewish and Christian thought and experience incorporate tendencies toward both poles, as illustrated by the diverse individual experiences expressed in part 2 of this book. While many of the Jewish participants expressed an orientation toward memory, and many of the Christians expressed an orientation toward the future, members of each tradition also expressed individual inclinations to the opposite pole as well.

While the eschatological focus of Judaism is strong and messianic hope central to Judaism, Jewish thought and practice is deeply rooted in communal memory, for which the biblical narrative serves as the primary historical anchor. This memorial orientation allows the focus to be directed toward events that have already occurred in history, whether as events documented by the modern sense of history or within mythical history.[12] This is seen in the liturgical festivals discussed in this book, all of which are significantly memorial. While eschatological elements are also present in most liturgical festivals, the eschatological focus is often more subtle than the memorial focus. We see this in Passover, which is

[11] See von Balthasar, *A Theology of History*, 18–19; Daniélou, *The Lord of History*, 24.

[12] The historical veracity of these past events is not of consequence in this context, for what matters is that they are envisioned to exist within history and memory, which allows Jewish tradition to maintain a generally sequential, linear vision of time.

firmly centered on the memory of leaving Egypt and yet also has attendant eschatological overtones. Likewise, even the more overtly eschatological celebration of Shabbat is primarily based on the remembrance of God's rest after the act of creation; the eschatological associations, although strong, arise secondarily from this memorial foundation.

Jewish thought also emphasizes the continuity between the past and the present, particularly as it impacts the notion of the Jewish community. There is a strong identification within Jewish thought and practice between the present Jewish community and that of the past. This is evidenced in the Passover obligation to identify with those who were set free from Egypt, to the extent that one must see oneself as one having been there. This identification with the past is, more specifically, an identification with the generations that preceded the present; that is, the identification is not only with past events but also with a people.[13]

This is discussed in the thought of Soloveitchik, who writes of a sense of continuity with the past—specifically, with the generations: "The Jew who prays sees himself as integrated with those who have carried the burden over the generations, as connected to the past and the future like a link in one long chain."[14] Again, he observes: "In reading the *Shema*, by contrast, we enter the presence of those persons who walked with Him, we stand in their shadow . . . in an act of self-identification with the history and destiny of our people, in the experience of oneness of ages and events, the merger of the multidimensional time-feeling into one focal point, a point that is, *eo ipso*, the center of my own self."[15] Here, we see that the process of identification with the past is also an identification of one's own self. This suggests that the Jewish memorial orientation allows individual identity to partake in a communal identity that stretches across time.

[13] Biblical references to past and future generations are voluminous. In just the first two books of the Hebrew Bible, see Gen 9:12; 17:7, 9, 12; Exod 12:14; 16:32; 17:16; 20:5, 6; 27:21; 29:42; 30:8, 10, 21, 31; 31:13, 16; 34:7; 40:15.

[14] Joseph B. Soloveitchik, *Worship of the Heart: Essays on Jewish Prayer*, ed. Shalom Carmy (New York: Toras HoRav Foundation, 2003), 155.

[15] Ibid., 112.

Christian thought, on the other hand, although both memorial and anticipatory, maintains a focus directed largely toward the future. More specifically, it focuses on the eschatological future, which does not fall within the chronological sequence of time. Eschatological anticipation, unlike memory, projects into the unforeseen future, through time and beyond time. According to Jürgen Moltmann, Christianity is in essence eschatological: "From first to last, and not merely in the epilogue, Christianity is eschatology, is hope, forward looking and forward moving, and therefore also revolutionizing and transforming the present. The eschatological is not one element *of* Christianity, but it is the medium of Christian faith as such, the key in which everything in it is set, the glow that suffuses everything here in the dawn of an expected new day."[16]

It must be clarified that the eschatological focus of Christianity is also paired with a memorial focus, just as Judaism is focused on both.[17] This is seen in the Eucharist, which is both memorial and eschatological, linking the remembered past to the anticipated future. It ritually remembers the Last Supper and makes it mystically present. At the same time, it ritually "remembers" the future, for the Christian vision of the future is contained within the person of Jesus Christ.[18]

Like Judaism, Christian thought and practice also envisions a continuity between the past and present. The Christian identification with the past, however, is highly theological and spiritual and much less related to a sense of community, identity, and historical heritage than it is in Judaism. Granted, in Christianity, the individual identifies as a member of the Body of Christ through faith and thus as a member of a "universal" family.[19] Yet, this universal

[16] Jürgen Moltmann, *Theology of Hope*, trans. James Leitch (New York: Harper and Row, 1967), 16.

[17] Robert Taft argues that "*history* and *eschatology* are not mutually exclusive. The eschatological tension between the present age and the age to come is too obvious in the Early Church to need elaboration here." Robert Taft, "Historicism Revisited," in *Liturgical Time*, ed. Wiebe Vos and Geoffrey Wainwright (Rotterdam: Liturgical Ecumenical Center Trust, 1982), 97–109, here 98.

[18] The Amidah similarly is both memorial and focused on eschatological redemption.

[19] The universality of this family is limited by the fact that it includes only those of Christian faith, even when articulated by inclusivist theologies such

family does not maintain the strong sense of identity of the Jewish community, which is perhaps attributable to Christian claims to universality, as exemplified by the injunction "Go therefore and make disciples of all nations" (Matt 28:19). In Jewish thought and practice, by contrast, the identification with the past is particularist and communal, as a people who carries the past into the present.

THE EXPERIENCE OF TIME: A SITE OF INTERRELIGIOUS CONVERGENCE

Despite the considerable differences between Jewish and Christian visions of time, the fundamental experience of the passing of time remains both deeply individual and communally shared in both traditions. Jewish and Christian thinkers return to the subject of time in theological reflection, as they contemplate the perception of the passing of time and the indeterminacy of the categories of the past, present, and future. We return now to Soloveitchik, this time in conversation with Saint Augustine. This first excerpt is from Augustine's *Confessions*, and the second is from a lecture by Soloveitchik about Passover:

> What is by now evident and clear is that neither future nor past exists, and it is inexact language to speak of three times—past, present, and future. Perhaps it would be exact to say: there are three times, a present of things past, a present of things present, a present of things to come. In the soul there are these three aspects of time, and I do not see them anywhere else. The present considering the past is the memory, the present considering the present is immediate awareness, the present considering the future is expectation.[20]

> Man's time-awareness is elusive and paradoxical. In grammar we have three tenses: present, future, and past. Experientially, however, the present can never be isolated and perceived; the point of time we call present lies either in the past or in the future. In a word, we

---

as Karl Rahner's "anonymous Christian." See Gavin D'Costa, "Karl Rahner's Anonymous Christian: A Reappraisal," *Modern Theology* 1, no. 2 (1985): 136.

[20] Augustine, *Confessions*, trans. Henry Chadwick (Oxford: Oxford University Press, 1992), 11.19.25.

experience time either as retrospection-recollection or as prospection-anticipation. What we call the present is nothing but a vantage point from which we look either forward or backward.[21]

The thought of both Augustine and Soloveitchik is formed and driven by the religious traditions and eras of which they are each a part. Each tradition maintains a temporal landscape shaped by the narrative of the Hebrew Bible, but each develops and interprets it differently, and each holds different understandings of the nature of the present and future. Yet despite the differences in the temporal landscape of each tradition, each tradition inspires meditation on the interior experience of time. Whereas Augustine focuses on the insubstantiality of the past and the future, and Soloveitchik notes the fleetingness of the present, both are concerned with the same conundrum, and both are captivated by the experience of time. Both ponder the way that time is experienced in the mind, contemplating the infinite from within the element of time.

THE VIRTUE OF IMPOSSIBILITY
The distinctiveness of Christianity and Judaism may pose a challenge to equally understanding each in their uniqueness and relatedness, particularly when the understanding concerns experiential liturgical phenomena. Liturgical experience can only be fully known by the experiencing subject; in other words, one must do it to know it. Liturgy is an "insider" activity in multiple ways: the full experiential depth of liturgical performance cannot be readily accessed by an objective observer, and in addition, it can only be experienced in complete integrity by a committed member of the religious tradition in which it is situated.

This is the paradox of liturgical performance as a locus of interreligious and comparative learning. This paradox, however, is beneficial through the cognitive limits to which it points: one of the greatest benefits of interreligious learning may be the recognition

---

[21] Joseph B. Soloveitchik, "Counting Time," in *Festival of Freedom: Essays on Pesah and the Haggadah*, ed. Joel B. Wolowesky and Reuven Ziegler (Jersey City, NJ: Ktav Publishing House, 2006), 175.

of the inaccessible depth of another religious tradition. That is, a comparative study of liturgical experience gestures toward the unattainable, toward the collective experience of a community and a tradition other than one's own. The most profound insight to be gained may be, paradoxically, the realization of the inaccessibility of an experience other than one's own and the recognition of the dignity of the "other" through all the rich layers of convergence and divergence with one's self.

This has valuable implications for interreligious relations. The assumption that the full truth of another religious tradition is not incommensurable but rather accessible and fully understood can signal a failure of properly receptive understanding. It can lead to a dismissal of the validity or internal coherence of another's experience, or even of a whole tradition, predicated on the hubristic assumption of its transparency. The humility engendered by the recognition of the inaccessibility of another's experience is thus invaluable to interreligious relations. This points to the virtue of impossibility: the study of the liturgical experience of the religious other may yield as much through the limits to understanding that it reveals—limits that acknowledge the dignity and ultimate mystery of the other—as through the concrete observations and conclusions it reaches.[22]

The study of the liturgical experience of time is similarly ultimately incomplete and also suggests the virtue of the impossible. In exploring the transformation of the experience of time within liturgical performance, this book has contemplated an elusive experience that shapes our understandings of our lives and ourselves. The experience of time is deeply internal, and this creates both great challenges and potentials for its study. The subjectivity of its experience resists objective observation, and yet this very condition allows its study to have the potential to be meaningful and profound, for it touches on one of the most intrinsic and intimate aspects of consciousness.

[22] The notion of the virtue of impossibility is indebted to Cornille's study of the virtues required for interreligious dialogue. See Catherine Cornille, *The Im-Possibility of Interreligious Dialogue* (New York: Herder and Herder, 2008).

Motivated by the notion that the experience of time is an integral aspect of faith, this book has demonstrated that the concept of a liturgically transformed experience of time sheds light on essential aspects of religious experience and identity. The experience of time is an intimate part of the experience of faith and of one's perception of self and world. It cannot be extricated from subjectivity, and this quality is precisely what grants its study a meaningfulness that speaks to the most internal aspects of the experience of faith.

The intimacy of the experience of time grants it the particular gift of being able to communicate across the boundaries of religious traditions. Although shaped by religious narrative, tradition, and practice, the experience of time is also intrinsic to human experience, and as such, is capable of subtly transgressing obstacles to interreligious understanding.

Why Remember, Why Hope?

*Time is important to me now, I tell myself. Not that it should pass
quickly or slowly, but be only time, be something I live inside and fill
with physical things and activities that I can divide it up by, so that it
grows distinct to me and does not vanish when I am not looking.*

—Per Petterson, *Out Stealing Horses*[1]

In his Nobel Lecture in 1986, "Hope, Despair and Memory," Elie
Wiesel retells a Hasidic legend that speaks of the desire to reach
the future and of the power of memory. In Wiesel's telling:

A Hasidic legend tells us that the great Rabbi Baal Shem Tov, Master
of the Good Name, also known as the Besht, undertook an urgent
and perilous mission: to hasten the coming of the Messiah. The Jewish people, all humanity were suffering too much, beset by too many
evils. They had to be saved, and swiftly. For having tried to meddle
with the history, the Besht was punished; banished along with his
faithful servant to a distant land. In despair, the servant implored
his master to exercise his mysterious powers in order to bring them
both home. "Impossible," the Besht replied. "My powers have been
taken from me." "Then, please, say a prayer, recite a litany, work a
miracle." "Impossible," the Master replied, "I have forgotten everything." They both fell to weeping.

Suddenly the Master turned to his servant and asked: "Remind
me of a prayer—any prayer." "If only I could," said the servant. "I

[1] Per Petterson, *Out Stealing Horses*, trans. Anne Born (New York: Picador,
2003), 6.

too have forgotten everything." "Everything—absolutely everything?" "Yes, except—" "Except what?" "Except the alphabet." At
that the Besht cried out joyfully: "Then what are you waiting for?
Begin reciting the alphabet and I shall repeat after you." And together the two exiled men began to recite, at first in whispers, then
more loudly: "*Aleph, beth, gimel, daleth* . . ." And over again, each
time more vigorously, more fervently; until, ultimately, the Besht regained his powers, having regained his memory.[2]

In the context of this lecture, Wiesel interprets this legend as a
meditation on the power of memory, expressing the capacity of
memory to save: "I love [this story] most of all because it emphasizes the mystical power of memory. Without memory, our existence would be barren and opaque, like a prison cell into which no
light penetrates; like a tomb which rejects the living. Memory
saved the Besht, and if anything can, it is memory that will save
humanity."[3] As Wiesel observes, this legend does indeed indicate
the capacity of memory to lift us out of captivity, but like many
Hasidic legends, this legend can be interpreted in many ways, revealing layers of meaning and associations, and it speaks to a number of notions discussed in this book.

The legend shows that memory saves, but more specifically, it
suggests that memory has the capacity to save through its ritual
enactment. In this legend, the fact that the Besht's servant remembered the alphabet did not, in itself, change their situation. It was
only in their act of repeated recitation, as they recited the alphabet
again and again, growing more fervent with recitation, that the
Besht's memory returned. The recitation of the alphabet became liturgical as it stood in place of the prayers that they could not remember. They could not pray the proper prayers, and so they
prayed memory, so to speak. They performed the act of memory,

[2] Elie Wiesel, "Hope, Despair and Memory," Nobel Prize Lecture, December
11, 1986, http://www.nobelprize.org/nobel_prizes/peace/laureates/1986
/wiesel-lecture.html.
[3] Ibid.

reciting the sole content of their memory until their full memory was restored; they are saved by the ritual performance of memory.

We must now ask from what, exactly, the two characters in this legend are saved. They are saved from exile in a distant land, and this punishment is a result of trying to hasten the future and for intervening in history. More terrible than the exile, however, is the punishment of the loss of memory. Memory, then, saves them from the loss of memory.

This legend expresses the desire to transform time, inspired by the specifically religious content of hope, that is, the hope for messianic redemption. It also speaks of the strength of the desire to harness time, to seize the religiously envisioned future. It also expresses, of course, the necessity of being able to access the past, which becomes clear once the Besht and his companion have realized that they have lost their memory and thus have lost their connection to the past. This reveals a linkage between the future and the past, for as the Besht tried to "steal" the future, he paid for it by having the past, in the form of memory, stolen from him. Here, the past and future are connected as if linked by a cord: as the Besht pulled prematurely close to the future, he lost the past.[4]

The past and the future are indeed linked in the activities of memory and hope. In response to the question posed in the title of this section, "Why remember?" we can offer at least a provisional answer: we remember so that we may hope. Without memory, there can be no hope. We see this in the work of psychologists and neurologists who have determined that the sense of the past is needed for the sense of the future, and furthermore, that even the

---

[4] In a Christian context, Hans Urs von Balthasar presents a related concept of the punishable desire to transcend time. Referring to the third chapter of Genesis, in which Adam and Eve eat the forbidden fruit, Von Balthasar identifies the sin to lie in their impatience. Jesus Christ, he writes, restores order through disciplining the desire to transcend time and returning them to the steady progress of time: "Hence the restoration of order by the Son of God had to be the annulment of that premature snatching at knowledge, the beating down of the hand outstretched toward eternity, the repentant return from a false, swift transfer into eternity to a true, slow confinement in time." Hans Urs von Balthasar, *A Theology of History* (San Francisco: Ignatius Press, 1994), 37.

fundamental capacity to experience time is dependent on the capacity to remember and to contemplate the future.[5]

Many of the people interviewed in part 2 of this book speak of remembering the past in order to have hope and direction in the future. Rabbi Bill finds this in the narratives of biblical history in which the past provides a template for the future. He comments, "[The ancient narratives] continue to be not only relevant but continue to provide us with a path to the future, about how we make choices and exercise our freedom in ways that allow for the arc of our lives and the arc of history to actually bend toward justice and goodness." He sees the future as a place of freedom, imbued with hope and directed by the memories of the past: "For me there's always a vast and expansive widening of possibilities that comes with the future. That's where hope lies, and that's also where the lessons from the past [lie] that I try to operationalize today. The hope that's imbued to them suggests that the future can be different."

Mother Clara, the cellarer of the monastery, experiences a similar relationship between memory and hope. As a Benedictine nun, she is very much in touch with layers of tradition, from the tradition of the biblical narrative to the monastic traditions of Benedictine life, and she observes, "The handing on of the tradition is a gift from the past that helps stabilize you and helps you keep oriented, and keep your feet on the ground, and keep faith, really. Memory is associated with hope; it gives you hope because you feel the strength of all those people who've come before you, and you feel the oneness with them, you feel the presence of Christ in the moment." Mother Clara finds strength in the past through a sense of identification with people throughout the generations. This sense of identification with previous generations is also seen in many of the Jewish interview subjects, but Mother Clara enunciates this sense in specifically Christian terms, connecting to the past through experiencing Christ in the present moment. Through this spiritual

---

[5] Claudia Hammond, *Time Warped: Unlocking the Mysteries of Time Perception* (New York: Harper Perennial, 2013), 214–15.

experience, therefore, her sense of the past and present are interwoven.

Memory determines the content of hope, and yet hope must be fed and continually reinvigorated through ritual return to remembrance. This is the role of the liturgical calendar and of daily prayer, which allow the liturgical community to pass again and again through cycles of remembrance and hope. This is expressed by Hannah, who describes her response to the last phrase of the Torah service, which is recited when the Torah scroll is returned to the ark. The phrase *"chadesh yameinu ke-kedem,"* "renew our days as of old," speaks of transforming the present moment in continuity with the remembered past. Hannah confesses, "There have been moments when I've almost wanted to weep [when we recite that] because of the extent of the longing and the way that that's linked to the stories of God's presence." She sees this as a liturgical merging of memory and hope. She continues, "I think that [the recitation of] that phrase is a moment [when] the magnitude of what was had and lost intermingles with the longing for what could be restored."

In the religious imagination, both Jewish and Christian, the present is interpreted and defined by the religious narrative of the past. As sociologist Daniele Hervieu-Leger observes, the religiously envisioned past is idealized and mythologized and is seen to exist outside of mundane chronology: "To the extent that the entire significance of the experience of the present is supposed to be contained, potentially at least, in the foundational events, the past is symbolically constituted as an immutable whole, situated 'outside time,' that is, outside history. In the Jewish and Christian traditions, the religious wresting of the past from history is given privileged significance by the core events being magnified in time; and this at once opens up the possibility of the utopian anticipation of the end of time."[6] The religious perspective, therefore, entails a restructuring of time. This temporal shift also lends itself to eschatological anticipation, for the concept of a religiously shaped

[6] Daniele Hervieu-Leger, *Religion as a Chain of Memory* (New Brunswick, NJ: Rutgers University Press, 2000), 124.

past outside of the bounds of mundane time lends itself to a utopian vision of the future. Seeing the past to be more than what is contained within history—that is, understanding the past to be a realm that is remembered rather than historicized, richly layered with myth, narrative, archetypes, revelation, and mystery—opens up the potential for seeing the future to be more than simply the historical events yet to come. In this perspective, the future is a realm of hope and is as rich with myth and narrative and revelation as the past.

A number of the people interviewed in this book understand the preservation and continuation of the religiously envisioned past to be a goal or mission to work toward. In discussing her own experience of Jewish collective memory in the context of Passover, Adira remarks, "I don't just consciously experience [communal memory], but I *work* towards it. I think part of the challenge of the Passover tradition is for parents to teach it to children and then for children to work on it themselves until they can then teach it to their children. . . . Like it says in the Seder, '*l kol dor v dor*,' 'in every generation,' and some people say that's the primary obligation of the Passover Seder, and the whole purpose of the Passover Seder. . . . It's a process of trying to connect." She continues, "That's part of the charge, to remember what came before us, recognize it as good, and then carry it onward."

Members of the Benedictine community also speak of the task of bringing the past, present, and future together as a goal in their religious life. Mother Clara observes, "I feel like our whole life is about knitting [the past, present, and future] together . . . all day long every day we're in this work of knitting it together, or bringing it together." Sister Revelatia also sees the interweaving of the past, present, and future as a spiritual mission, but she specifically identifies it in christological terms. First she speaks of this temporal interpenetration in the nature of Jesus Christ: "I think that union of past, present, future, is why Christ 'works,' because he can unite past, present, and future." She also understands this temporal interpenetration to be something that she is invited to participate in, through faith: "That's how we are connected to the future, by simply doing the next thing that Christ is asking us to do, and that union only comes about through Christ." This echoes the words of Fr. Frank, who speaks of the union of the past, present, and future in Jesus Christ and the capacity to partake in that union through faith: "Christ is the one who is, who was, and who is to come. . . . Insofar as we are one with him . . . all time becomes one. All time becomes now."

In his Nobel Lecture, Wiesel speaks of the reciprocal relationship between memory and hope: "For me, hope without memory is like memory without hope."[7] In other words, to have one without the other would be as if one had neither. Hope deprived of memory is woefully impoverished, and memory without hope is akin to spiritual death. And so, to attempt an answer to the second part of the question posed in the title of this epilogue, "Why hope?" we can say that we hope so that we may remember. Through hope, we anchor ourselves in the future and open up the dimension of the past.

We return now to Rabbi Joseph B. Soloveitchik, who sees the future to be substantial enough to serve as an anchoring point. He writes, "The future is real, tangible; it can be experienced. . . . The genuine historical reality is to be found along the uncharted lanes of a silent, enigmatic future."[8] Soloveitchik sees the future to be more than just a dream; it is real enough to function as a vantage point from which we can see the time in which we now live. The fullest reality of time and existence is found not in the observable present, he suggests, but in hope. Another suggestion is implicit in this passage: the reality discovered through the future is "genuine historical reality"; that is, it is not purely a futuristic reality but is composed of the past, present, and future. Here we see that we remember so that we may hope, and we hope so that we may remember.

As we have seen, memory and hope each need the other, and furthermore, we need both in order to make sense of ourselves in the present and to make ethical decisions to move from the present

---

[7] Wiesel, "Hope, Despair and Memory."

[8] Joseph B. Soloveitchik, *Festival of Freedom: Essays on Pesah and the Haggadah*, ed. Joel B. Wolowesky and Reuven Ziegler (Jersey City, NJ: Ktav Publishing House, 2006), 177.

into the future.[9] In this lecture, Wiesel writes about memory and hope in the context of the memory of the Holocaust, for which the ethics of remembrance are particularly crucial. "The opposite of the past," Wiesel writes, "is not the future but the absence of future; the opposite of the future is not the past but the absence of past. The loss of one is equivalent to the sacrifice of the other."[10] He calls for a retrieval of the memory of the horrors of the past so that we may have hope for our future. Wiesel speaks of a memory that, for many, has proved too acute to bear and has been pressed down into the tomb of forgetfulness. Yet Wiesel reminds us that still we must remember, as he recalls a certain young man, likely himself, who in the aftermath of the war believed "that the memory of evil will serve as a shield against evil; that the memory of death will serve as a shield against death."[11] Even when hope seems impossible, memory is vital, for only memory can allow for hope.

The ethical implications of memory are also addressed by David, who is interviewed in chapter 3. He identifies multiple senses of the past and distinguishes between the past as documented by history and the past as remembered by ethical consciousness: "I have a desire to go beyond a historical past. I think there [also] is an ethical past, a consciousness past, which is not exactly a chronological one. History judges what I do in one way, but the ethical and spiritual consciousness that I have has to take that into account

---

[9] See John F. Baldovin, "The Liturgical Year: Calendar for a Just Community," in *Between Memory and Hope: Readings on the Liturgical Year*, ed. Maxwell Johnson (Collegeville, MN: Liturgical Press, 2000), 429–44, here 429. Baldovin argues that "the Christian vision of the fullness of the end times—the eschatological vision—is intrinsically social or communal. No Christian community, which means no worshipping community, can afford any longer to stick its corporate head in the sand of individualistic salvation at the expense of concerns about society and the culture at large." See also Bruce T. Morrill, "Time, Absence, and Otherness: Divine-Human Paradoxes Bonding Liturgy and Ethics," in *Sacraments: Revelation of the Humanity of God*, ed. Philippe Bordeyne and Bruce T. Morrill (Collegeville, MN: Liturgical Press, 2008). In this essay, Morrill points to the ethical dimensions of liturgical anamnesis.

[10] Wiesel, "Hope, Despair and Memory."

[11] Ibid.

and to step out of the box and see that it has to be perspectivized by other forms of consciousness." The evaluative criteria of the historical past differ from that of ethical and spiritual memory, and he identifies the latter as a spiritual goal, encouraging himself to re-evaluate his consciousness of time, memory, and ethics.

Given the significance of memory and hope to existential awareness, religious faith, and the capacity to live in ethical integrity, what then is the significance of the transformation of the experience of time which has served as the subject of this book? When memory and hope bring the past into the present moment and usher in the future, the distinctiveness of the dimensions of time collapses, as the "then" becomes the "now." As proposed in the introductory chapter, this disintegration of the boundaries between the past, present, and future is fruitful, for it creates a reintegration of time.

This reintegration expresses the humanity of time. It is not a sense of time marked by a secular calendar, in which the days are crossed off one after another and the pages of each month ripped off and discarded. Nor is it the time of a clock, in which every second passes at a calculated rate, regardless of the ebb and flow of the very human life that at times leans toward reflection and asks for slowness, and at other times requires the space to leap toward the future. It is a sense of time formed by the necessity of memory and the necessity of hope.

In this reintegrated sense of time, the past, present, and future knit together in a way that is both personal and communal, and most importantly, meaningful. It is personal, for it is formed in negotiation with the experience of each individual, drawing on a personal reserve of memory and hope. And yet, as this book has argued, it is also communal, particularly as it is formed by liturgical experience and shaped by the contours of religious tradition and liturgical performance. The reintegration of time through memory and hope allows us to understand the events of our lives as cohesive; not as disconnected events but as parts of a narrative with a beginning, a present, and a future. Finally, it creates a sense of time that is ultimately meaningful, for in this sense of time, the past, present, and future of the person, the community, and the tradition become integrated into a cohesive present moment brought into fullness through memory and hope.

Bibliography

Ashtekar, Abhay. "Space and Time: From Antiquity to Einstein and Beyond." *Resonance* 11, no. 9 (2006): 4–19.

Assmann, Jan. *Moses the Egyptian: The Memory of Egypt in Western Monotheism*. Cambridge, MA: Harvard University Press, 1997.

Atkins, Peter. *Memory and Liturgy: The Place of Memory in the Composition and Practice of Liturgy*. Hants, UK: Ashgate, 2004.

Attridge, Harold W., and Margot Elsbeth Fassler, eds. *Psalms in Community: Jewish and Christian Textual, Liturgical, and Artistic Traditions*. Leiden: Brill, 2004.

Augustine. *Confessions*. Translated by Henry Chadwick. Oxford: Oxford University Press, 1992.

Baghos, Mario. "St. Basil's Eschatological Vision: Aspects of the Recapitulation of History and the 'Eighth Day.'" *Phronema* 25 (2010): 85–103.

Baldovin, John F. "The Liturgical Year: Calendar for a Just Community." In *Between Memory and Hope: Readings on the Liturgical Year*, edited by Maxwell Johnson, 429–44. Collegeville, MN: Liturgical Press, 2000.

———. "*Pignus Futurae Gloriae*: Liturgy, Eschatology, and Hope." In *Hope: Promise, Possibility and Fulfillment*, edited by Richard Lennan and Nancy Pinena Madrid, 142–54. New York: Paulist Press, 2013.

———. *Reforming the Liturgy: A Response to the Critics*. Collegeville, MN: Liturgical Press, 2008.

Barnett, Jo Ellen. *Time's Pendulum: The Quest to Capture Time—From Sundials to Atomic Clocks*. New York: Plenum Trade, 1998.

Basil. *On the Holy Spirit*. Translated by David Anderson. Crestwood, NY: St. Vladimir's Seminary Press, 2001.

———. *Exegetical Homilies*. The Fathers of the Church Series. Translated by Agnes Clare Way. Washington, DC: The Catholic University of America Press, 2003.

Beckwith, Roger T. *Calendar, Chronology and Worship: Studies in Ancient Judaism and Early Christianity*. Leiden: Brill, 2005.

Begbie, Jeremy S. *Theology, Music and Time*. Cambridge, UK: Cambridge University Press, 2000.

Bell, Catherine. *Ritual: Perspectives and Dimensions.* New York: Oxford University Press, 1997.

———. "Ritual Tensions: Tribal and Catholic." *Studia Liturgica* 32 (2002): 15–28.

———. *Ritual Theory, Ritual Practice.* New York: Oxford University Press, 1992.

Benedict. *Rule of St. Benedict 1980.* Edited by Timothy Fry. Collegeville, MN: Liturgical Press, 1981.

Benedict XVI. *Spe Salvi.* Encyclical Letter. November 30, 2007.

Bergin, Liam. "Between Memory and Promise: Sacramental Theology Since Vatican II." In *Faith, Word and Culture,* edited by Liam Bergin, 80–97. Dublin: The Columbia Press, 2004.

———. *O Propheticum Lavacrum: Baptism as Symbolic Act of Eschatological Salvation.* Rome: Editrice Pontificia Università Gregoriana, 1999.

Bindler, Paul. "Meditative Prayer and Rabbinic Perspectives on the Psychology of Consciousness: Environmental, Physiological and Attentional Variables." *Journal of Psychology and Judaism* 4 (1980): 228–48.

Bokser, Baruch M. *The Origins of the Seder.* Berkeley, CA: University of California Press, 1984.

Bradshaw, Paul F., and Lawrence A. Hoffman, eds. *The Making of Jewish and Christian Worship.* Notre Dame, IN: University of Notre Dame Press, 1991.

Brettler, Marc. "Memory in Ancient Israel." In *Memory and History in Christianity and Judaism,* edited by Michael A. Signer, 1–17. Notre Dame, IN: University of Notre Dame Press, 2001.

Campbell, Stanislaus. *From Breviary to Liturgy of the Hours.* Collegeville, MN: Liturgical Press, 1995.

———. "Liturgy of the Hours." In *The New Dictionary of Sacramental Worship,* edited by Peter E. Fink, 562–75. Collegeville, MN: Liturgical Press, 1990.

Carruthers, Mary. *The Book of Memory: A Study of Memory in Medieval Culture.* Cambridge, UK: Cambridge University Press, 1992.

Chauvet, Louis-Marie. *Symbol and Sacrament: A Sacramental Reinterpretation of Christian Existence.* Translated by Patrick Madigan and Madeleine Beaumont. Collegeville, MN: Liturgical Press, 1995.

Childs, Brevard S. *Memory and Tradition in Israel.* London: SCM Press, 1962.

Chilton, Bruce. *Redeeming Time: The Wisdom of Ancient Jewish and Christian Festal Calendars.* Peabody, MA: Hendrickson Publishers, 2002.

Collins, Mary. "Liturgy of the Hours: Some Ritual, Ecclesial and Monastic Considerations." *Benedictines* (Spring/Summer 1977): 7–13, 50–53.

Connerton, Paul. *How Societies Remember*. Cambridge: Cambridge University Press, 1989.

Cornille, Catherine. "Conditions for Interreligious Dialogue." In *Wiley-Blackwell Companion to Interreligious Dialogue*, edited by Catherine Cornille, 20–33. Chichester, UK: John Wiley and Sons, 2013.

———. *The Im-Possibility of Interreligious Dialogue*. New York: The Crossroad Publishing Company, 2008.

Cornille, Catherine, and Christopher Conway, eds. *Interreligious Hermeneutics*. Eugene, OR: Cascade Books, 2010.

Cox, Dermot. *The Psalms in the Life of God's People*. Slough, England: St. Paul Publications, 1984.

Csikszentmihalyi, Mihaly. *Flow: The Psychology of Optimal Experience*. New York: Harper and Row, 1990.

Cunningham, Philip A., Joseph Sievers, Mary C. Boys, Hans Hermann Henrix, and Jesper Svartik, eds. *Christ Jesus and the Jewish People Today: New Explorations of Theological Relationships*. Grand Rapids, MI: Eerdmans, 2011.

Daley, Brian E. *The Hope of the Early Church: A Handbook of Patristic Eschatology*. New York: Cambridge University Press, 1991.

Daniélou, Jean. *The Lord of History*. Chicago: H. Regnery, 1958.

D'Costa, Gavin. "Karl Rahner's Anonymous Christian: A Reappraisal." *Modern Theology* 1, no. 2 (1985): 131–48.

De Clerck, Paul. "'*Lex orandi, lex credendi*': The Original Sense and Historical Avatars of an Equivocal Adage." *Studia Liturgica* 24 (1994): 178–200.

Derrida, Jacques. "Structure, Sign, and Play in the Discourse of the Human Sciences." In *A Postmodern Reader*, edited by Joseph Natoli and Linda Hutcheon, 223–42. SUNY Press, 1993.

Dix, Dom Gregory. *The Shape of the Liturgy*. London: Dacre Press, 1975.

Dodd, C. H. *The Apostolic Preaching and Its Developments*. London: Hodder and Stoughton, 1936.

Dohrn-van Rossum, Gerhard. *History of the Hour: Clocks and Modern Temporal Orders*. Translated by Thomas Dunlap. Chicago: University of Chicago Press, 1996.

Dolgopolski, Sergey. *The Open Past: Subjectivity and Remembering in the Talmud*. New York: Fordham University Press, 2012.

Dudai, Yadin, and Mary Carruthers. "The Janus Face of Mnemosyne." *Nature* 434, no. 7033 (2005): 567.

Durkheim, Emile. *Elementary Forms of the Religious Life*. Translated by J. W. Swain. New York: Free Press, 1965.

Ehrlich, Uri. *The Nonverbal Language of Prayer*. Translated by Dena Ordan. Tubingen, Germany: Mohr Siebeck, 2004.

Eliade, Mircea. *The Quest: History and Meaning in Religion.* Chicago: University of Chicago Press, 1969.

Epstein, Isidore, trans. *The Babylonian Talmud.* London: Soncino Press, 1948.

Epstein, Marc Michael. *The Medieval Haggadah: Art, Narrative, and Religious Imagination.* New Haven, CT: Yale University Press, 2011.

Fagerberg, David W. *Theologia Prima: What Is Liturgical Theology?* Chicago: Hillenbrand Books, 2004.

———. *What Is Liturgical Theology? A Study in Methodology.* Collegeville, MN: Liturgical Press, 1992.

Fletcher, Jeannine Hill. "Religious Pluralism in an Era of Globalization: The Making of Modern Religious Identity." *Theological Studies* 69, no. 2 (2008): 394–411.

———. "Shifting Identity: The Contribution of Feminist Thought to Theologies of Religious Pluralism." *Journal of Feminist Studies in Religion* (2003): 5–24.

Flood, Gavin. *The Ascetic Self: Subjectivity, Memory, and Tradition.* Cambridge: Cambridge University Press, 2004.

Gadamer, Hans Georg. *Truth and Method.* Translated by Joel Weinsheimer and Donald G. Marshall. New York: Crossroad, 1991.

Geertz, Clifford. *The Interpretation of Cultures: Selected Essays.* New York: Basic Books, 1973.

———. "Making Experience, Authoring Selves." In *The Anthropology of Experience.* Edited by Victor Turner and Edward Bruner. Urbana, IL: University of Illinois Press, 1986.

General Instruction on the Liturgy of the Hours. Collegeville, MN: Liturgical Press, 1975.

Gimenez, Maxime. "La liturgie et le temps." *Irenikon* 4 (1980): 473–82.

Ginn, Richard J. *The Present and the Past: A Study of Anamnesis.* Eugene, OR: Pickwick, 1989.

Goldberg, Sylvie Anne. "Accounts and Counts of Jewish Time." *Bulletin du Centre de recherche francais a Jerusalem* 7 (2000): 92–108.

———. "Questions of Times: Conflicting Time Scales in Historical Perspective." *Jewish History* 14 (2000): 267–86.

Gort, Jerald D., Hendrik M. Vroom, Rein Fernhout, and Anton Wessels, eds. *On Sharing Religious Experience: Possibilities of Interfaith Mutuality.* Grand Rapids, MI: Eerdmans, 1992.

Grant, John, and Colin Wilson, eds. *The Book of Time.* North Pomfret, VT: Westbridge Books, 1980.

Grimes, Ronald L. *Beginnings in Ritual Studies*. Columbia, SC: University of South Carolina Press, 1995.

———. *Ritual Criticism: Case Studies in Its Practice, Essays on Its Theory*. Columbia, SC: University of South Carolina Press, 1990.

Guiver, George. *Company of Voices: Daily Prayer and the People of God*. New York: Pueblo Publishing Company, 1988.

Halbwachs, Maurice. *The Collective Memory*. Translated by Francis J. Ditter and Vida Yazdi Ditter. New York: Harper and Row, 1980.

———. *On Collective Memory*. Edited and translated by Lewis A. Coser. Chicago: University of Chicago Press, 1992.

Hammond, Claudia. *Time Warped: Unlocking the Mysteries of Time Perception*. New York: Harper Perennial, 2013.

Hayes, Zachary. *Visions of a Future: A Study of Christian Eschatology*. Collegeville, MN: Liturgical Press, 1992.

Hervieu-Leger, Daniele. *Religion as a Chain of Memory*. New Brunswick, NJ: Rutgers University Press, 2000.

Heschel, Abraham Joshua. *God in Search of Man: A Philosophy of Judaism*. New York: Noonday Press, 1955.

———. *Man's Quest for God: Studies in Prayer and Symbolism*. New York: Scribner, 1954.

———. *The Sabbath: Its Meaning for Modern Man*. New York: Farrar, Straus and Giroux, 2005.

Hoffman, Eva. *Time*. New York: Pickador, 2009.

Hoffman, Lawrence A. *Beyond the Text: A Holistic Approach to Liturgy*. Bloomington, IN: Indiana University Press, 1989.

———. "Does God Remember? A Liturgical Theology of Memory." In *Memory and History in Christianity and Judaism*, edited by Michael A. Signer, 41–72. Notre Dame, IN: University of Notre Dame Press, 2001.

———, ed. *My People's Prayer Book*. Vol. 10. *Shabbat Morning*. Woodstock, VT: Jewish Lights Publishing, 2007.

———, ed. *My People's Prayer Book*. Vol. 1. *The Sh'ma and Its Blessings*. Woodstock, VT: Jewish Lights Publishing, 1997.

Idel, Moshe. "Sabbath: On Concepts of Time in Jewish Mysticism." In *Sabbath: Idea, History, Reality*, edited by Gerald J. Blidstein, 57–93. Beer Sheva: Ben Gurion University of the Negev Press, 2004.

Jacobson, B. S. *Meditations on the Siddur: Studies in the Essential Problems and Ideas of Jewish Worship*. Translated by Leonard Oschry. Tel Aviv: Sinai, 1978.

———. *The Sabbath Service: An Exposition and Analysis of Its Structure, Contents, Language and Ideas*. Translated by Leonard Oschry. Tel Aviv: Sinai, 1981.

———. *The Weekday Siddur: An Exposition and Analysis of Its Structure, Contents, Language and Ideas.* Translated by Leonard Oschry. Tel Aviv: Sinai, 1978.

Johnson, Maxwell E., ed. *Benedictine Daily Prayer: A Short Breviary.* Collegeville, MN: Liturgical Press, 2005.

———, ed. *Between Memory and Hope: Readings on the Liturgical Year.* Collegeville, MN: Liturgical Press, 2000.

Kavanagh, Aidan. *On Liturgical Theology: The Hale Memorial Lectures of Seabury-Western Theological Seminary.* New York: Pueblo Publishing Company, 1984.

Kepnes, Steven, ed. *Interpreting Judaism in a Postmodern Age.* New York: New York University Press, 1996.

———. *Jewish Liturgical Reasoning.* New York: Oxford University Press, 2007.

Kimelman, Reuven. "The Literary Structure of the Amidah and the Rhetoric of Redemption." In *The Echoes of Many Texts: Reflection on Jewish and Christian Traditions; Essays in Honor of Lou H. Silberman,* edited by William G. Dever and J. Edward Wright, 171–218. Atlanta: Scholars Press, 1997.

———. "The Messiah of the Amidah: A Study in Comparative Messianism." *Journal of Biblical Literature* 116, no.2 (1997): 313–24.

———. "The Shema and Its Rhetoric: The Case for the Shema Being More than Creation, Revelation and Redemption." *Journal of Jewish Thought and Philosophy* 2, no. 1 (1993): 111–56.

Knuuttila, Simo. "Time and Creation in Augustine." In *The Cambridge Companion to Augustine,* edited by Eleonore Stump and Norman Kretzmann, 103–15. Cambridge, UK: Cambridge University Press, 2001.

Kolbet, Paul R. "Athanasius, the Psalms, and the Reformation of the Self." *Harvard Theological Review* 99, no.1 (2006): 85–101.

Kraemer, David. *The Mind of the Talmud: An Intellectual History of the Bavli.* New York: Oxford University Press, 1990.

Kurtzer, Yehuda. *Shuva: The Future of the Jewish Past.* Waltham, MA: Brandeis University Press, 2012.

Lakeland, Paul. *Postmodernity: Christian Identity in a Fragmented Age.* Minneapolis, MN: Fortress Press, 1997.

Langer, Ruth. "The Liturgical Parting(s) of the Ways: A Preliminary Foray." In *A Living Tradition: On the Intersection of Liturgical History and Pastoral Practice,* edited by David A. Pitt, et al., 43–58. Collegeville, MN: Liturgical Press, 2012.

———. "Liturgy and Sensory Experience." In *Christianity in Jewish Terms*, edited by Tivka Frymer-Kensky, et al., 189–95. Boulder, CO: Westview Press, 2000.

———. "Prayer and Worship." In *Modern Judaism: An Oxford Guide*, edited by Nicholas de Lange and Miri Freud-Kandel, 231–42. Oxford: Oxford University Press, 2005.

———. *To Worship God Properly: Tensions between Liturgical Custom and Halakhah in Judaism*. Cincinnati, OH: Hebrew Union College Press, 1998.

Levenson, Jon D. *Creation and the Persistence of Evil: The Jewish Drama of Divine Omnipotence*. Princeton, NJ: Princeton University Press, 1988.

———. *Sinai and Zion: An Entry into the Jewish Bible*. New York: Harper and Row, 1985.

Lindbeck, George A. "The Gospel's Uniqueness: Election and Untranslatability." *Modern Theology* 13:4 (October 1997): 423–50.

———. *The Nature of Doctrine: Religion and Theology in a Postliberal Age*. Philadelphia: Westminster Press, 1984.

The Liturgy of the Hours: According to the Roman Rite. New York: Catholic Book Publishing, 1975.

Lyotard, Jean Francois. *The Postmodern Condition: A Report on Knowledge*. Translated by Geoff Bennington and Brian Massumi. Minneapolis, MN: University of Minnesota Press, 1984.

Marion, Jean-Luc. *God without Being: Hors-Texte*. Chicago: University of Chicago Press, 1991.

Martimort, A. G., I. H. Dalmais, and P. Jounel, eds. *The Liturgy and Time*. Translated by Matthew J. O'Connell. Collegeville, MN: Liturgical Press, 1986.

Mateos, Juan. "The Origins of the Divine Office." *Worship* 41 (1967): 477–85.

Mays, J. L. *The Lord Reigns: A Theological Handbook to the Psalms*. Louisville, KY: Westminster Jon Knox, 1994.

McCall, Richard D. *Do This: Liturgy as Performance*. Notre Dame, IN: University of Notre Dame Press, 2007.

———. "In My Beginning Is My End: Remembering the Future Shape of Liturgy." *Anglican Theological Review* 82, no. 1 (Winter 2000): 17–27.

———. "Liturgical Theopoetic: The Acts of God in the Act of Liturgy." *Worship* 71, no. 5 (S 1997): 399–414.

McCutcheon, Russell T., ed. *The Insider/Outsider Problem in the Study of Religion*. London: Cassel Press, 1999.

Michaels, Axel. "Ritual and Meaning." In *Theorizing Rituals: Classical Topics, Theoretical Approaches, Analytical Concepts*, edited by Jens Kreinath, Jan Snoek and Michael Stausberg. Leiden: Brill, 2008.

Moltmann, Jürgen. *Theology of Hope*. Translated by James Leitch. New York: Harper and Row, 1967.

The Monastic Hours: Directory for the Celebration of the Work of God and Directive Norms for the Monastic Liturgy of the Hours, edited by Anne M. Field. Collegeville, MN: Liturgical Press, 2001.

Mooij, J. J. A. *Time and Mind: The History of a Philosophical Problem*. Translated by Peter Mason. Leiden: Brill, 2005.

Morrill, Bruce T. *Anamnesis as Dangerous Memory: Political and Liturgical Theology in Dialogue*. Collegeville, MN: Liturgical Press, 2000.

———. "Time, Absence, and Otherness: Divine-Human Paradoxes Bonding Liturgy and Ethics." In *Sacraments: Revelation of the Humanity of God*, edited by Philippe Bordeyne and Bruce T. Morrill, 137–52. Collegeville, MN: Liturgical Press, 2008.

Mourant, John A. *Saint Augustine on Memory*. Villanova, PA: Villanova University Press, 1980.

Moyaert, Marianne. "Absorption or Hospitality: Two Approaches to the Tension between Identity and Alterity." In *Interreligious Hermeneutics*. Edited by Catherine Cornille and Christopher Conway. Eugene, OR: Cascade Books, 2010.

———. "Postliberalism, Religious Diversity and Interreligious Dialogue: A Critical Analysis of Lindbeck's Fiduciary Interests." *Journal of Ecumenical Studies* 47, no. 1 (2012): 64–87.

Munk, Rabbi Dr. Elie. *The World of Prayer*. 2 vols. New York: Feldheim, Inc., 1961.

Nakamura, Jeanne, and Mihaly Csikszentmihalyi. "The Concept of Flow." In *Handbook of Positive Psychology*, edited by Shane J. Lopez and Charles R. Snyder, 89–105. Oxford: Oxford University Press, 2002.

Nasuti, Harry P. "The Sacramental Function of the Psalms in Contemporary Scholarship and Liturgical Practice." In *Psalms and Practice: Worship, Virtue, and Authority*, edited by Stephen Breck Reid, 78–89. Collegeville, MN: Liturgical Press, 2001.

Patai, Raphael. *The Messiah Texts*. Detroit, MI: Wayne State University Press, 1979.

Petterson, Per. *Out Stealing Horses*. Translated by Anne Born. New York: Picador, 2003.

Pickstock, Catherine. *After Writing: On the Liturgical Consummation of Philosophy*. Oxford: Blackwell Publishers, 1998.

———. "Radical Orthodoxy and the Mediations of Time." In *Radical Orthodoxy: A Catholic Enquiry*, edited by Lawrence Paul Hemming, 63–76. Burlington, VT: Ashgate, 2000.

Rashkover, Randi, and C. C. Pecknold, eds. *Liturgy, Time and the Politics of Redemption.* Grand Rapids, MI: Eerdmans, 2006.

Ratzinger, Joseph. *Eschatology: Death and Eternal Life.* 2nd ed. Washington, DC: The Catholic University of America Press, 1988.

———. *The Spirit of the Liturgy.* San Francisco: Ignatius Press, 2000.

Rau, Catherine, and Lucy Rau. *Saint Augustine's Theory of Time.* Berkeley, CA: The Gillick Press, 1952.

Rausch, Thomas. *Eschatology, Liturgy, and Christology.* Collegeville, MN: Liturgical Press, 2012.

Regan, Patrick. "Pneumatological and Eschatological Aspects of Liturgical Celebration." *Worship* 51, no. 4 (1977): 332–50.

Ricoeur, Paul. *Time and Narrative,* Vol. 3. Translated by Kathleen Blamey and David Pellauer. Chicago: University of Chicago Press, 1988.

Rosenfeld, Gavriel D. "A Flawed Prophecy? *Zakhor,* the Memory Boom, and the Holocaust." *The Jewish Quarterly Review* 97, no. 4 (Fall 2007): 508–20.

Rosenzweig, Franz. *The Star of Redemption.* Translated by William W. Hallo. Notre Dame, IN: University of Notre Dame Press, 1985.

Sacks, Jonathan. "Counting Time." In *Shabuot Reader: Torah Readings and The Book of Ruth with Laws and Commentaries,* edited by Nathan M. Dweck, 15–22. New York: Tebah Educational Series, 2008.

———. "Time as a Narrative of Hope." In *Rabbi Jonathan Sacks' Haggadah,* 75–83. New York: Continuum, 2006.

———, ed. *The Koren Siddur.* Jerusalem: Koren Publishers, 2009.

Schechner, Richard. *Performance Theory.* New York: Routledge, 2003.

Scherman, Nosson, and Meir Zlotowitz, eds. *The Complete ArtScroll Siddur: Weekday/Sabbath/Festival.* Brooklyn, NY: Mesorah Publications, 1986.

Schmemann, Alexander. *Introduction to Liturgical Theology.* Translated by Asheleigh E. Moorhouse. Crestwood, NY: St. Vladimir's Seminary Press, 1966.

———. "Liturgy and Eschatology." *Sobornost* 7, no.1 (1985): 6–14.

———. *Liturgy and Life: Christian Development through Religious Experience.* New York: Orthodox Church in America, 1974.

Scholem, Gershom. *The Messianic Idea in Judaism.* Translated by Michael A. Meyer. New York: Schocken, 1971.

Schweid, Eliezer. *The Jewish Experience of Time: Philosophical Dimensions of the Jewish Holy Days.* Translated by Amnon Hadary. Northvale, NJ: Jason Aronson, Inc., 2000.

Second Vatican Council. *Nostra Aetate* (Declaration on the Relation of the Church with Non-Christian Religions). In *Vatican Council II: The Basic*

Sixteen Documents; Constitutions, Decrees, Declarations. Edited by Austin Flannery. Collegeville, MN: Liturgical Press, 2014.

———. *Sacrosanctum Concilium* (The Constitution on Sacred Liturgy). In *Vatican Council II: The Basic Sixteen Documents; Constitutions, Decrees, Declarations.* Edited by Austin Flannery. Collegeville, MN: Liturgical Press, 2014.

Seeskin, Kenneth. *Jewish Messianic Thought in an Age of Despair.* New York: Cambridge University Press, 2012.

Segal, Robert. "Myth and Ritual." In *Theorizing Rituals: Classical Topics, Theoretical Approaches, Analytical Concepts,* edited by Jens Kreinath, Jan Snoek, and Michael Stausberg, 101–21. Leiden: Brill, 2008.

Signer, Michael A. "The Poetics of Liturgy." In *The Changing Face of Jewish and Christian Worship in North America,* edited by Paul F. Bradshaw and Lawrence A. Hoffman, 184–98. Notre Dame, IN: University of Notre Dame Press, 1991.

———, ed. *Memory and History in Christianity and Judaism.* Notre Dame, IN: University of Notre Dame Press, 2001.

Soloveitchik, Joseph B. *Festival of Freedom: Essays on Pesah and the Haggadah.* Edited by Joel B. Wolowesky and Reuven Ziegler. Jersey City, NJ: Ktav Publishing House, 2006.

———. *The Lord Is Righteous in All His Ways: Reflections on the Tish'ah be-Av Kinot.* Edited by Jacob J. Schacter. Jersey City, NJ: Ktav Publishing House, 2006.

———. "Sacred and Profane: Kodesh and Chol in World Perspectives." *Gesher* 3, no. 1 (June 1966): 5–29.

———. *The Seder Night: An Exalted Evening: The Passover Haggadah.* Edited by Menachem Genack. New York: Orthodox Union Press, 2009.

———. *Worship of the Heart: Essays on Jewish Prayer.* Edited by Shalom Carmy. New York: Toras HoRav Foundation, 2003.

Spiegel, Gabrielle. "Memory and History: Liturgical Time and Historical Time." *History and Theory* 41 (May 2002): 149–62.

Staal, Frits. "The Meaninglessness of Ritual." *Numen* 26, no. 1 (June 1979): 2–22.

Steinsaltz, Adin. *A Guide to Jewish Prayer.* New York: Schocken Books, 2000.

Stern, Sacha. *Calendar and Community: A History of the Jewish Calendar, Second Century BCE to Tenth Century CE.* Oxford: Oxford University Press, 2001.

Taft, Robert. "Historicism Revisited." In *Liturgical Time,* edited by Wiebe Vos and Geoffrey Wainwright, 97–109. Rotterdam: Liturgical Ecumenical Center Trust, 1982.

———. "The Liturgical Enterprise Twenty-Five Years after Alexander Schmemann (1932–1983): The Man and his Heritage." *St. Vladimir's Theological Quarterly* 53, nos. 2–3 (2009): 139–63.

———. *The Liturgy of the Hours in East and West.* Collegeville, MN: Liturgical Press, 1986.

———. "Liturgy as Theology." *Worship* 56, no. 2 (1982): 113–17.

———. "*Quaestiones Disputatae* in the History of the Liturgy of the Hours: The Origins of Nocturnes, Matins, Prime." *Worship* 58, no. 2 (1984): 130–58.

Talley, Thomas. "History and Eschatology in the Primitive Pascha." *Worship* 47 (1973): 212–21.

Thekla, Sister. "The Service of Vespers: Prayers of the Day." *Library of Orthodox Thinking* 3 (1976).

Turner, Victor W. *The Ritual Process: Structure and Anti-Structure.* New York: Aldine Publishing Company, 1969.

———. "Ritual, Tribal and Catholic." *Worship* 50 (1976): 504–26.

Van Gennep, Arnold. *The Rites of Passage.* Translated by Monika B. Vizedom and Gabrielle L. Caffee. University of Chicago Press, 2011.

Von Balthasar, Hans Urs. *The Glory of the Lord: A Theological Aesthetics.* Vol. 7. *Theology: The New Covenant.* Translated by Brian McNeil, San Francisco: Ignatius Press, 1989.

———. *Theo-Drama: Theological Dramatic Theory.* Vol. 3. *Dramatic Personae: Persons in Christ.* Translated by Graham Harrison. San Francisco: Ignatius Press, 1992.

———. *Theo-Logic: Theological Logical Theory.* Vol. 2. *Truth of God.* Translated by Adrian J. Walker. San Francisco: Ignatius Press, 2004.

———. *A Theology of History.* San Francisco: Ignatius Press, 1994.

Vos, Wiebe, and Geoffrey Wainwright, eds. *Liturgical Time.* Rotterdam: Liturgical Ecumenical Center Trust, 1982.

Wainwright, Geoffrey. *Doxology: The Praise of God in Worship, Doctrine and Life: A Systematic Theology.* London: Epworth Press, 1980.

———. *Eucharist and Eschatology.* Oxford: Oxford University Press, 1981.

———. "Sacramental Time." *Studia Liturgica* 14, nos. 2–4 (1982): 135–46.

Wiesel, Elie. "Hope, Despair and Memory." Nobel Lecture, December 11, 1986. http://www.nobelprize.org/nobel_prizes/peace/laureates/1986/wiesel-lecture.html.

Yerushalmi, Yosef Hayim. *Zakhor: Jewish History and Jewish Memory.* Seattle: University of Washington Press, 1982.

Yuval, Israel Jacob. *Two Nations in Your Womb: Perceptions of Jews and Christians in Late Antiquity and the Middle Ages.* Translated by Barbara

Harshav and Jonathan Chipman. Berkeley, CA: University of California Press, 2008.

Zerubavel, Eviatar. "The Benedictine Ethic and the Modern Spirit of Scheduling: On Schedules and Social Organization." *Sociological Inquiry* 50 (1980): 157–69.

———. "The Jewish Week: Its Origin and Essence." *Reconstructionist* 50, no. 8 (1985): 16–20.

———. *The Seven Day Circle: The History and Meaning of the Week*. Chicago: University of Chicago Press, 1989.

Index